AF264723

Carbondale After Dark was first published in the USA
by Dome Publications, a Browne-Koplowitz Collaboration, 1982

25th anniversary limited edition reprint published by Dome Publications, 2007

Print-on-demand expanded third edition paperback published by Dome Publications, 2022

Print-on-demand expanded third edition hardcover published by Dome Publications, 2022

Expanded eBook and Kindle editions published by Dome Publications, 2022

Expanded PDF edition published by Dome Publications, 2022

Certain stories and pictures, as noted, were previously published
in the *Southern Illinoisan*, *Daily Egyptian* and *nonSequitur* magazine.

Design and layout by Deb Browne
Cover illustration by Marvin L. Hill

Made in USA

ISBN 978-0-9791393-6-9

Preface

Carbondale's Long Strange Trip

In the 1960s and '70s, Southern Illinois University and Carbondale transmogrified from a quiet little college town in the Midwest into a cauldron of countercultural revolution, artistic renaissance and alternative lifestyles. Some say that was Carbondale's golden age, while others call it the city's hippie phase. Either way, it left a permanent mark on the town and those who lived through those tumultuous times, and it remains a period of interest to those who came after.

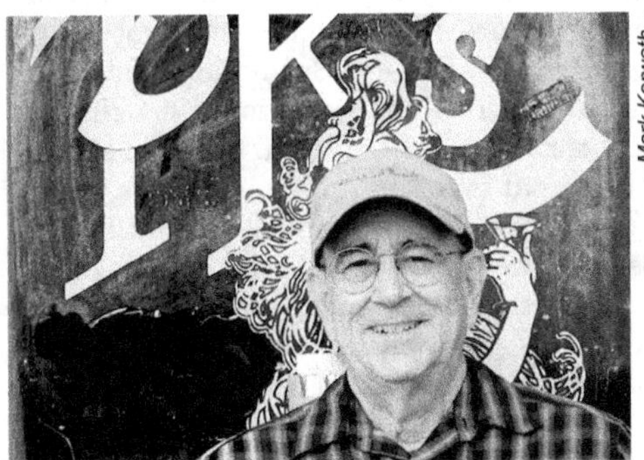

H.B. Koplowitz
Carbondale, 2017

Carbondale After Dark, first published in 1982, was my attempt to capture the essence of that era, and to preserve a slice of local history that city and university officials might try to suppress. Actually, it was an unabashed vanity project that somehow became a touchstone for those who were there and a revelation for those who were not. A quarter-century later, *CAD* co-creator Deb Browne and I collaborated on a 25th anniversary limited edition reprint. Both editions are now out of print.

In 2018 I released expanded print-on-demand paperback, hardcover, and e-book editions (updated in 2019 and 2022), and a PDF that is available exclusively at my Dome Publications website, hbkoplowitz.com. This expanded edition preserves the original text and layout, warts and all, although Yolan Presley has been credited for the Devil's Kitchen band photo on page 35. Sorry Doon. There's also an addendum with four additional stories. "Carbondale Before Dark" is about growing up in the town in the 1950s and '60s. "Bucky's Dome" is about living in futurist Buckminster Fuller's dome home in the early 1980s. "Ghosts of Carbondale Past" is about a 2017 reunion concert of Carbondale bands from the 1970s. "I Killed a Man" is a poem I wrote circa 1959, when I was in about 4th grade at U-School, old enough to type, but young enough not to know how to spell the n-word.

Over the past half century, much has changed in Carbondale and the world. In 1966, *Playboy* magazine named SIU the nation's top party school, and by 1991, enrollment had grown to nearly 25,000 students. But by 2018, SIU's party-school image was long gone, and enrollment had shrunk to under 13,400 students, a level not seen since, well, 1966.

Following Halloween melees on the strip in the 1990s, the city and university tried to ban the holiday by restricting alcohol sales and closing the school over Halloween. In the aughts, students started a new tradition, officially called Unofficial Halloween, which entailed roving revelry and boisterous house parties the weekend before the Halloween break. In part to mitigate the perennial problem of raucous partying in residential neighborhoods, in 2015 the city tried luring students back to the strip by repealing its Halloween ordinance and sanctioning the first downtown street festival since 1988.

After 15 years in Los Angeles, where I edited for City News Service and taught journalism at Los Angeles Southwest College, in 2011 I moved to Boca Raton and became a writing tutor at Florida Atlantic University. In August 2017 I returned to Carbondale to experience two-and-a-half minutes of a total eclipse of the sun (and open containers of alcohol allowed on the strip the weekend of the blackout). I returned again in 2019 to attend my 50th high school class reunion.

Revisiting my hometown was happy-sad. Except for the Dairy Queen and PK's, much of the strip was unrecognizable. South of PK's was a new Hilton hotel, and south of that, another block of stores had been replaced by a new city hall and civic center. Across from PK's, the former Golden Gauntlet/Merlin's/T.J. McFly's nightclub had been flattened into a parking lot that stretched south past the 1988 train station to Pagliai's Pizza. Mary Lou's and PK's founders, Mary Lou Trammel-Staffey and Gwen Hunt, had passed away, and the last of the Karayiannis family businesses, Pinch Penny Pub, had closed.

PK's and Hangar 9 were for sale. Jim's Pub, Silverball, Gatsby's, The Club and Booby's, all gone. The last of the original bagel men, Winston Mezo, retired in 2017. Across the tracks, ABC Liquor and Tres Hombres were still there, but the former Tuscan Lodge and Jeremiah's restaurant had become a community garden. Even 710 Bookstore had been replaced by a boxy student apartment building, and the iconic, 18-story Brush Towers -- Schneider, Mae Smith and Neely residence halls -- were almost demolished.

SIU and Carbondale had fallen on hard times. A budget crisis in Springfield had forced cuts in state spending on higher education, causing tuition and fees to go up, causing enrollment to go down, with negative ripple effects throughout the region. Carbondale saw the eclipse as a chance to rehab its image. In anticipation of an influx of visitors, downtown sidewalks and curbs, including the Dairy Queen wall, were replaced, and the strip looked cleaner than it had in years. The city restored the old train station and some of the original town square around Main Street and the tracks. It also made efforts to preserve some of the older homes and downtown buildings. The Varsity Theater, in particular, became a center for performing arts. Beyond Carbondale, a vineyard and winery industry had sprung up, revitalizing rural communities like Makanda, Cobden and Alto Pass. Two other things Carbondale did to transform itself into Fun City again was to drop the bar entry age to 19 and allow pot dispensaries.

The country had also been transforming. In 2008, America elected president a young, liberal black man named Barack Hussein Obama, who embodied many of the ideals of the counterculture of the 1960s, like peace, equality and inclusion. In a stunning reversal, eight years later the voters replaced him with an old populist con man, Donald Trump, who in the 1980s epitomized what was then called yuppie scum. As president, Trump seemed hell-bent on dismantling not just the humanist legacy of his predecessor, but of a generation, and perhaps a planet. The internet and social media also warped the world.

The 2013 not-guilty verdict in the Trayvon Martin case in Florida, the death of Michael Brown a year later in Ferguson, Mo., and other unarmed blacks killed by cops ignited a Black Lives Matter movement that agitated for social justice. In response to men behaving badly in Hollywood, politics and the media, a #MeToo movement arose to combat sexual harassment and assault. In 2018, yet another mass shooting, at a high school in Parkland, Florida, sparked a children's crusade for gun control. And Swedish teen climate activist Greta Thunberg tried to shame OK Boomers into saving the environment. They all sought a safer, saner society, but it's too soon to say whether they will change the world or, as generations before them, be subsumed by materialism. America, indeed, all of humanity, is caught between the forces of modernity and the lures of chauvinism, and it is unclear whether we will embrace a global village or cling to the tribalism of our DNA.

In 2015, Buckminster Fuller's dome home, where much of *CAD* was written and laid out, was designated a Carbondale Historic Landmark. That same year, John "Mike" Henry, owner of Henry Printing, where the original book was typeset and produced, was elected mayor. His long association and assistance with *CAD* is much appreciated.

Finally, my deepest gratitude and admiration for my dearly departed parents, Deb Browne, and all the "freaks, geeks and uniques" who made *CAD* possible.

-- H.B. Koplowitz
Boca Raton, Fla., 2022

Foreword

Dennis Franz, actor

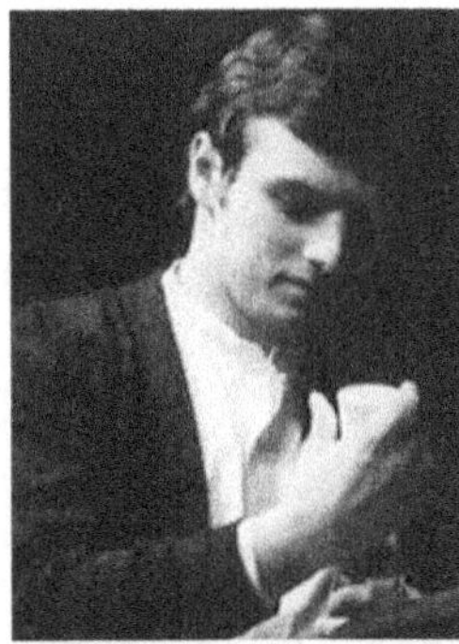

"Long Day's Journey"
Dennis Franz, SIU 1966
*-- Photo courtesy of
SIU Theater Department--*

Carbondale was probably my happiest, free-spirited, soul-searching time. It was an experience that has remained lifelong. It was far enough away from my home in the Chicago area, so I felt removed. It was wonderful to be able to do things like go to this old pond where we would spend days swimming with a lot of the other students.

I used to love to go to the record stores. At the time, everybody was into music, and that was the Beatles era, so a lot of people were growing their hair long and wearing beads and bells on their clothes. And there were two factions at the school -- the ones going in that direction and those who hated anybody going in that direction. So you had to defend yourself if you chose to grow your hair long and wear beads and bells.

When I went I think it was rated the number-two party school in the country. And that had a great deal to do with my choice in going there. I had gone down to spend a weekend with a buddy of mine who was enrolled and we went to a party that lasted all weekend. I told my parents, "This is the place for me. Send my transcripts." I didn't go back home.

I was there during the riots, too. I was there, but I could never find them. We'd hear about things, and I'd be at home and hear all this commotion was going on, and it would have busted up. Even though I was there, I never was a part of any of it. That probably was for the better.

I remember in town going to all the stores that were geared toward students ... Moo 'n' Cackle ... Varsity Theater ... Italian Village ... Many a night was spent there eating pizza and salad with Italian dressing. Much of my time was spent at the McLeod Theatre being in plays, rehearsing plays. In fact, I did the very first play at the theatre, *Long Day's Journey into Night*. That was my very first theatrical experience at SIU. My name back then was Dennis Schlacta.

After I graduated, I spent a year in Vietnam. That was a rude awakening to manhood. I think up until then I was a carefree, irresponsible young man. But the direct opposite -- the shit hit the wall when I went into the service. That experience, the military, changed my personality quite a bit. I became much more serious and focused in life and realized the things I had to do as a young man instead of nothing, and owing nothing to anybody. I started a different type of soul-searching then, and when I came back to Chicago I got involved in a few theater companies and started studying people.

Somewhere along the way I came into possession of a copy of *Carbondale After Dark*, and loved it. The book brought back so many memories of that idyllic town, and that wonderful, growing time in my life.

One of my teachers, Darwin Payne, years ago he said, "If you are going to be serious about this business, you will suffer some things." Those words always stuck in my head. I enjoy movies and good television. I enjoy being challenged -- but I do like all kinds. I like cartoons on Saturday morning, too, but I say my appreciation of entertainment started in that direction back in Carbondale.

-- Dennis Franz, SIU class of 1970
As told to Carbondale Nightlife, *August 2006*

Backword

P.S. Mueller, humorist

When I arrived in Carbondale in the fall of 1969, SIU was druggies, jocks, frat rats and ratettes, clueless party people like myself, and a whole lot of folks really pissed off about a ruinous war on people we didn't know anything about. Today I'm a middle-aged white guy really pissed off about a ruinous war against people we don't know anything about, as well as at my fellow boomers, who blithely tell me to "get over it."

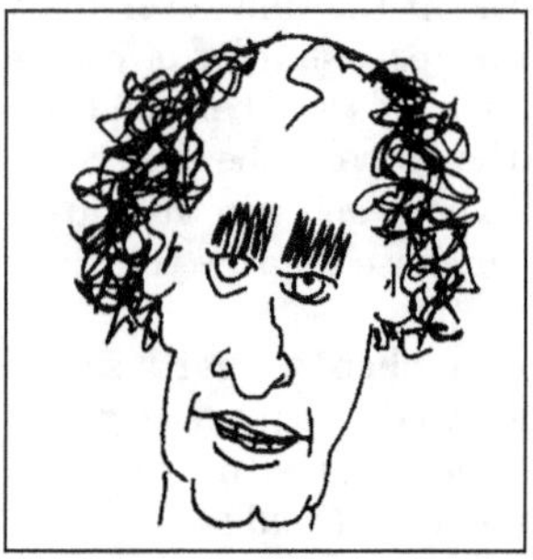

I certainly got over any faith I had in *Leave It To Beaver* America in the spring of 1970, when police stormed my Italian language class in the basement of Wheeler Hall, the upstairs of which was home to the ROTC. I was beaten for attending class, gassed when I returned to my dorm, and given little choice but to take my place amid thousands of confused, frightened, angry kids in the streets. Days of hell, well chronicled in this little book, followed.

Then again, I was 18 and liked to draw cartoons, and the *Daily Egyptian* published my cartoons, and I also learned radio -- I still do both today. I also made great friends and had fine adventures. I stole the hands off the north face of the Pulliam clock, I blew up my hand in an abortive college prank, just the usual stuff.

In 1974 I met H.B. Koplowitz, or "H" as I call him -- he of the wily mustache and Mykonos hat. I became great friends with the late Marvin Hill, whose cover drawing did perfect justice to the text in this book. I hid out from bloodthirsty state troopers at Little Caesar's and ate strawberry pie with acidhead prison guards who worked the night shift at the bighouse in Marion. I cooked at Charlie Pickle's, where the local constable Art V. arrived nightly to sell amphetamines to the waitresses. While renting a small trailer from the remarkable Goffrey Hughes, I learned to avoid my neighbor, a cross-dressing something calling itself Joe Scorpio. I swam in old strip mines, sold records to hippies, went broke, moved away, came back, and eventually departed forever for Wisconsin, all while managing to draw and sell my silly cartoons.

One cold afternoon in Carbondale, I was riding in a car with a guy in possession of a huge chunk of hashish. A police siren erupted behind us and I was handed the chewy brown nugget and advised to eat it fast. The cop car sailed on by, and a couple of hours later yours truly sailed on into the Carbondale night, so high I became convinced that a long desperate walk around town was the only way to save my life. So I walked. And walked. Until the middle of the night, when, as I passed the old graveyard on Logan Street, a snowball nailed me on the side of my already bald head.

There were kids in the graveyard! Young black kids hiding out and having a little fun with people like me who happened along. I suddenly forgot about the existential pall of my drugged-up situation and went back at 'em. Soon enough, we picked teams and launched into the mother of all snowball fights, there, in the Logan Street boneyard, among the headstones and beneath the January stars. We slid and slammed and splooshed our way to soaked exhaustion at 3 a.m. Then it was time for all of us to go home. I will never get over Carbondale after dark.

-- P.S. Mueller, SIU class of 1976
Madison, Wisconsin, July 2006

Reacknowledgments

H.B. Koplowitz, writer

Carbondale After Dark tells the story of how a sleepy little teacher's college in the Midwest called Southern Illinois University earned a reputation for being a party school and radical outpost.

Written on a manual typewriter in Bucky Fuller's funky dome home, which I was renting at the time, it provides a blow-by-blow account of the political and cultural upheavals that led to the May 1970 riots in Carbondale -- how panty raids became political movements, and riots evolved into a Halloween street party.

It also chronicles streakers, bands, bars, hangouts, protest movements and street people, and efforts by city and school officials to control the madness. In other words, all the things that get left out of official histories and Chamber of Commerce brochures.

It didn't start out that way. I intended to publish an anthology of my early writings, which mostly explored the world of teenage angst. But I soon realized that wasn't going to sell. So I decided

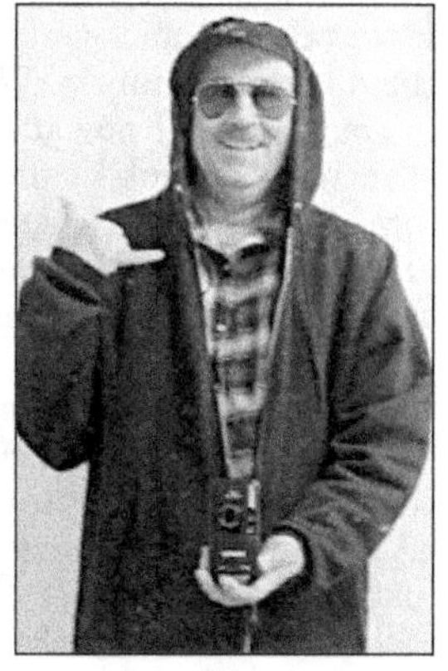

H.B. Koplowitz
Halloween in L.A. 2005

to tack on a history of Carbondale's notorious strip, which ended up taking me another year to "research" and write. It also occurred to me that people like pictures, so with the help of collaborator Deb Browne, the book was profusely illustrated with photos and drawings by local artists, most notably the late Marvin Hill, who created the evocative cover art.

As it turned out, *CAD* chronicled a period that was a turning point in the history of Carbondale and SIU. It became a touchstone for those who lived there during the 1960s and '70s, and a reference for those who came later. Its reissue brings not just the events, but the spirit of the times to a new generation.

Hippies, freaks, counterculture and revolution, was it just another passing fad? Recreational drugs never seem to go out of style, and on those rare occasions when I step into a bar nowadays, it seems the band is always playing some Beatles or Chuck Berry tune, which would be like Devil's Kitchen doing Frank Sinatra, or Big Twist covering Rudy Vallee. Certainly the music lives on. Every other TV commercial samples some song from the golden age of rock, and Tony Bennett sings duets with Shawn Colvin. But Led Zeppelin for Cadillac and Bob Dylan for Victoria's Secret? Gimme a frickin' break!

Ironically, places like Eastern Europe and the Middle East are more stuck in the '60s than we are. The Velvet Revolution in Czechoslovakia and Iranian "students" taking over the U.S. embassy took some of their cues from protest movements in America, just as Palestinian intifadas and riots over cartoons are a warped version of "no justice, no peace" and "the whole world is watching."

Could it happen again? Should it? Righteous indignation is the most seductive drug of all, especially for those still young enough to view the world in black and white, instead of darker shades of pale. It can cloud reason, unloose savagery and send armies of children marching into the night. Sometimes it's righteous and sometimes it's not, and sometimes it's really hard to tell the difference.

Americans felt righteously indignant after 9/11, as did the "greatest generation" after Pearl Harbor. The free world united to invade Afghanistan and fight terrorists, just as the Allies came together to defeat the Nazis. But then Afghanistan turned into Iraq, and World War II morphed into Vietnam. Bush lied and people died. When there's a credibility gap between what our leaders tell us and objective reality, the conditions are ripe for a generation to turn on, tune in and drop out. The '60s are just a draft call away.

Did the antiwar, civil rights, gay, feminist and other liberation movements of the '60s change anything? America is more diverse, but there is still racism, or classism as they like to call it today. Gays still can't get married, pot is still illegal, and many of us have forgotten the hard lessons of Vietnam -- the limits of power, the folly of nation-building and the dangers of hubris. We weren't supposed to get fooled again.

They say that nowadays, Carbondale is dead on Halloween because SIU is closed and students are sent home, lest they rise up again. Even though it's not meant to be, the school's quirky Halloween break is a testament to the student power movement, an annual reminder of what happened in Carbondale and around the country in the '60s and '70s.

Me? After Carbondale I moved to the Illinois state capital, Springfield, where I got a master's degree, became a flack for a state agency, ghostwrote a book for then-Gov. Jim Thompson and had some serious relationships. But after 10 years I escaped to Los Angeles, where I've tried to get back into writing. I took screenwriting classes, wrote columns for a weekly, taught journalism at a community college in South-Central and edited for a news wire service. I never hit the big-time, but I've done a lot of writing and you just may see it yet.

I wish to thank Michael Batinski, Pete Emmett and everyone who encouraged me to do a 25th anniversary reprint, especially those who purchased advance copies. Thanks also to Sue Leonard and McNaughton & Gunn for their quality printing, as well as to Henry Printing for once again providing technical assistance. A special thanks to Dennis Franz and Pete Mueller for providing the Foreword and Backword (BTW, Pete's third from the left on the front cover and I'm second from the left -- Marvin is second from the right; Dennis is on reruns of *NYPD Blue*).

Finally, I wish to thank my parents, Julius and Audrey Koplowitz, for being there no matter what, and Deb, without whom there never would have been a *Carbondale After Dark*, or a 25th anniversary reprint, which is dedicated to Jim and Melissa, Booburt and Boots, Cousin Mike and Mary Lou. The original book has been left intact, warts and all. For the record, a certain photo caption should read Spyros Karayiannis; Kelly VanLaningham also proofread the original manuscript; and it's eminent sted imminent domain.

A lot has changed in Carbondale and the world since the 1960s, when America was fighting an unpopular war and young people liked to party in the street. Then again, the more things change . . .

-- H.B. Koplowitz, SIU class of 1977
Los Angeles, January 2007

CARBONDALE AFTER DARK

And Other Stories

by HBKoplowitz

DOME
PUBLICATIONS   CARBONDALE, ILLINOIS 62901

A BROWNE—KOPLOWITZ COLLABORATION

Acknowledgments

First and foremost, I wish to express my deepest gratitude and love to Deborah Browne, who encouraged me to turn an idle fantasy into a reality. In addition to designing and pasting up all the pages, Deb did the typesetting, created the sales brochures and display ads, handled negotiations with the printer and bookstores, and still found the energy and patience to love me.

My parents, Audrey and Julius Koplowitz, thought we were crazy, but they helped to finance the venture anyway, for which I am extremely grateful.

Gary Marx copy-edited most of the text, and he is responsible for all the words that are spelled correctly (I'm responsible for the ones that aren't). Gary also gave me valuable editorial advice, not enough of which did I accept.

All you folks who purchased books before they were printed helped me raise the capital to pay the bills, and I appreciate your trust and your checks.

In addition, I wish to thank Marvin Hill for the cover illustration; Gordon Olmsted, Harry Klein and Wendi (Carroll) Hill for addressing brochures; Lester Magee for addressing envelopes and advice on layout; Norma Colyer for teaching Deb how to operate the typesetting machine; Henry Printing for letting Deb use the typesetting machine; the entire Henry staff for putting up with our pre-publication jitters; the Observer Press in Peoria for their quality printing and prices; David Pichaske of Spoon River Publishing in Peoria for explaining how to publish a book; and Mark Kerwath for coming up with the title I didn't use -- "A Koplowitz Now."

Lastly, I wish to credit all those outrageous Carbondale geeks, freaks and uniques without whom there would not have been enough material for this book.

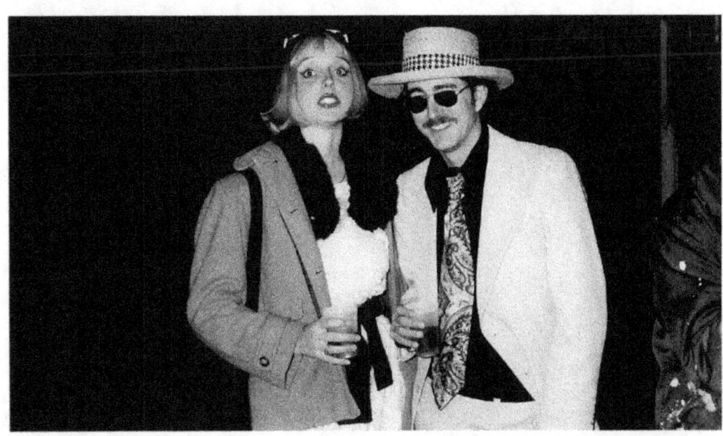

H.B. and Deb
Halloween 1981
--Harlan Mendenhall--

Contents

*T*he two adventurous grade school kids dragged a couple of chairs over to a nickel pinball machine called "Slick Chick." Oblivious to the bemused stares from a group of tray-carrying college kids filing through the cafeteria line, the younger of the two boys, a high-strung fifth grader named Harold, climbed on his chair and peered over the glass. His eyes grew wide as he gazed at the brightly lit rows of intersecting bumpers spelling out

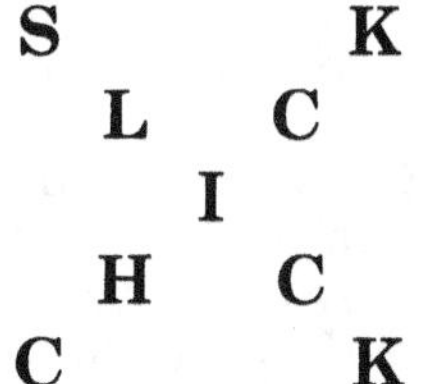

The other boy, Tom, a prematurely pubescent sixth grader, climbed on his chair and pushed a quarter into the machine.

"Pop pop pop pop pop," popped the machine.

With practiced hands, Tom tested the flipper buttons. He thumbed a ball out of the chute and shook the machine.

"Clang clang, clack clack clack, flip clang clack, flip thunk, ding, ding, te-te-te-te-te."

He guided another ball into the chute and had Harold change places with him. Patiently he reminded the novice to wait for the ball to come to the flipper and to try to use just one flipper at a time.

Gingerly, Harold pulled back the spring and let it go. Spreading his spindly arms wide, he gripped the sides of the machine.

"Clang, clang, clack clack . . . "

When the ball was still a foot from the flippers, he flailed his fingers on both flipper buttons.

"Flap flap flap flap thunk flap flap te-te-te-te-te."

Tom repeated his instructions, and Harold practiced one flipper at a time. He rubbed his hands along the wood rubbed smooth by a thousand sweaty palms. He could smell the grease. It smelled like grownups. He shot another ball, and as it came down the board, he timed his flip perfectly. The vibration of the ball colliding with the flipper echoed through his body. He was hooked.

After the pinball lesson, Tom led Harold up the street to a small cafe. They bought a couple of vanilla Cokes, Tom fed a dime to the jukebox and Harold's eyes went misty as he listened to the twanging notes of the instrumental, "Apache," by Jorgen Ingmann and his guitar . . .

That giddy experience on a crisp autumn Saturday morning in 1960 was my first exposure to what a decade later would officially become known as "cruising the strip." The pinball machine was in a hamburger joint called U.D.'s at 901 S. Illinois, and the jukebox was in the Alibi Cafe at the northwest corner of College and Illinois.

Soon my childhood friend, Tom Small, would move away. But I would continue to haunt the hangouts as they evolved on the strip. Pizza restaurants, cafes, pool halls, and later the bars. Places with names like Crazy Horse, Moo 'n' Cackle, Dunk 'n' Dip, Spudnut's, Jim's Pizza Palace, The Purple Mousetrap, Tiffaney III, the Golden Gauntlet, Charlie Pickle's, the Zodiac Club and Papa Caesar's.

Often I would carry a notebook when I went uptown, and as the protesting, partying and proselytizing whirled around me, I'd steal away to the back booth of a cozy cafe and write about the passing parade. I would pretend my diary entries and half-completed essays were the beginnings of the Great American Novel, which I somehow envisioned as being all about a skinny introverted teenager growing up in the middle of the Midwest in the 1960s.

In 1969 I left Carbondale to attend college in California. By May 4, 1970, I had dropped out of school and was bumming around the country, experimenting with drugs and plotting to overthrow the government.

And, keeping a lot of notes.

Between 1967 and 1975 I continued to ink up notebooks with diaries, essays, short stories and rambling narratives. Some of it was about Carbondale and some about the politics and culture of the '60s. But alas, most of it was about myself. Such was not the stuff of The Great American Novel, and besides, another insecure neurotic Jew had beat me to the title.

So I became a journalist. I crash landed on my parents' driveway, asked Dad for some money and enrolled in journalism school at SIU. Journalism held the promise of a steady income, and it forced me to get out of my own head and into the lives of other people. And it taught me discipline. At least in my writing.

Soon I was writing about Carbondale again, the Carbondale of the mid-1970s, and getting read by more people. My first journalism experiences were rather idyllic: With the help of some pretty talented friends I founded and edited nonSequitur, a news-feature magazine published in Carbondale 14 times between 1975 and 1977; in 1976 I was a columnist and student editor for the Daily Egyptian; and in 1977 I worked for the Illinois Times, an alternative weekly newspaper in Springfield.

In 1979 it was back to Carbondale, this time as a feature writer for the Southern Illinoisan. A year later I was reassigned to the news staff, and shortly thereafter given the Murphysboro beat. It was then that I discovered what journalism is really all about -- daily deadlines, endless assignments, constant pressure and details, details, details.

A beat reporter on a middle-sized daily newspaper is the epitome of journalism. It ain't what you'd call glamorous, but it's real. Being a newspaper reporter has given me an identity and a respectability I could never have achieved writing fiction. Thousands of people a day may read my words. I even have my own business cards.

It's nice to be respectable, for a change, and news reporting is a thoroughly challenging occupation. But as I eclipsed the untrustworthy age of 30, I began to wonder about the writing I had done before they taught me not to use *adjectives. The stuff about an earlier Carbondale and the "children's crusade" of the '60s and early '70s. Was that just a lot of wasted motion, or was some of it worth preserving in some more enduring form than the dog-eared notebooks hybernating in my dresser drawers?*

It was curiosity, as much as vanity, that prompted me to one day open the dresser drawer and take a critical look at my early writings. But it was definitely vanity that motivated me to transform the rough drafts into a book. There were two main obstacles in trying to do that. One was the tricky editing job of making the stories coherent and grammatical without diluting the original "rawness" of style. The other problem was picking stories that would be compatible with each other.

I tried to find a middle ground during the editing -- so the feelings as well as the events of the late '60s and early '70s would shine through. But that period was also pretty raunchy, and I took some (but not all) of the raunchiness out of the stories in deference to the more refined expectations of today's readers.

To give the book some continuity I divided the stories into three sections. Part I, "The Strip," traces the evolution of downtown nightlife in various period pieces, including "Carbondale After Dark I," a high-school-eye view of pre-strip Carbondale in 1967; "Carbondale After Dark II," a tour of downtown nine years later, when the bar scene was in full bloom; and "The Last Street Takeover," written in 1979 when the strip was starting to die. Also included are "Seven Days in May," a blow-by-blow account of the May 1970 riots in Carbondale; and "A Layman's History of the Strip," which provides a synopsis of events in downtown Carbondale from 1852 to the present.

Part II, "Pontifications," includes a collection of columns written for the Daily Egyptian in 1976. The D.E. columns tackle such thorny social issues as meditation, women's lib, doctors, disco and a white people's disease called "Afrophobia." Also included are several columns written for nonSequitur magazine, and a new journalism treatment of the 1976 Republican National Convention, "The Rubbish and the Rubies."

Part III, "A Koplowitz Now," is a potpourri of short stories, personal reflections and imaginations, several of which have earned me rejection slips from some of America's most prestigious magazines. Included are two chapters out of my maybe-someday-to-be-completed novel, "Kid Clyde, An Existentialist's Horror Story." Also, a letter, "Kidnapped by Jesus Freaks," and a short story, "Occurrence in August Heat," on the subject of contemporary religion; and an explicit stream-of-consciousness poem "The Horny Blues," meant to be read aloud to the accompaniment of bongo drums and snapping fingers.

In spite of what has now become a rather lengthy explanation and justification for this book, I have yet to answer the obvious question, namely, why didn't I try for real fame and sell my manuscript to a legitimate publishing house in New York rather than go through the expense of publishing it myself? The obvious answer is that the big city publishers could probably give a hoot about life in Carbondale. But for co-publisher Deb Browne and myself, the satisfaction of being in control of every aspect of the book, from the editing to the layout and marketing, has more than compensated for the ego thrills of selling it to a publisher.

It's only fitting that this bound offering be known in the trade as a "vanity book." For this book was conceived in unabashed vanity. I take no shame in that. No matter what they say about social responsibility, the artistic endeavor is essentially an act of self-gratification, and don't let anyone ever tell you different.

The Strip

It lacks the neon of Las Vegas, the soul of Harlem and the culture of Greenwich Village. And it takes only a couple of minutes to walk from one end to the other. But the five blocks between Walnut and College streets have done more to establish Carbondale's reputation than Walt Frazier, Bucky Fuller and Delyte Morris rolled into one. Murphysboro has its tornado, Williamson County has its blood and Carbondale has its strip.

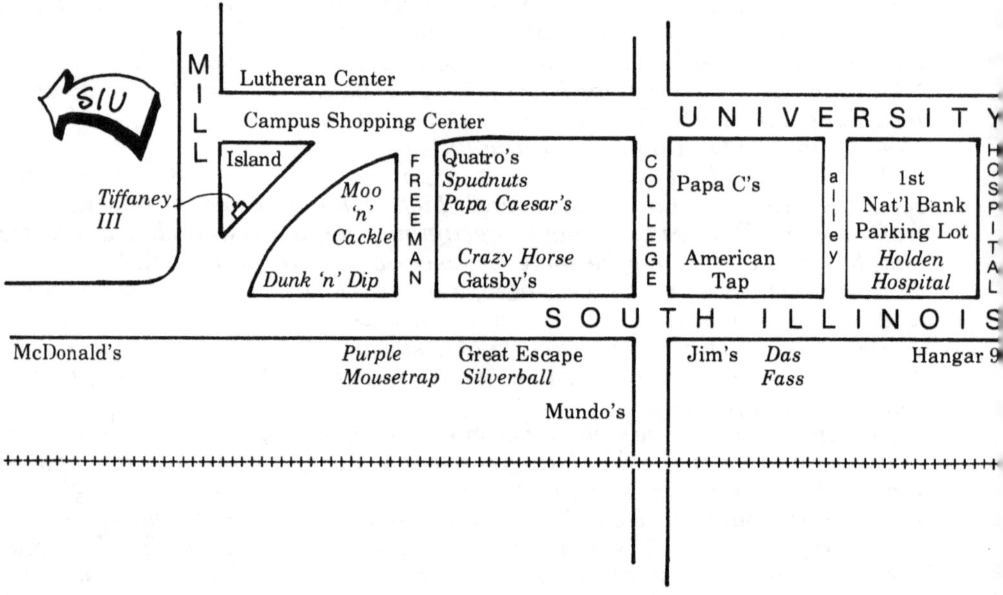

KEY: *italic - former places*
regular - 1982 places
Map is not to scale

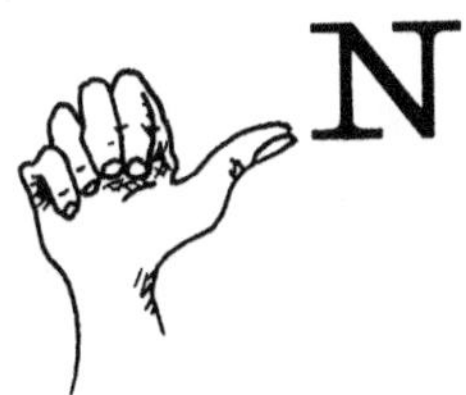

N

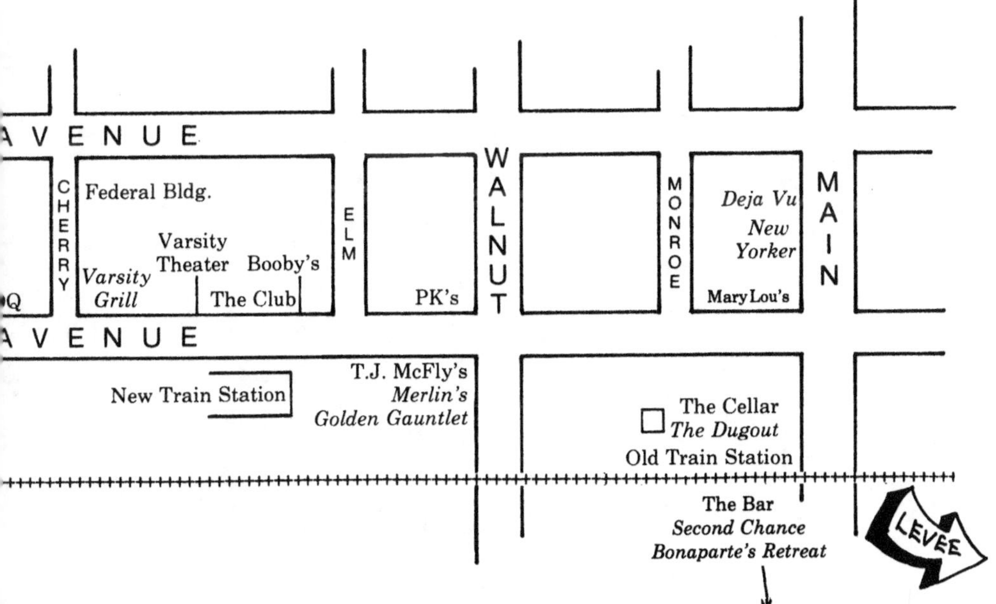

A V E N U E
CHERRY
Federal Bldg.
Varsity
Theater
Booby's
Varsity
Grill
The Club
Q
ELM
PK's
WALNUT
MONROE
Deja Vu
New
Yorker
Mary Lou's
MAIN
A V E N U E
New Train Station
T.J. McFly's
Merlin's
Golden Gauntlet
The Cellar
The Dugout
Old Train Station
The Bar
Second Chance
Bonaparte's Retreat
LEVEE

The Strip

Part **1**

1852-1982

A Layman's History of "The Strip"

The following is not a fable -- it all really happened, and it has no morals. Nor is it a comprehensive history of Carbondale. Rather, it is a chronology of events that have contributed to Carbondale's reputation as a party town, drug den and radical outpost. The methodology employed was time-consuming but simple. I started with real histories of Carbondale, then digested years of Southern Illinoisan and Daily Egyptian newspapers, and filled in the gaps with interviews and personal recollections.

Certainly "the strip" names a specific place, and therefore might more properly be written, "The Strip." But the term also refers to a harder-to-define state of mind, and an atmosphere of crowdedness, intoxication and decadence that occurs at different times in different places. Hence the lower case. No attempt was made to put a value judgment on the strip. What I set out to do was to compile, for the first time, all of the events that have played a role in the evolution of Carbondale's strip.

The readers may draw any conclusions they wish as to why the strip developed, and whether it is good, meaningless or evil. But one thing is for sure: Carbondale certainly earned its reputation.

Several years ago *Chicago* magazine published an article by former SIU student Lynn Emmerman titled "Burned Out in Carbondale." The story was widely criticized for showing only the negative side of town. But what is undeniable is that the article faithfully portrayed Carbondale's stereotyped image; an image largely defined as "the strip."

Murphysboro has its tornado, Williamson County has its blood and Carbondale has its strip. Unlike the other two examples, however, Carbondale has come by its dubious reputation only lately. As recently as 15 years ago there was no strip, except perhaps the levee, a historic neighborhood on North Washington Street in the predominantly black side of town, and the term "the strip," as it applies to Carbondale, is only about 10 years old.

When Carbondale was founded by Daniel H. Brush in 1852, the sale of alcohol within the city limits was prohibited, and violators forfeited their land to the public schools. Brush acquired a distaste for the liquor scene in the 1840s while he was a youthful storekeeper in the original county seat of Brownsville. Brownsville allowed the sales of bottled liquor, but not liquor by the drink. So to have a shot of whiskey a fellow would have to buy a whole quart. As often as not he would pass the bottle around to his "cronies," who would return the favor, and pretty soon everyone was blottoed. In Brush's memoirs he describes the "drunken set" of Brownsville with "bunged-up eyes and swollen noses" from fighting, and he was determined to keep "spiritous liquor" out of Carbondale.

Ironically, it was Carbondale's teetotaler image that contributed to Southern Illinois Normal University being established there in 1869. SINU was a small and conservative teachers' college with strict rules governing student behavior, including dress codes, chaperones and a curfew for female students. But as the town and the college grew, more liberal people were attracted to the area, and in 1895 the voters narrowly approved a referendum legalizing alcohol. The voters changed their minds and voted the town dry again in 1899, then voted it wet again

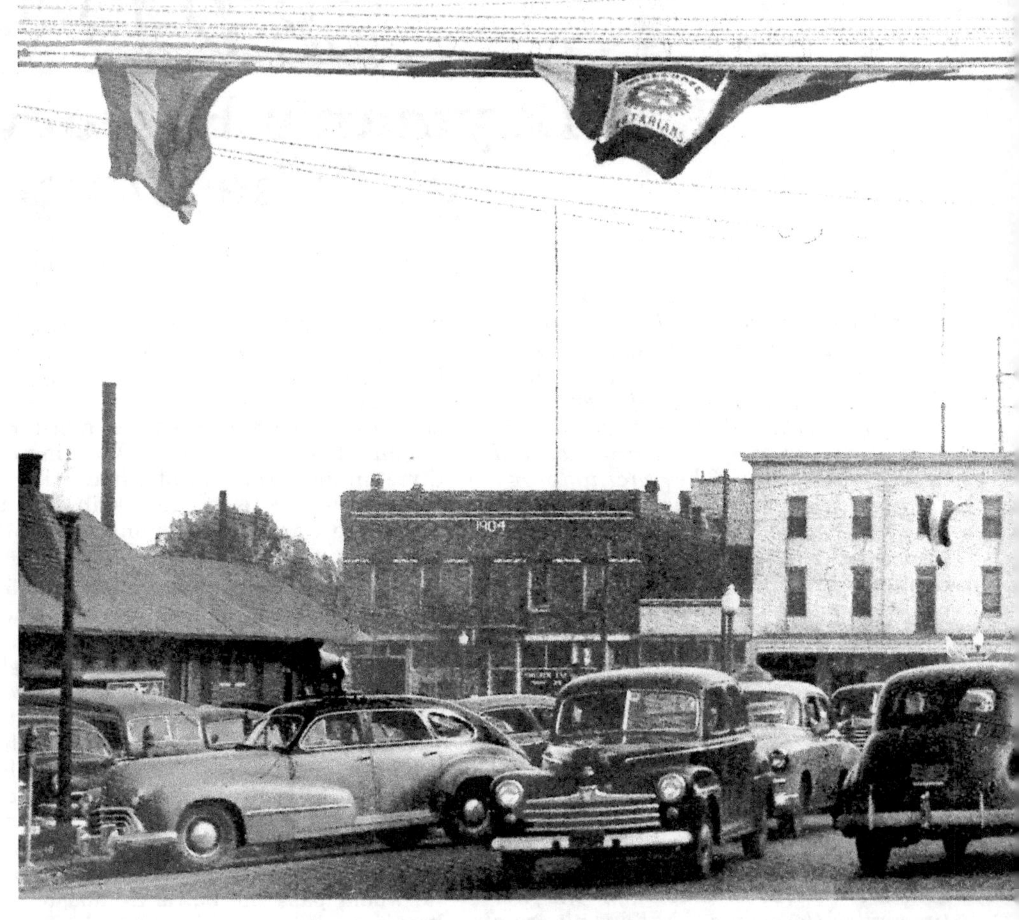

Carbondale 1952:

in 1902 and dry again in 1907, all to the frustration of the community's four saloon owners. It wasn't until the repeal of Prohibition in 1933 that Carbondale became wet again, although there were unsuccessful attempts in 1942 and 1952 to make it dry again.

Carbondale and its college remained pretty much "normal" until 1948 when Delyte W. Morris became SIU president. With vision and political finesse, Morris created new departments, new graduate programs, new buildings and new campuses. Between 1950 and '60 SIU's 5,000-student enrollment doubled, and between 1960 and '70 it more than tripled-- from 10,000 students to 23,000 students at Carbondale and 10,000 at Edwardsville.

Student activities in the '50s and early '60s were not unusual, centering around Homecoming in the fall, a Greek-sponsored spring festival topped off by the Theta XI variety show, and basketball games starring Sweet Charlie Vaughn and Walt Frazier. In May of 1952 there was one night of disruptions when, according to the *Southern Illinoisan*, "1,000 frenzied male students stormed sororities and Anthony Hall (then a women's dorm) destruction-bent and in quest of panties." The panty raids were imitative of a wave of panty raids at other universities that had gotten a lot of press coverage, and there were no political overtones. The "raiders" were met with giggles and, in some cases, field hockey sticks from alarmed coeds. At 11 p.m.

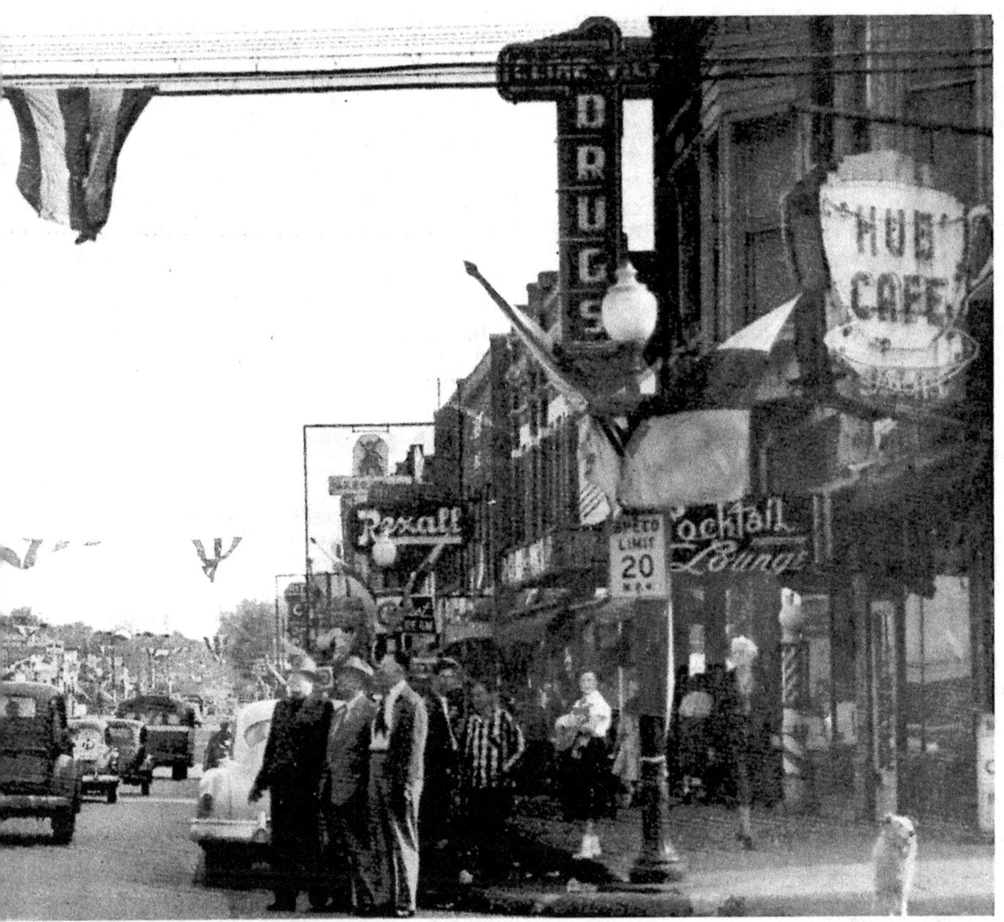

Illinois Avenue looking south from Main Street, note two-way traffic.   *--Southern Illinoisan--*

President Morris confronted the raiders and said, "We've all read about the raids at other schools. It's been fun. Now let's all go home and go to bed."

They did.

The growth of the university was not matched by a growth in the bar scene, however. Through the administrations of mayors John I. Wright and D. Blainey Miller in the 1950s and '60s, there were only a few more bars than at the turn of the century, and none of them were on South Illinois Avenue. The bars were mostly clustered on North Washington Street -- the levee -- and they were closed at midnight and on Sundays. Downtown Carbondale consisted of a few small shops and a lot of trees and frame houses. By state law the sale of alcohol was prohibited within 1,500 feet of the university, roughly to College Street, and a city ordinance prohibited liquor establishments within 100 feet of Holden Hospital, which was on South Illinois Avenue between College and Cherry, where today's First National Bank parking lot is.

Part of the reason for the non-proliferation of bars was the conservative nature of the community. But it was also said the cozy relationship between Mayor and Liquor Commissioner Miller and the Bill Budslick family, who owned or had interests in ABC Liquor, LBJ Steakhouse, Cypress Lounge and the Longbranch Saloon, also inhibited competition in the liquor business. When affable, if naive, "reform" candidate David Keene was elected mayor in 1967, the only other package liquor store-lounge besides ABC was Leo's Place, next to the old train station, owned by the Palmier family. The only other bars were the Flamingo Lounge and Rumpus Room at 211 and 213 E. Main; Nick Master's Rathskeller in the basement of The Hub at Main and Illinois; Stan Hoye's newly opened Five O'Clock Club in the new Holiday Inn; and the Stumble Inn and Palm Tavern, two black bars on the levee. Three establishments, The Club at 408 S. Illinois, Ernie Fligor's Southern Barbecue, then at 217 N. Illinois, and the recently moved Pizza King, owned by Tom and Gwen Hunt at 308 S. Illinois, were licensed to sell beer with meals; and Colletti's on the west side and Engel's on the east side could serve liquor with meals. The five remaining liquor licenses were owned by private clubs: the Elks, VFW, American Legion, Eagles and Moose.

Under Keene the city made the transition from a commission to a city manager form of government, and the mayor also promised to open up the liquor business. Between April 1967 and May 1969, Liquor Commissioner Keene issued 11 new licenses. The majority of the new bars were adult lounges east of downtown, but two, Bonaparte's Retreat at 213 E. Main and The Golden Gauntlet at 315 S. Illinois, were large bars with loud rock music that attracted growing crowds of college students.

Still, the city resisted turning Illinois Avenue into a strip by rejecting licenses for The American Tap at 518 S. Illinois, Papa Caesar's in the Campus Shopping Center and the Purple Mousetrap at Illinois and Freeman. The reason given for the denials was that the locations were too near the school or the hospital. However, when the Purple Mousetrap applied for its license in April 1968 there was also some discussion of "law enforcement problems" in the area of the Campus Shopping Center on Freeman Street. Police Chief Jack Hazel noted the area had become a popular hangout for college students (see Carbondale After Dark I) and that it was "policed more than any other area of the city." Liquor Advisory Board Chairman Ward Morton added that it was a "very sensitive and highly explosive section of the city."

While the city was liberalizing some of its policies, the SIU Board of Trustees and the university administration still tended to treat students as if they were attending a parochial teachers' college. SIU's *in loco parentis* policies had changed little from the 1920s when coeds weren't allowed off campus without escorts. In the early '60s, "girls" living in dorms had an 11 p.m. curfew; freshman and sophomore males had to participate in Air Force ROTC; undergraduates weren't allowed to live off campus; and no one living on campus could have a car. As late as 1970 the only time members of both sexes were allowed in the same dorm room was every other Sunday afternoon.

But times were changing, and so were the students, who were becoming more liberal in their lifestyles as well as their politics. There was a growing interest in the great social issues of the day -- Vietnam and civil rights -- and also the major social issue at SIU -- visitation hours in the dorms. Morris was unprepared for -- and some said out of touch with -- the new breed of students who had descended on his school. Students who smoked pot, "cohabitated" and demonstrated on his lawn. Many of the new students were from Chicago and had come to SIU to get away from their parents, dodge the draft, or because they couldn't get accepted at any other school. A lot of them were brats; there is no other way to put it. Although SIU had not tightened its admission requirements, it had improved its curriculum, and thus had also attracted a lot of bright, idealistic students and teachers who wanted to build a new system as much as they wanted to tear down the old one.

One of the first activist groups at SIU was the Student Non-Violent Freedom Committee, a local chapter of the Student Non-Violent Coordinating Committee, a civil rights group founded by Julian Bond, Andrew Young and Stokely Carmichael, among others. SNFC was formed in 1962 to investigate race discrimination in Southern Illinois, especially Cairo. In 1963 a contingent of SNFC members spent the summer in Mississippi, setting up "freedom schools" and registering black voters. And in 1965,

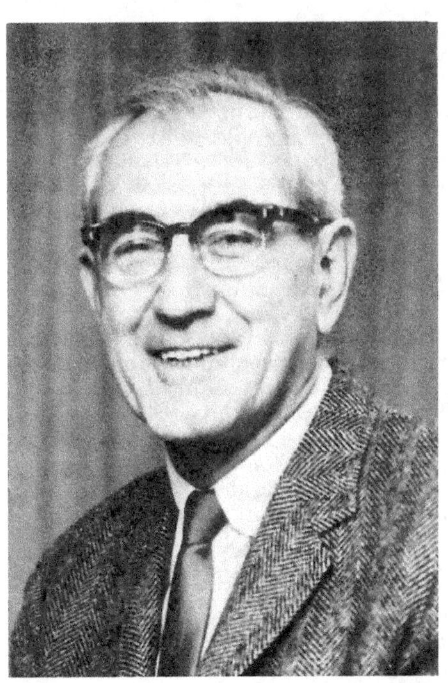

Morris and Old Main

When Delyte W. Morris became SIU's president in 1948, he rapidly transformed a small teacher's college into a major university, and Old Main symbolized the university's traditions. But in the late 1960s both Morris and Old Main became victims of the political unrest on campus.

--Southern Illinoisan--

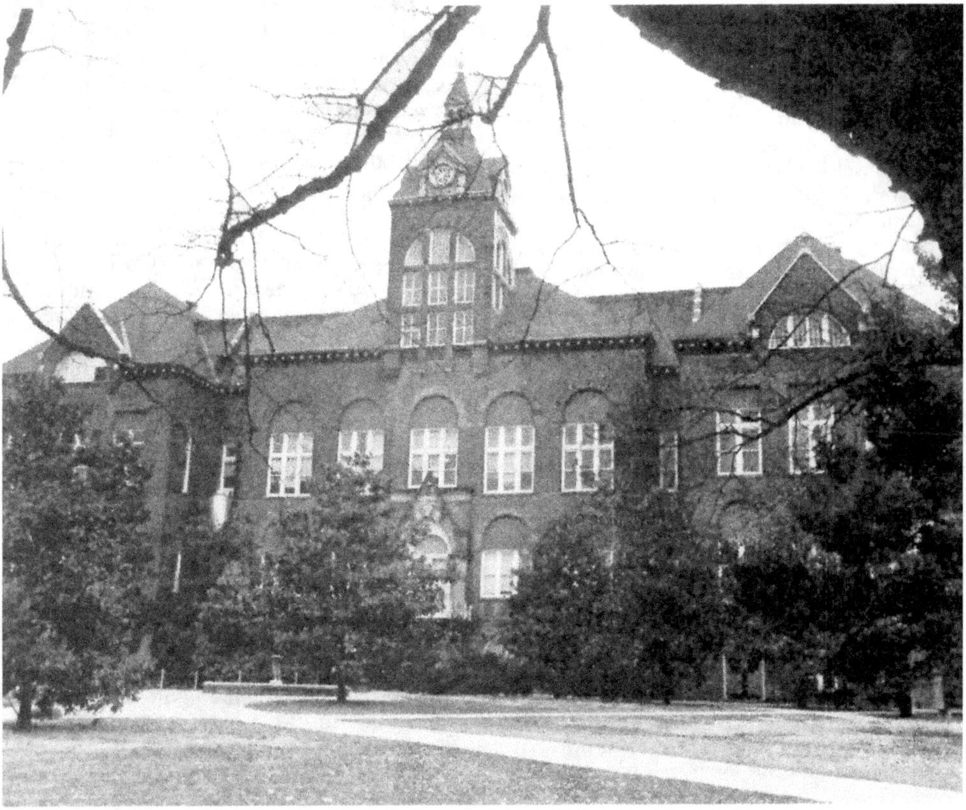

SNFC gave Carbondale its first taste of organized political protest.

1965

SNFC made front-page headlines in February that year when the group picketed the Family Fun drive-in restaurant (now J.R.'s restaurant, next to the Holiday Inn) for hiring "Negroes" to work only in the kitchen and not where they would be in contact with the customers. Hecklers shouted "nigger lovers" at them, and after a week of picketing, eight SNFC members were arrested for trespassing.

SNFC made an example out of Family Fun and was investigating the hiring practices of other businesses by sending "salt-and-pepper" teams around to apply for jobs. If a merchant hired the white but not the black, he was threatened with a picket and boycott, a classic civil rights tactic. The tactic worked for a while, but once the merchants caught on to SNFC's methods they became adept at spotting the phony jobseekers and would hire the black ones, knowing they would never show up for work.

SNFC's tactics were resented by the townspeople, but they also prompted a lot of people to re-examine race relations. More blacks were hired, and the city's advisory Human Relations Commission became more active.

Shortly after the Family Fun picketing, civil rights demonstrators were attacked in Selma, Ala., and the national SNCC decided to adopt the philosophy of "black power" advocate Stokely Carmichael, which was to create an autonomous black society without the help of whites. Carmichael was elected SNCC president and the white members were ousted. Some of the Carbondale SNFC members then formed a new group, the Radical Action Movement, which was a spinoff of the Free Speech student power movement at Berkeley.

1966

RAM attracted a broader cross-section of students than SNFC, as Greeks and dormies were just as upset as the radicals about female curfew hours and car restrictions. In the spring RAM held its first mass rally at what would become the staging area for a lot of student protests over the next four years -- the lawn in front of Morris Library. The rally, attended by several hundred people, was to protest the university's *in loco parentis* policy, and to demand the university adopt a student bill of rights and freedoms, which was endorsed by the American Association of University Professors.

The university didn't.

In addition to the new "radical" groups on campus, the sheer numbers of students attending SIU had changed the atmosphere of the community. Students had always hung out downtown, but by 1966 there were 20,000 of them, with long hair, raggedy clothes and God knows what sorts of chemicals in their bloodstreams.

In June, the week of final exams, there occurred an innocent water fight that would escalate into several nights of near rioting and foreshadow the more violent clashes between police and students in coming years. The disruption was apolitical, and it started with a spontaneous and spirited water fight between several hundred dormies in the area of the student housing on Wall Street. The festivities lasted from 10:30 p.m. to 2 a.m. Police arrived when some neighbors complained, and the water fight ended. There was an element of rebellion against the university's coed curfew rule, but it was mostly just a party, and a good time was had by all.

So good a time, in fact, that the next night, Monday, several hundred males staged a panty raid of sorts at Woody Hall, which at the time was a women's dorm. According to press accounts, some of the coeds egged the males on by shouting unspecified "obscenities" from their windows. When police arrived at the scene, the crowd scattered and re-formed at another women's dorm, Neely Hall, where it was greeted by women's undergarments sailing out of 17th story windows. The crowd swelled to more than a thousand people as someone pulled a fire alarm in the women's dorm, requiring an evacuation of the building. The police responded with tear gas and some shoving. Similar incidents occurred that night at U-City, 600 Freeman and the Egyptian dorm on University Avenue, with the cops always in close and ever more irritated pursuit. No major injuries or property damage were reported, although 120 student I.D.s were taken by police, and the university summarily suspended seven students and "disciplined" 50 others. In a special edition of the *Daily Egyptian*, President Morris deplored the "mob action of 2 percent," and called for the students to desist.

It might seem cliche today, but in 1966 it was very much in vogue to claim "police brutality," and that is exactly what the students did. By 10 p.m. Tuesday, a rowdy crowd of 600 young people had congregated in the area of the Campus Shopping Center. The area was further congested by thousands of curious townspeople and college students who were "scooping the loop" in their automobiles. Some of the students in the crowd began to chant "cops eat shit" and others threw eggs and rocks at the cars of the gawkers and the police, who had come to investigate. A short section of University Avenue west of the island was taken over by the students, garbage cans were tipped over and a trash fire was started in the street.

The police arrested five people who allegedly set the fire, but they did not try to break up the crowd. Angered by the arrests, and emboldened by the restraint exhibited by the police, the mob moved up Illinois Avenue and staged a "sit-down" at the intersection of Main and Illinois. The cops rerouted traffic and would not be provoked, so some of the students blocked the IC tracks. Sure enough, along came a freight train, and the students scattered just in time to avoid a senseless tragedy.

Next, the students "marched" several blocks east to the police station, which at the time was next to the old City Hall at Main and Marion, to demand the release of the five students arrested earlier. At 4 a.m., the state police stepped in. Troopers with yellow helmets and long riot sticks formed a line across Main Street, and backed by city and university police they drove the protesters back toward campus.

No major injuries or property damage were reported, but the city took a number of precautions the next day, one of which was to cancel the live music for the University High School "last fling" yearbook party outside Pulliam Hall, which was near the riot area. It never made the newspaper, but as the 15-year-old rhythm guitarist for the Breakaways, the band scheduled to play that night, I never forgot.

Canceling the live music may have been a good idea, however, because by 10 p.m. Wednesday an unruly crowd of 2,000 students again had congregated near University and Mill streets. This time the police quickly moved into the crowd, swinging their riot sticks. The melee lasted for an hour as lines of police stalked fleeing students back and forth across the Moo 'n' Cackle parking lot near the Campus Shopping Center. Police arrested 23 people, and, according to press accounts, a fire department pumper truck was ready to be used if the crowd had attempted another march downtown.

The disturbances fizzled out as a cold spell set in and school ended. But in the wake of the panty raid, the city and university did some soul searching and decided that to avoid a repeat occurrence they should provide students with some enjoyable activities to relieve the pressure of final exam time. Hence the concept of "Fun City, Carbondale style," was born. The next time final exam time rolled around, the coed curfew was extended to 2 a.m., the library and the Student Center were open until midnight, there was free coffee, free Three Stooges movies and free outdoor rock band concerts.

1967

The next year, Illinois Avenue and University Avenue became one-way streets, and SIU elected its first black Homecoming queen. There were no mass disturbances that year, but student unrest continued to grow -- and become more organized. In May, sophomore Ray Lenzi was elected student body president as a member of the RAM-backed Action Party. (Lenzi was one of the founders of the innovative SIU Free School in 1966.)

The school newspaper, the *Daily Egyptian,* reflected the views of the administration and ran cartoons on its news pages such as one from Shoemaker of *Chicago American* showing a scruffy folksinger with a guitar and goatee standing in front of two pictures of a scruffy Lenin and a scruffy Trotsky. The caption reads, "Notice any family resemblance?"

However, the "KA" page, an independent student-edited opinion and satire page published once a week in the *DE,* was devoting more space to anti-war views and increasingly critical attacks on university administrators. In May KA published an article by The Local Anarchist, an already controversial and anonymous KA writer, urging the students to rebel against the university's dorm visitation rules. The column suggested the students express their protest individually and chided them for being too "apathetic" to "take to the streets" as they did the year before.

Morris hit the roof. After KA editors refused to reveal the identity of The Local Anarchist, Morris put a hold on their enrollment and suspended publication of the page. There followed a short legal squabble involving the First Amendment and the American Civil Liberties Union. Eventually the students were allowed to re-enroll, and KA was allowed to publish, though not in the *DE.*

The following fall several members of RAM, including black Marxist Bill Moffett, formed an anti-war group called the Southern Illinois Peace Committee. The SIPC's first action was reported as a "small but cheerful" protest of Navy recruiters at the student center. Later that fall the SIPC held a silent vigil and march through downtown Carbondale to mourn the dead in Vietnam, and organized a bus ride for about 50 SIU students to Washington, D.C., to participate in one of the more famous anti-war demonstrations, the march on the Pentagon.

1968

In 1968 the university took a number of steps to deal with student unrest, many of which backfired. For instance, in February the campus TV station, WSIU, bowed to political pressure and canceled the telecast of a PBS documentary called "Inside North Vietnam." The cancellation raised a storm of protest from the faculty as well as the students, and WSIU later aired the show. Shortly before Schneider and Mae Smith towers opened in April, the administration announced less restrictive curfew hours for sophomore, junior and senior coeds. The

students responded by staging a mass rally to demand that all students be allowed to determine their own hours.

In April the SIPC staged another march through downtown, and May 2 they again protested the presence of military recruiters in the Student Center. Only this time the protesters weren't so "cheerful" and locked arms to keep people away from the recruiters. There was a near confrontation between the SIPC and hecklers, and SIU security made the demonstrators leave.

The recruiter protest was overshadowed by a sit-in at Morris' office the same day by a dozen SIU students with bags over their heads. On the bags were written their student I.D. numbers, and the demonstration was intended to protest the administration's impersonal attitude toward students and the lack of student rights on campus.

Five days later, Monday night, May 7, several hundred members of the various student groups met on campus to try to form a coalition. The meeting was chaired by former student Stuart Novick, a 23-year-old anarchist with a flair for the theatrical. Grievances discussed at the meeting ranged from visitation hours in the dorms to student control of the *Daily Egyptian* and the campus police. The tone of the meeting was militant, and some speakers suggested burning down Morris' house.

Several hours later a bomb exploded in the Agriculture Building on the campus. To this day it is not known who set off the bomb. No radical group ever claimed responsibility, and some suspected the university had bombed its own building as an excuse to crack down on the activists. But at the time there were a lot of students on the fringes of the radical groups who just liked to make bombs, start fires and call in false bomb threats, so it's anyone's guess.

Tuesday afternoon Morris "banned" Novick from the campus for his "incendiary remarks," and he canceled plans for an appearance by black power advocate Stokely Carmichael. The Carmichael cancellation was a result of the high tensions on the campus and in the town: Less than a month before, Martin Luther King's assassination had sparked rioting across the country and disruptions on Carbondale's northeast side that were serious enough to put the National Guard on stand-by alert. The cancellation was viewed as racist by the students, and about 200 of SIU's 1,750 black students protested in front of Morris' office.

That night about 150 members of the newly formed Student Coalition met again, this time off campus at the Wesley Foundation so Novick wouldn't be arrested. The group was discussing issues and tactics when SIPC member Bill Moffett stirred up the crowd with a high-powered speech, challenging the mostly white audience to show their support for the blacks who were sitting in at Morris' office. There was some disagreement by coalition leaders as to whether to join the sit-in, but the rank and file voted with their feet and headed over to Morris' house.

Shortly after the additional bodies swelled the crowd around Morris' house and office, several blacks bolted past police and into the office. According to the *Southern Illinoisan*, the seven-or-so students were "milling around" inside when a police officer shouted, "Are we going to let them get away with this? Hell no!" The police chased the students out using their clubs, and dispersed the rest of the crowd. Five blacks were arrested, and two were treated for head and rib injuries.

The next morning Morris issued a terse statement for which he would be elected man of the year by the Chamber of Commerce: "An unruly mob broke into my office. They were driven out by security officers. Some are in jail, some are in the hospital. All are expelled."

The blacks demanded amnesty for those arrested and continued their protest by jamming the president's office switchboard with nuisance calls and threatening a mass withdrawal from school. Friday, four SIPC members went to Morris' office and tried to present a list of demands that included banning military recruiters and ROTC from campus and providing information about whether the university was conducting any military-subsidized research.

The administration, feeling besieged from all sides, refused to accept the list of demands saying the proper channel to voice student grievances was through student government. Dean of Students Wilbur Moulton convened the Student Senate and requested that it "reaffirm" its role as "the appropriate channel for student petitions, requests and grievances." Moulton said the university was making a good-faith effort to set up an orderly mechanism for presenting student complaints to the administration, but the SIPC argued the university was trying to muzzle student dissent by using the senate as a bottleneck, where students would be making their protests to each other rather than to the administration.

The senate had seldom been asked by the administration to take itself seriously, and it could not resist the temptation to approve Moulton's resolution. But Student Body President Ray Lenzi vetoed it, and the senate subsequently passed an amended resolution that granted students the right to "go outside the channels when necessary to gain students' rights." The senate also passed a resolution urging the administration to "take all steps to remove" the court cases pending against the students arrested for breaking into Morris' office.

As May turned to June, things began to quiet down, but June 2, President Morris had Stuart Novick arrested for trespassing after he went to the Student Center at the invitation of SBP Lenzi to address the Student Senate during its annual banquet.

The university then denied Novick's registration for summer quarter because of his "incendiary" remarks at the May 2 Student Coalition meeting, and the ACLU filed a federal lawsuit alleging the university was violating Novick's First Amendment right to free speech.

In the midst of Novick's hassles with the university, he made headlines again when his van was discovered burned on a rural road. Novick told reporters the van was burned by someone who said he was a "professional killer" and wanted Novick to leave town. But he told intimates that the burning of the van was his "contribution to the revolution" -- he had burned it himself.

The summer of 1968 was the time of the "Days of Rage" and the Democratic

National Convention in Chicago. That summer the university reorganized its governing structure and made Robert MacVicar chancellor of SIU-C and John Rendleman chancellor of SIU-E. Morris kept his title as SIU system president, but in his new role he was not supposed to be as directly involved in operations at either campus. Despite the shuffling of titles, the administration continued its "hawkish" policies toward student dissidents. Publication of the KA page was suspended again (this time permanently), the SIPC was denied the use of campus facilities, and the board of trustees expelled 11 students who had blocked Army recruiters at the Student Center May 2. After a private *tete-a-tete* between Novick and Morris, the federal lawsuit was settled out of court and Novick was allowed to enroll for the fall term, on probation.

As if President Morris hadn't had enough aggravation, in August the SIU Board of Trustees announced it was going to build him a $250,000 mansion (which he would never live in and eventually would cost $1 million). The biographers and historians may haggle over whose idea University House was, but it couldn't have come at a worse time. Even though it would have allowed Morris to live somewhere else besides the favorite campground of protesters, the mansion became a symbol of Morris' alleged cavalier attitude toward students, and it also gave the Illinois Board of Higher Education the opening it was looking for to diminish Morris' influence in the General Assembly.

1969

In 1969 an underground newspaper, the *Big Muddy Gazette*, started publishing in Carbondale. The motto of the paper was "If we ain't got news, we'll make it," which it did in March by printing a caricature of President Morris in the nude on the front page. SIU responded by banning the paper from the campus, causing another First Amendment squabble, which the university lost.

Following the pattern of previous years, as the spring riot season rolled around, campus unrest increased. On April 25 about 500 students turned out for an afternoon rally to demand the abolishment of coed hours. In the past the curfew issue had mostly been a student desire to nookie after midnight, but now a newly formed Women's Liberation Front, headed by Judy Michaels, was addressing the obvious but previously unprotested fact that the curfew was a blatant case of sex discrimination.

On May 5 about 150 students protested at a "salute to Morris" banquet, which was to honor him for his 20 years of service to the university, by marching through the Arena where the dinner was being held shouting "Sieg Heil." May 14 the Student Senate passed a resolution calling for the end of coed hours, and on May 16 there was an anti-war rally. On May 21 about 2,000 students protested coed hours by staying outside Brush Towers an hour after the 11 p.m. curfew.

Then, on May 26, about 1,500 students took their curfew protest onto President Morris' lawn. The protesters decided to hold a vigil outside Morris' house until the administration agreed to let coeds

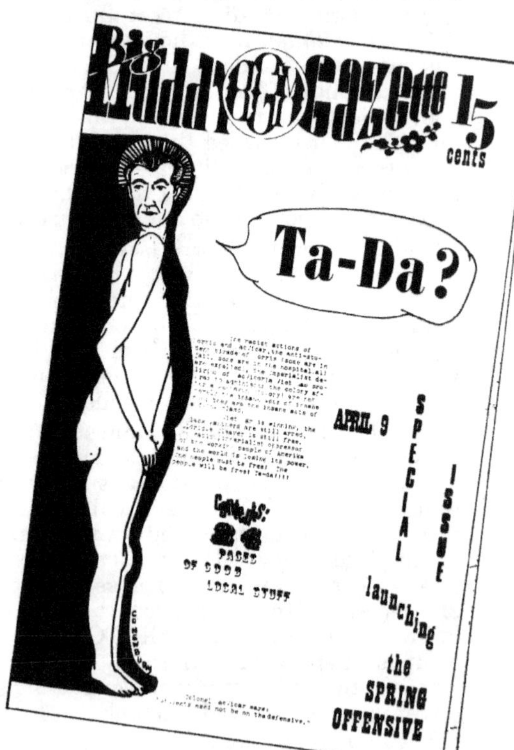

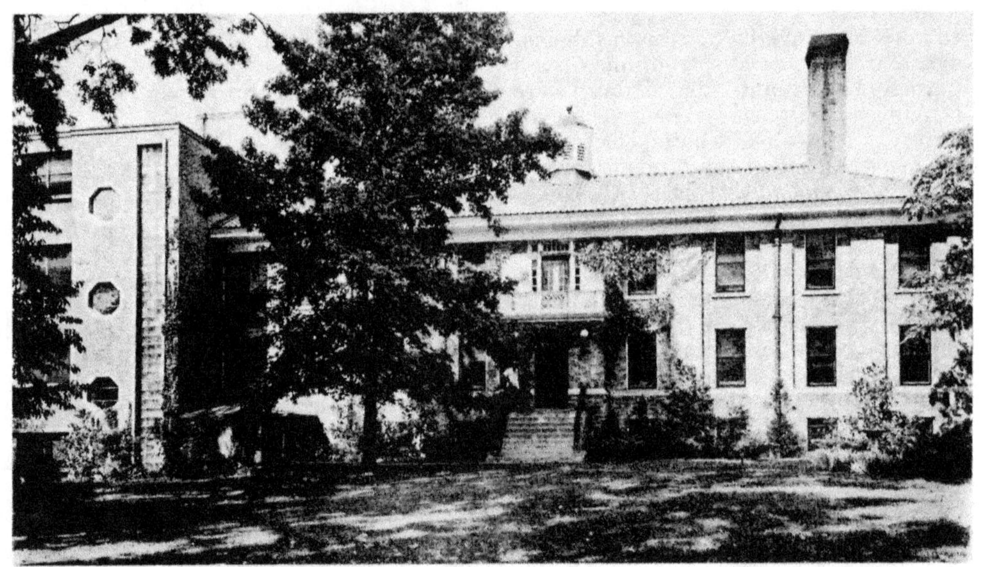

Holden Hospital was the town's first health facility. In the late 1960s the hospital's spacious lawn became a popular place for young people to hang out. Shortly after the May 1970 riots the hospital was closed and a fence erected around the grounds. The First National Bank bought the property and uprooted the trees to construct a parking lot.   *--Southern Illinoisan--*

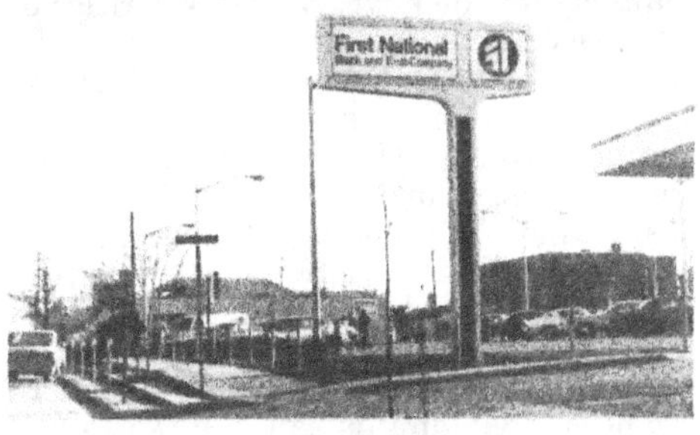

determine their own hours. A band began to play, joints were rolled and bottles of wine were opened. At 10:30 p.m. the administration announced the protesters could stay through the night if the band stopped playing. About 30 police with helmets and sticks waited behind Morris' house in case students attempted another break-in. The band left, as did all but about 75 of the protesters.

The next day, Monday, the vigil continued as several hundred demonstrators returned to Morris' lawn. Someone started a hunger strike and a dummy of Morris was burned in effigy. To head off a confrontation, Chancellor MacVicar announced two days of "voluntary discussions" in which teachers were encouraged to depart from their prepared lectures to allow discussion of current events in their classes. As "voluntary discussions" had been occurring in classes for some time, the announcement had little impact.

The vigil, which was really more like a party, continued until June 2 when the SIU chapter of Students for a Democratic Society (SDS) and other student leaders withdrew their support because some crowd members were becoming rowdy and carrying molotov cocktails. School ended, and it appeared the disruptions would subside for a while, but on June 8 SIU's most revered building, Old Main, was destroyed by fire. The cause was arson, and on a third-floor chalkboard were scrawled some obscenities and the words "Old Main is burning." (Indeed, the whole town had been burning. Between the fire at Old Main and the bombing of the Ag Building the previous year, there had been more than a dozen attempted or threatened bombings and at least as many arson fires or false alarms in campus buildings or houses on the east side.) It was never determined who burned Old Main, but many were convinced the fire was a result of student unrest, and the already hateful feelings of townspeople, police and officials toward student activists increased.

A month later, the university's acceptance of a $1 million grant from the U.S. Agency for International Development for a Center for Vietnamese Studies Programs on the Carbondale campus would outrage the campus activists as much as the burning of Old Main had angered the townspeople. AID funded a variety of social service programs in underdeveloped nations, including an SIU mission in Southeast Asia to train teachers. But AID had also served as a front for the CIA, and the cry "off AID" would be heard a lot on the campus for the next five years. Critics of the Viet center could never prove it was assisting in the war effort. In fact, its activities were mostly academic, compiling a library of Vietnamese books and periodicals, starting one of the first Vietnamese language classes in the country, writing a dictionary and history of Vietnam, publishing a journal and bringing in speakers to talk about the history and culture of the region. But some of the administrators hired to run the center, and especially Wesley Fishel, were associated with a University of Michigan project, funded by AID, which allegedly had trained South Vietnamese police in counter-insurgency tactics. And it could be argued that constant pressure put on the SIU center by its critics prevented it from ever implementing those sorts of "programs."

1970

The riot season started early in 1970 and school ended early. At the end of January the SIPC held a mock trial of Viet center advisor Wesley Fishel at the Student Center. "Fishel" was found "guilty," and the sentence was a pie in the face. The guerrilla theater event was a publicity stunt to create interest in an anti-Viet center rally to be held several weeks later. But after the incident several plain-clothes SIU security officers asked one of the participants to step upstairs to the Student Center director's office. The student attempted to flee, a scuffle ensued, fists were thrown, and six people were arrested.

The next day, on Jan. 30, a crowd gathered at the Student Center at noon to protest the arrests. They marched to Woody Hall, where the Viet Center was housed on the third floor, to demand information about the center. The *Southern Illinoisan* gave a blow-by-blow account of what happened next: Center officials hemmed and hawed, and at 1 p.m. a false fire alarm was set off. As the employees filed out of Woody about 100 protesters entered the building and took over three of the six rooms used by the Viet center. About 2 p.m. SIU police ordered the protesters out of the building. The crowd exited and the police entered the building. A scuffle between students and police broke out in the courtyard of Woody, and one person was arrested. Security Chief Thomas Leffler then requested assistance from Carbondale and state police, who showed up about 2:40 p.m. Some of the police appeared at the University Avenue entrance to Woody and the crowd came around to the front of the building. Three buses pulled up and parked in front of Woody, apparently to be used to cart off demonstrators.

Before the police were able to take any action, however, classes changed at 2:50 p.m. and the crowd grew to more than 500 persons. Some in the crowd threw apples and tomatoes at the police, who retreated inside the building. Shortly after 3 p.m. the administration decided to provide the information the demonstrators had requested, but asked for an hour to get it copied. At 3:45 p.m. student leaders Jon Taylor, Bill Moffett and Nick Fera climbed onto a second-floor overhang and through a bullhorn pleaded for patience. The crowd got restless as the 4 p.m. deadline passed, but at 4:15 p.m. it quieted when copies of the information were passed out. Next, the buses were driven away, but the protesters still did not disperse.

At 4:30 p.m. three Carbondale policemen decided to test the water. Boldly they strode out of Woody and got into their police car. The crowd gathered around the car, and Judy Michaels, head of the

Women's Liberation Front who had made headlines the previous year for disobeying the curfew, began to let the air out of a tire. Patrolman Jim Rossiter grabbed Michaels, who reportedly had to be carried off and placed in another police car. As the police strugged with her, the crowd began pushing and throwing mud. The remaining 40 police inside Woody then went to their comrades' aid.

At 4:50 p.m. police formed parallel lines across West Grand Avenue to clear the street for five o'clock traffic from the library parking lot. A half-hour later the protesters were still there, and the police formed another line. Elwyn Zimmerman, assistant dean of students, used a bullhorn to tell the students they had 15 minutes to disperse. "Hell no, we won't go," responded the students. As the clock ticked down, crowd leaders argued with police about how to resolve the Mexican stand-off peacefully. Jon Taylor suggested police leave first because they were the ones holding the clubs. The cops were skeptical, and at 5:50 p.m. they began to advance up West Grand Avenue, as if to arrest the protesters. The crowd retreated but did not break up, and after the police had advanced about 10 yards Zimmerman came running out of Woody Hall to confer with police again. At 5:52 p.m. Carbondale Police Chief Jack Hazel shouted "All Carbondale boys, let's go home," and the Carbondale police left the ranks. The crowd cheered, and then the state police left. In five minutes the area was almost completely cleared; and the campus temporarily returned to normal.

Several weeks later a coalition of anti-war groups calling itself the Coalition organized a weekend of "Off AID" activities, which included a march through downtown Carbondale and a talk by journalist I.F. Stone. The event drew about 300 protesters from out of town, and it got out of hand. Friday evening, Feb. 20, a march was staged through downtown Carbondale, which conference organizers later said was not on the agenda. Many of those who participated in the march were from out of town and they were protesting a variety of issues, including student rights and the decision in the Chicago 7 conspiracy trial, as well as the Viet studies center. The march started on the sidewalk but at several points surged into the streets as those in the front of the line chanted "the streets belong to the people." After parading up Illinois Avenue and down University Avenue the crowd seemed to be breaking up. But it re-formed in the Student Center while conference organizers tried to get them to attend a dance, which was on the agenda.

But someone started a fire in a trashcan in the hallway, and the police moved in and evicted about 300 people. The "protesters" stood outside the Student Center and chanted "kill the pigs." Violence erupted when firecrackers and rocks were thrown at the police. But police efforts to break up the crowd sent it heading toward downtown again, breaking windows along the way.

At noon Saturday, the Coalition held its scheduled march through downtown, which was peaceful and attended by about 1,500 people. Near the end of the march there was a minor confrontation as about 100 hecklers threw firecrackers at the protesters and shouted "off you." The 1,500 marchers then joined another 2,000 protesters in front of Morris Library where speakers condemned the Viet center. While the Coalition was holding its rally, city, university and police officials huddled and decided to request the National Guard, which sent about 140 soldiers. But the evening was uneventful, and the soldiers were not deployed.

At the end of March, Harold Calhoun, part-owner of the Golden Gauntlet bar, announced plans for a Woodstock-type rock festival just south of Carbondale off the Giant City Blacktop Road. Called May Fest, organizers were making preparations for 100,000 people. Concerned citizens filed a lawsuit, and a permanent injunction was granted May 2, just days before the festival was to begin. On May 1 President Nixon announced the incursion into Cambodia and on May 4 four people were killed during demonstrations at Kent State. Those events would set off a week of intense disruptions across the country, and in Carbondale would force SIU to close before the end of the term (see "Seven Days in May"). The disruptions included takeovers of campus buildings, riots in downtown, martial law, 600 National Guardsmen, police violence and more than 350 arrests. Some of the impetus for the rioting was anger over cancellation of the May Fest. But one can only wonder what would have happened if 100,000 hippies had been camped just outside of town when the riots erupted.

The night SIU closed, May 12, about 5,000 jubilant students, activists and street people had a street party on South Illinois Avenue. The event would mark a change in the type of disruptions that would plague downtown Carbondale in the future. The war would wind down, the university would drop the last of its *in loco parentis* policies, and student activities would change from protesting to partying.

After the riots, the city and university went through another round of soul searching. President Morris retired, Chancellor MacVicar made a lateral move to the University of Oregon, and Mayor Keene declined to run for re-election. The city passed a parade ordinance to control crowds without violating their rights, and SIU created an "interim policy on demonstrations" for the same purpose. The new policy prohibited rallies anywhere but in a special "free forum" area in front of Anthony Hall, and also set up a mechanism for disciplining protesters who violated university regulations.

In an effort to heal wounds, the city, university and student government made plans for a gala "Alternative '71" festival to be held in May. Alternative '71 was to be an alternative to rioting, and included a carnival on the campus, movies, dances and concerts. And in October the city council approved an ordinance allowing bars to be open on Sunday.

But not everyone was in a forgive-and-forget mood. The university put enrollment holds on 60 students involved in the May riots and the board of trustees denied tenure to philosophy professor and Viet center critic Doug Allen. Townspeople abandoned downtown, Jackson County Sheriff Ray Dillinger advised Carbondale merchants to arm themselves (some did), and in June local police agencies and the Illinois Bureau of Investigation arrested 29 persons, most of them students, on drug charges. Some heroin was found, but most of the charges were for medium amounts of marijuana, LSD and amphetamines. En mass drug busts would become commonplace in coming years, but this was the first, followed by a bust of 16 people in December.

Post-riot jitters also may have been partly responsible for a 90-minute shoot-out Nov. 12 between police and Black Panthers in which 10 persons were injured, nine arrested and none convicted. The shooting began about 5 a.m. when two SIU security police stopped a suspicious van at the corner of Grand and Illinois avenues. A black man in the van fired at the police, wounding one in the leg, and police said the man fled on foot toward the levee. Carbondale and SIU police converged on the levee, and several moments later a black man on foot wounded a Carbondale policeman parked near the Black Panther Community Center at 401 N. Washington St., just north of the levee. Two other Carbondale patrolmen chased the man down an alley and lost sight of him. But then they came across two armed blacks running from the Panther headquarters. More shots were fired and the two blacks were wounded and arrested. Then shots were fired from inside the house, and all hell broke loose.

In 1970 the Carbondale Police Department did not issue department weapons, so police officers had bought their own, and they had an arsenal, including large caliber pistols, rifles, shotguns and several automatic weapons, including a machine gun. The police surrounded the house, and using neighboring houses for cover, they peppered the Panther house with bullets and tear gas. From the second floor of the house, three Panthers returned the fire, and for the next hour and a half the neighborhood was a battle zone. Neighbors were trapped in cross fire, and one was wounded when he walked onto his front porch to see what was going on.

Meanwhile, back at the abandoned van at Grand and Illinois, two SIU police were guarding the vehicle, waiting for a tow truck. At about 7:30 a.m., a car cruised past and a black man jumped out and fired a shotgun, wounding the two officers in the legs. The man fled toward campus where he was later apprehended.

About 8 a.m. a neighbor living across the street from the Panther house, civil rights activist Elbert Simon, got permission from the police to enter the house and attempt to negotiate a surrender. A cease-fire was arranged, and three men on the first floor of the house came out in their underwear and were arrested for attempted murder and taken to jail. (The men, Jamaican SIU students, were later released when it was determined they were not Panthers but rented the apartment below the Panther headquarters, and were trapped when gunfire erupted.) Police also evacuated a woman and her 10 children who had been trapped in a home just north of the Panther center, which had drawn fire when a policeman used the kitchen for cover; and a man and six children were evacuated from behind the Panther house where they had been trapped when another officer used the cellar for cover.

For the next half hour Simon talked with one wounded Panther inside as two other Panthers sat on a second-floor porch and led the growing crowd in Black Panther cheers. At 8:30 a.m. the three Panthers surrendered and were charged with attempted murder.

Before the first of three scheduled trials on the case the next year, the two Panthers who had been shot while running from the house (one of whom was a high school student) had their charges reduced from attempted murder to unlawful use of weapons and were put on probation. At the second trial -- a long and well-attended jury trial in which the defendants were the three people who were in the house at the end -- State's Attorney Richard Richman tried to prove the shooting at the van and the shoot-out at the house were related, and that the Panthers in the house had fired at the police first. Defense attorneys argued the police fired first and that the defendants thought they were going to be killed and returned the fire in self-defense. After the longest trial in Jackson County history, 24 days, it took the jury only three hours to dismiss all 42 charges against the defendants.

Charges against the man who allegedly shot the police officers near the van were later dropped after he jumped bail and was imprisoned in another state for armed robbery.

There are a lot of maybes about the Nov. 12, 1970, shoot-out. But one thing is certain. It's a miracle no one was killed.

1971

Shortly after New Year's Day, SIU-E Chancellor John Rendleman opened the lid on the Paul Powell shoebox scandal, Secretary of Defense Melvin Laird announced the "Vietnazation" of the war and the Charlie Manson clan was convicted of ritual murders in California. In Carbondale, once again more than the temperature began heating up as spring approached, but this time the disruptions had a different twist. On the weekend of April 17 and 18, crowds of people who had gone downtown to drink, not to demonstrate, took over the street in an apparently spontaneous response to overcrowded bars and the midnight closing time.

About 300 people took over the street at midnight Friday in front of Merlin's, the former Golden Gauntlet at 315 S. Illinois. Police blocked off the street at Cherry and did not attempt to disperse the crowd. Word spread, and the next evening more than 1,000 students, street people and curious out-of-towners congregated on the sidewalks of downtown. At 10:30 p.m. the new mayor, Neal Eckert, ordered the bars closed, and everyone went into the street. No property damage or injuries were reported either night, although some glass was broken and small street fires were started.

Sunday, black folksinger Richie Havens and the most popular local rock band, Coal Kitchen, gave a free concert in the Moo parking lot, and police patrolled downtown on foot that evening. The concert, police and chilly weather were credited for averting another street takeover.

Although the crowds were definitely apolitical, there was a certain militancy about them, similar to the panty-raiders of 1966, that the city had to take seriously. So several days later the city and SIU announced a series of free weekend concerts and dances in the Moo parking lot and on campus to give the students something to do besides block the street. This, in addition to the elaborate Alternative '71 activities scheduled to start in May. (One of the Alternative '71 events was a "Pigs vs. Freaks" softball game pitting Carbondale police against student radicals.)

Meanwhile, Illinois Bureau of Investigation Director Mitchell Ware staged a clumsy publicity stunt to claim credit for "averting trouble between students," which further tarnished the town's reputation upstate. On the morning of April 23 about 120 area police and IBI agents raided houses in various Southern Illinois communities and arrested 44 people on illegal weapons and drug charges. Siezed were bazookas, machine guns, dynamite, drugs and drug paraphernalia. Eleven of the people arrested were SIU students. By Wednesday afternoon Ware had paraded the bazookas and hookas in front of the state media and boasted the raids had prevented student violence.

The next day, after the media had a chance to digest the information, they realized the students had all been arrested on drug charges only (and small amounts of drugs at that), and that the weapons had apparently come from White Hat-Ku Klux Klan types and were bound for Cairo, not Carbondale. But the damaging publicity had already been done.

The next week, chilly weather, police foot patrols on Illinois Avenue and a street dance in the Moo parking lot that lasted until 2 a.m. kept the strip open. Police mingled with the crowd and told drinkers to pour out their alcoholic beverages, but did not arrest them. About a dozen people were ticketed for under-age drinking and for urinating in the alley behind Pizza King, but there were no major incidents.

In conjunction with plans for national anti-war protests set for May, the SIPC and a new group, the Student Mobilization Committee, organized a week of anti-war, off AID and Kent State memorial activities on the anniversary of the Carbondale riots. To generate publicity for the event, the SIPC announced it would napalm a dog. The group decided to violate the new demonstration policy by holding rallies outside the free forum area, and made plans to form a human chain around Woody Hall to close down the Viet center.

The SIPC did not follow through with its promise to napalm a dog, but it did stage a candlelight parade through downtown May 5, after getting a parade permit from the city. About 250 people attended the march, which was uneventful. The students then sat for an hour on the lawn across from Woody Hall and listened to speakers, some of whom urged more violent action. SIPC leader Bill Moffett said, "The majority of us are here because we are genuinely concerned."

"I'm here to party," someone yelled from the lawn.

The SIPC invited the crowd to stay all night, but a light rain and lack of interest caused most of the people to leave before midnight. The next day a group of people joined hands and paraded through Woody Hall. The crowd was small and did not have much direction. After several hours of minor disruptions the rally broke up.

The city and university continued to hold multiple free concerts on weekends, which did keep the kids off the streets, literally. The largest of the free concerts in 1971 was held behind the Newman Center Friday, May 15, and featured Chuck Berry. More than 1,000 people showed up for the concert, which included several bands, a picnic and permission to drink alcohol.

But there were problems with the sound system, Berry showed up several hours late and left early, and women libbers objected to the sexist lyrics in the songs. During Coal Kitchen's set some women began accusing the band of being sexist. Carla Peyton, lead singer for the group, cut them to the quick. "This band ain't sexist," she shouted through the mike. "I should know because I'm a lesbian."

School ended peacefully, and on schedule.

The first weekend of the fall 1971 term, Sept. 24, about 1,000 students staged another street takeover on South Illinois Avenue. Again, the purpose was to party, not protest, and police said freshmen and sophomores too young to drink were the first people into the street.

During a city council discussion of the problem Oct. 22, Mayor Eckert referred to South Illinois Avenue as "the downtown strip," which may have been the first time a city official publicly used that term to describe the area.

Various suggestions for solving the crowd control problems were offered at the meeting, including fenced-in beer gardens, dispersing the bars, lowering the drinking age, establishing pubs on campus and making downtown into a mall. The council finally opted to continue its policy of trying to keep the street open, but closing it to avoid confrontations.

As more troops were withdrawn from Southeast Asia and more student rights were granted, the large student coalitions fragmented into smaller groups, and tactics changed from mass action to lobbying and service providing. The SIPC and Student Mobe continued to organize rallies, marches and teach-ins against the war and Viet center, but other student and community activists organized a women's center, a tenant union, a gay union, a Public Interest Research Group (Ralph "Nader's Raiders"); drug centers Aeon and Synergy; a halfway house, Hill House; a prison work release center, House of Glass; an environmental center; a sex counseling center; and a Christian coffeehouse, the Upper Room. Other student trends included a renewed interest in the "back-to-the-land" homesteading movement, Transcendental Meditation, Hari Krishna and Scientology. (The first meditation sect to organize in Carbondale was the Ananda Marga house, a yoga and social service commune that began in 1969 and is still active.)

But the university administration and board of trustees made a series of moves that gave the students -- and the faculty -- more reasons to take to the streets. The board reaffirmed its decision to fire Viet center critic Doug Allen, and denied a pay raise to another center critic, history professor C. Harvey Gardner. The administration tried to stop some allegedly pornographic films from being shown during a feminist conference, and plans were made to fire 104 teachers for reasons that were political, as well as financial. But perhaps the most inflam-matory action the board took was to hire David R. Derge as SIU president in December. Derge had a reputation for not getting along with students, and he was a political ally of President Nixon. (Shortly after Derge was hired by SIU he played a role in Nixon's "China initiative" by accompanying an American ping pong team to Red China on the first cultural exchange between the two countries since the revolution.) The board's actions would result in lawsuits, censure by the American Association of University professors, and in May 1972, another near riot.

1972

In February, Carbondale was designated an "All-American City," and in April, the man who would become the strip's most influential nemesis, Carroll Fry, became city manager. But it was also another big year for the counter culture.

The largest crowd that gathered in Carbondale in 1972 consisted of blacks from universities throughout the Midwest who came to town in April to attend the Kappa Karnival. The carnival was a spring festival put on by Kappa Alpha Psi, a black social fraternity. It had started in 1951 as a small party for black SIU students at the fraternity house. But by the 1970s, Kappa Karnival had become one of the largest black social events in the country, attracting more than 5,000 people a year, and in 1972 it drew a record 10,000.

The three-day festival included a concert, dance, beauty pageant and carnival in the Arena. (In 1972 and in several other years until 1978, the city extended the drinking hour until 6 a.m. for Kappa weekend in the spring and Homecoming in the fall.) The highlight of the festival was a mile-long motorcade Saturday afternoon of slick-looking aces driving motorcycles, recreation vans and customized Cadillac pimpmobiles through downtown.

Although Kappa-goers never engaged in mass protests or street takeovers, other kinds of activities occurred that gave the festival a bad name. Kappa brought a lot of money into the community, but the merchants also considered Kappa Saturday the biggest shoplifting day of the year. There were usually a number of robberies and thefts over Kappa weekend, and what might be called the "annual crap game and stabbing." (Kappa continued to draw large numbers of people through 1976, when rainy weather forced the cool-car parade to be canceled. After that, participation dropped to about 2,000 people a year until 1979 and '80 when it appeared to be making a comeback, attracting about 5,000 people. But in 1981 the fraternity was suspended by the university for falling behind $18,000 on rent payments, and the festival has not been held since.)

In addition to allowing the bars to stay open until 6 a.m. for Kappa Karnival in 1972, the city council also tried to head off confrontations with white students by approving a plan to officially close South Illinois Avenue and provide carnival-like street parties on the strip for seven consecutive weekends in April and May. (At the same time, the council put a temporary freeze on issuing new liquor licenses on the strip.) The university also proceeded with plans for "Alternative '72," which included several weeks of free concerts, movies, a Maypole dance and another "pigs vs. freaks" softball game.

The street closings of 1972 provided a preview of the Halloween festivities several years later: Thousands of restless and intoxicated youths meandered up and down the street consuming alcohol and drugs in the open, street vendors made some money, but not much, and there were few incidents. One of the more popular activities was a dunking booth manned by Mayor Eckert, Councilman Hans Fischer, Carbondale Police Chief Jack Hazel and student radical Roger Leisner, among others. Another of the booths was rented by the New Burnside Community Church, a fundamentalist group. The church placed a haywagon in the middle of the street, and as partiers wandered past them they performed amplified Jesus music and delivered fire-and-brimstone sermons beseeching passersby to abandon their sinful ways.

They didn't.

The street parties and other diversions went well. Everyone -- students, townspeople, city and university officials -- seemed to be cooperating to avoid a repeat of 1970. But there was one person who did not cooperate. On May 6, President Richard M. Nixon announced a resumption of bombing in North Vietnam and the mining of Haiphong Harbor.

Campuses across the country erupted almost as they had after Kent State. Two protesters were shot by police at the University of New Mexico, and at the University of Illinois, students rampaged through downtown, breaking windows and looting.

At SIU, plans were made for marches, rallies and a boycott of classes, and several protesters began a 24-hour-a-day vigil at the new location of the Viet center, 511 S. Graham. The vigil was non-violent, but there were a lot of other protesters who apparently wanted to see a repeat of 1970.

Wednesday, May 10, about 1,000 people participated in a march through downtown. Parade organizers had intended it to be a quiet candlelight march, but things started to get out of hand when the group reached Walnut and Illinois. The marchers were supposed to head west on Walnut to the Viet center. But about 150 hot-heads broke away from the group and ran toward Main and Illinois, as student leaders tried to get them to stop. About 40 protesters sat in the intersection where the riots had started two years before, and police and student leaders worked together to get them to move without having a confrontation.

Student Body President-elect Jon Taylor grabbed a bullhorn and said, "We gotta work this out some way or we will be divided." He was jeered by the crowd, but eventually the group moved out of the intersection and headed down Washington Street toward the Viet center.

Once at the Viet center, rocks were thrown through windows as student leaders tried to persuade people from using violence. Bill Moffett made an emotional appeal for restraint, saying, "We cannot trash because we are going to lose and alienate a lot of students who are against the war." Convinced his appeal had worked, Moffett asked rhetorically, "Do you want to trash?" The crowd roared an affirmative reply.

One man in the crowd shouted, "Let's get to the nitty gritty, let's close the school," and about half the crowd headed to Brush Towers to get more people. That crowd grew to 1,000 people and headed back downtown, breaking windows along the way. They were tear-gassed by police, and then ran back to the Viet center. Police gassed there, and the crowd regrouped at Brush Towers.

At about 11:20 p.m., the students armed themselves with rocks and charged the SIU security office, then located in a frame house behind Brush Towers at the pedestrian overpass. The police counter-charged and drove the students behind the blue barracks where they collected more rocks. The students charged again, the police charged again, rocks were hurled, tear gas was released, clubs were swung and 15 people were arrested.

The next night, Thursday, it seemed violence might be averted, but tactical errors and indecision by a rookie mayor and university president resulted in five hours of confrontation, police violence and 90 arrests. During the day the anti-war groups agreed to hold their vigil in the prescribed place for protests, the free forum area in front of Anthony Hall. By 8 p.m. about 600 students had gathered there, and Assistant Dean of Students Ed Hammond told them they could stay the night if they did not attempt to go downtown. At 8:45 p.m. about 150 of the protesters headed across the overpass to Brush Towers to recruit more people. Soon the crowd grew to 1,500 people. Then, about 150 of the protesters decided to cross the line the university had drawn. They blocked U.S. 51 even though others in the crowd tried to dissuade them. The group refused a police order to move, until a show of force by the police sent them scurrying back to the free forum area.

Shortly after that, about 10 p.m., Mayor Neal Eckert lost his cool and declared a state of emergency and a curfew to go into effect in 30 minutes. The curfew had no effect on the protesters in the free forum area because they were on university property, which was not in the city limits. But the curfew did force the bars to close, which sent hundreds of non-protesting drinkers into the streets.

City and university officials later gave contradictory accounts of who did what and when, but apparently Eckert declared his emergency before conferring with the university. Once Derge was informed of the situation in the town, it was decided that it was "unfair" to have kicked the partiers out of the bars without penalizing the protesters on the campus. So the university revoked its permission for the all-night vigil and set a midnight curfew on the campus. Besides feeling betrayed, the students who lived off-campus were caught in a Catch 22 situation -- they could be arrested for violating the city's curfew if they attempted to go home, and if they stayed they would be busted for violating the university's curfew.

Shortly before midnight the 50 or so city, state and university police prepared to charge the 300 hardcore protesters who had stayed around for the finale. According to press accounts, as the police donned their masks and raised their clubs, the students recited the Pledge of Allegiance and sang the National Anthem and "Give Peace a Chance." The students planned to sit quietly and let the police arrest them. But instead, the police uncorked smoke bombs, which the students at first thought was tear gas, and then the police waded into the crowd swinging their clubs. The students fled toward Campus Lake with the police in pursuit. The police then used tear gas, and some students sought refuge in the dorms at Thompson Point while a few dove into the lake trying to escape. Police went into the dorms after protesters and plucked others out of the water. Before the night was over, 90 people had been arrested. Most of the charges were later dropped.

Eckert canceled Friday's scheduled street party, but in a gutsy decision allowed Saturday's party to go on. SIU also canceled its curfew and the protesters who weren't in jail proceeded with their plans for an overnight vigil in the free forum area. But most of the partiers and protesters stayed inside over the weekend because of a steady downpour of rain.

The next week 25 to 40 people continued their vigil in the free forum area. Although the sleep-in was peaceful, at 4:30 a.m. Tuesday, police made the protesters take down their tents and extinguish the campfires. The vigil petered out around the end of the week.

Over the summer there was another

major fire in Carbondale, only it wasn't a campus building. On July 25 the most popular student bar, Merlin's club bar, burned to the ground. Merlin's predecessor, the Golden Gauntlet, had originally been intended to be a ritzy nightclub with dinners and show bands. But from the beginning spirits out-sold steaks and rock 'n' roll bands outdrew the lounge acts. In 1971 Bill Hitchcock bought the Gauntlet and turned it into Merlin's, and in May 1972 he expanded the operation into a building to the north which had been the location of the Fettish head shop, and before that, the Zodiac Club, a black nightclub. (Merlin's is now T.J. McFly's.)

After the fire, Merlin's started having bands in the small bar and opened a beer garden outside. In the fall of 1973 the rebuilt nightclub reopened with a 55-foot-long bar, said to be the longest in Southern Illinois.

1973

Indeed, by Oct. 1, 1973, when the state lowered the drinking age for beer and wine to 19, the strip was well-equipped to handle the new business. Between 1969 and 1973 a number of new bars had popped up on the strip, and several restaurants had gotten liquor licenses and had become more bar-like. The new liquor businesses on or near the strip included Jim's Pizza Palace, The Club, Pizza King, Charlie Pickle's, Booby's, Buffalo Bob's and Papa Caesar's. In addition, the closing hour for bars had been pushed back from midnight to 2 a.m., and to keep a better eye on the strip, a Police Community Relations Center was opened in a vacant storefront next door to P.K.'s.

In January the Vietnam peace treaty was finally signed, bringing to an end the era of mass protests. But the passing of political unrest was hardly noticed, as the city and university had their hands full adjusting to the latest student trend, which was hard-core partying. In February the university threatened to stop holding rock concerts in Shryock Auditorium unless the students stopped smoking pot and drinking liquor inside, and in the fall, drug agents busted 13 SIU students and confiscated 30 pounds of marijuana and enough downers to sedate half of SIU's 18,000 students. Later, a PCP lab was raided in Cambria. A state Health Department study reported Jackson County had the highest incidence of venereal disease in the state; area liquor stores reported increased sales of wine, tequila and the ingredients for Harvey Wallbangers; and the drug crisis center Synergy reported a sudden increase in the abuse of Quaaludes and other tranquilizers.

In the Spring, the city and university continued their annual series of outdoor concerts and street closings, changing the name from "Alternative" to "Spring Fest," and the growing colony of born-again Christians held a Jesus Fest at the same time at Old Main park on the campus. Another religious leader who adapted to changing student interests was Rabbi Earl Vinecour, the head of the Jewish student organization, Hillel House, located on the island at University and Mill streets. Vinecour had come to Carbondale in 1972 after being kicked out of South Africa for preaching against apartheid. To publicize the fact that Israel was observing its 25th anniversary, on May 17, 1973, Vinecour got permission to close the University Avenue spur west of the island to hold a street party featuring Coal Kitchen. And when the Yom Kippur Mideast war erupted in October, Vinecour's response was to have an Israel Solidarity Rally, which boiled down to another street party.

Later in October there was a pro-Palestinian rally that marked the beginning of a new trend in campus politics. As the American students became less active in politics, the increasing number of foreign students from places like the Mideast, Taiwan and Iran became more outspoken.

The summer was relatively quiet, but in the fall there was a panty raid on Brush Towers. The concept of a panty raid in 1973 was rather superfluous as 24-hour visitation was by then allowed in the dorms. But the timing of the panty raid -- in October rather than April or May -- indicated a shift from spring protests to fall parties. Another omen was a Halloween costume dance in conjunction with Homecoming activities.

1974

It was truly a banner year for the strip. A governor, massage parlors, topless go-go girls, nearly-bottomless go-go guys, and completely naked streakers all made an appearance, and the first Halloween street party occurred.

The governor, Dan Walker, proved he was just one of the guys June 23 by sauntering into Merlin's, ordering a beer and glad-handing the flabbergasted patrons. Another dark horse, Dennis Sullivan, was elected student body president by 430 of SIU's 18,000 students for promising to bring the Grateful Dead to SIU to play a concert. (As with a lot of campaign promises, Sullivan was unable to keep his, though he tried.)

The streakers made their debut in March. Like the SIU panty raiders of 1952, the streakers were aping a fad that was sweeping the nation. Only this time SIU had a reputation to uphold.

It did.

March 5, a day after 50 streakers were reported at the University of Illinois, 12 masked streakers cavorted on the SIU

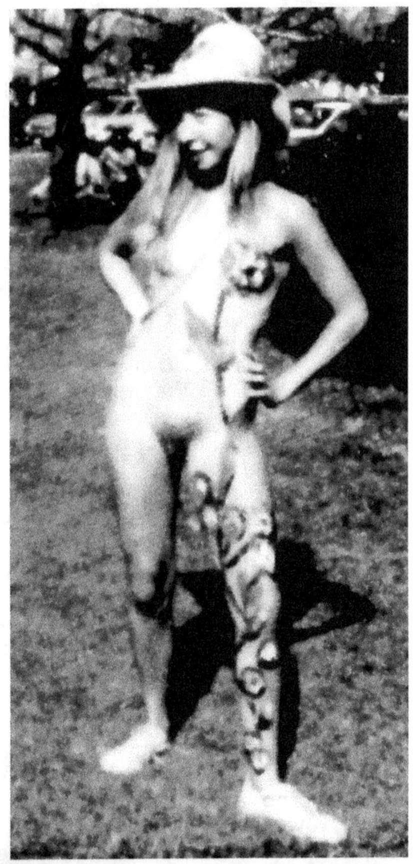

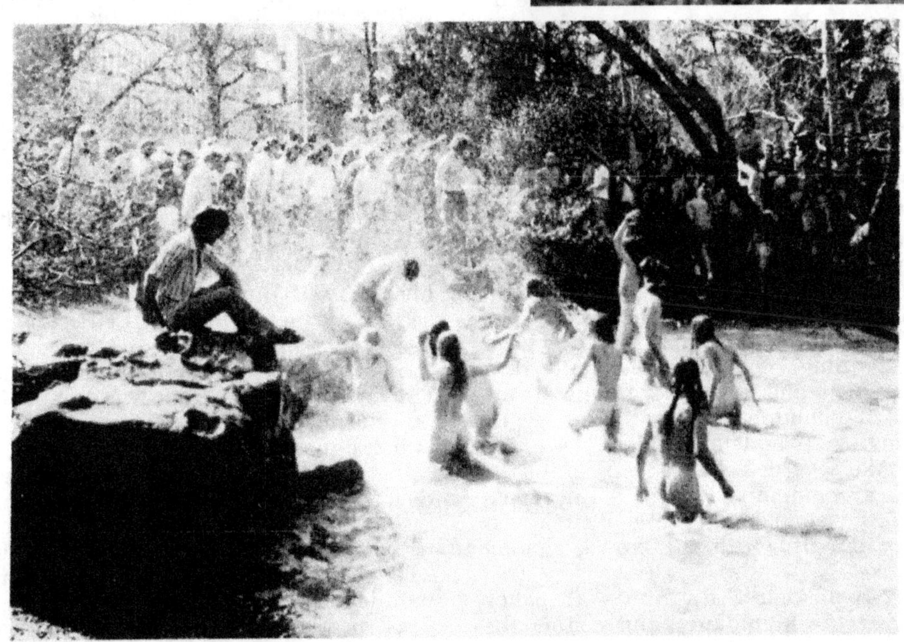

Streakers invaded the SIU campus March 7, 1974.   *--Photos courtesy of Spiros Karayiannis--*

campus and at the Murdale Shopping Center. The next evening, Wednesday, the first female streaker, a married student whose husband drove the getaway car, was arrested after running around Brush Towers. Police had been tipped she would be there, and they charged her with disorderly conduct for almost creating a mob scene at Neely Hall.

Then, Thursday, the streakers really cut loose. The festivities got under way about 2:30 p.m. on the campus where a crowd of several thousand people had gathered at the old protest rally site, the lawn in front of Morris Library, in response to fliers announcing a "streak-in." The crowd grew restless as everyone had their clothes on. But suddenly all eyes looked upwards at the Faner Building where four nude males were frolicking on the roof. A short time later nine naked men ran through the library. Then, about a dozen students of both sexes stripped off their clothes and splashed around in the pond in front of the library, while other streakers darted through the crowd.

There were other incidents of streaking that evening at Thompson Point and Brush Towers, and at 2 a.m. about 1,000 people closed South Illinois Avenue as about two dozen streakers entertained the crowd. At one point four male streakers carrying a female streaker accidentally dropped her on the street. The largest group of streakers, about 30 of them, ran around the Illinois and Grand inter-section about 1:30 a.m.

Friday afternoon the craziness continued. A few streakers ran around the campus, but most of the action occurred on the strip from late afternoon until midnight. About 3,500 people closed the street at 6 p.m. as groups of streakers did their thing. One streaker suffered a broken rib and wrist after falling off the roof of a building south of Merlin's while doing a handstand. That evening streakers "struck" inside Merlin's and the Police Community Relations office. And after the streakers got tired of streaking, they mingled with the crowd, sipping drinks.

The police followed a "hands-off" policy during the night, arresting neither the streakers nor the many people who were drinking and smoking in the street. Indicative of police behavior that night was an incident between police and two streakers on a motorcycle. SIU security stopped the motorcycle and gave the riders a warning -- for not wearing goggles.

The next day rain kept streaking to a minimum, and by the end of the next week the fad had ended. Nevertheless, area clergymen condemned the streakers for being immoral, and the police for not arresting anyone.

Barely a month after the streaking had died down, network TV news crews descended on the strip to do an expose on male go-go dancers at the Peppermint Lounge. It seems the Peppermint (formerly Leo's Place, now the Cellar, a basement bar next to the old train station) was alleged to be the first bar in the country to have male go-go dancers. Several months before, the Peppermint and several other Carbondale lounges had started having go-go girls. (At Whitt's Restaurant the girls were topless.) When women demanded equal time, the Peppermint called their bluff and offered a "Ladies Night" with two male SIU students shaking their tooshes in tiny tight swim trunks. The Ladies Nights were well attended by spirited, squealing females. At the request of the go-go guys, males were not allowed in on Ladies Night, and it got to be quite the thing for males to sneak in, which usually required going in drag.

Apparently even high level SIU administrators were not immune to the naughtiness that had swept the community. Over the summer President Derge, his assistant, Danilo Orescanin, and SIU security chief Thomas Leffler were accused of improperly using university funds to buy booze for parties at University House. No one was ever put in jail, but by the end of the year all three had resigned their positions.

In the fall, the city attempted to keep South Illinois Avenue open, with violent results. Homecoming weekend, which was several days before Halloween, about 7,000 people attended the Homecoming parade Saturday afternoon, and about 1,000 partiers took over the street that night after a Sly and the Family Stone concert. The police let the kids have their way, but when about 500 partiers attempted to close the street again Sunday night, the police decided to enforce the law. The partiers resisted, bottles and punches were thrown, tear gas or mace was sprayed (police denied they were the ones to spray the gas), and between 1:30 and 3 a.m. 10 people were arrested.

Nobody realized it at the time, but Thursday, Oct. 31, 1974, the bizarre Halloween street party tradition was born. At about 9:30 a.m. that night, about 1,000 young people, many of them in outrageous home-made costumes that ranged from the abstract to the obscene, took over the street between Merlin's and P.K.'s. Some in the crowd had toy pistols as part of their costumes, and edgy police began confiscating them to avoid an accidental shooting.

At 11 p.m., after the crowd had ballooned to as many as 5,000 people and the party was really starting to cook, Mayor Eckert lost his cool again and ordered the bars to close. The partiers took their anger out on the police, especially in the area of the Police Community Relations Center next to P.K.'s, where a rock was thrown through the front window. Five people were arrested, but property damage was relatively small.

Friday night Eckert changed his mind again, and when a smaller crowd of 500 people flowed into the street, the police dutifully put up a barricade at College Street. The party broke up before 3 a.m. Saturday it rained and the streets were clear.

In a rather obtuse analysis of the weekend's events, Police Chief Kennedy suggested the street party was a result of overcrowded bars and Homecoming activities. Halloween was not mentioned.

Another institution born in 1974 was the Metropolitan Enforcement Group (MEG), a secret police drug enforcement agency. Seven MEGs were set up across the state, incuding the Southern Illinois Enforcement Group (SIEG) in Carbondale. Headed by steely-eyed Rick Pariser and staffed by plainclothed officers from area police departments, SIEG's professed goal was to go after the major

suppliers of hard drugs. But especially during its first years, standard operating procedure for many SIEG agents was to hang out on the strip for several months, and then shortly before final exam time, bust the people they had partied, purchased and used drugs with.

Over time SIEG developed a network of informants, or narcs, some of whom were sleazier and more involved in the drug world than the people they were ratting on. The typical SIEG bust was an Abscam type affair, with narcs setting up sales between suspected drug dealers and undercover agents. Several weeks to months later there would be an early morning raid in which dozens of small-time druggies and maybe one or two dealers were arrested. Sometimes houses would get trashed during execution of a search warrant, and things like cash, guns, stereos, address books and photograph albums would get confiscated along with drugs. Recently SIEG has taken to seizing the vehicles allegedly used in drug crimes, and, as a result of a new state law, it will be able to keep cash, bank accounts and other assets of convicted drug dealers.

SIEG has enjoyed strong community support, in spite of several faux pas, including a civilian license plate that ended up on an unmarked SIEG vehicle; a change of administration from Carbondale to Murphysboro as a result of alleged accountability problems; and a heroin-related murder of a former Carbondale police dispatcher by a sometime SIEG narc. Although judges frequently give light sentences, SIEG can boast of a 90 percent conviction rate.

In some ways, SIEG has been beneficial to everyone, except the careless small-time drug-user. The community is happy SIEG busts so many druggies, the police are happy they can focus on more important law enforcement problems, and the major drug traffickers are happy SIEG so seldom gets to them.

In November 1974, a groundswell of opposition to the two "local" massage parlors was started not by a born-again church group, but by the *Southern Illinoisan*. Using an investigative technique seldom, if ever, employed by the newspaper, a male and female reporter, posing as a customer and job applicant, respectively, infiltrated one of the parlors. In anonymous articles, the reporters described the massage parlor operation, which included dirty books and films, waterbeds, nude masseuses and "locals," stimulating male sex organs to a climax.

The first Carbondale massage parlor, Deja Vu, had opened 11 months earlier on Main Street, just northwest of the strip. For $25, Deja Vu's scantily clad masseuses would provide a full body massage culminating in a handjob. Several months later a dirty book store, Triette Enterprises, moved in two doors away, at the former location of the Carbondale Chamber of Commerce office. Triette expanded into the New Yorker massage parlor, which provided extras, including nude masseuses and porno films. Sometime after that, Jerry Bryant, a fundamentalist Christian who had started the Upper Room Christian coffeehouse on the strip, opened a religious bookstore, Upon This Rock, in the storefront between the two massage parlors.

By the time the *SI*'s four-part series had run its course, Bryant and another fundamentalist, the Rev. Ben Glinn of the Lantana Baptist Church, had organized a group called Citizens For Decency, which started a petition drive to outlaw the parlors. To beef up interest in the April 1975 election, the city council decided to hold an advisory referendum on the issue, the results of which were inconclusive: The voters narrowly approved a measure to prohibit locals, but narrowly defeated a provision to outlaw massages entirely.

The council proceeded to enact a puritanical ordinance that in addition to banning handjobs for money, also required separate bathroom and locker facilities for men and women, and customers to have their sex parts covered at all times. Masseuses had to go through a state licensing examination, wear opaque clothing from the shoulders to the knees, and nametags -- enabling the perverts who came into the parlors to find them later. Soon, just about every other municipality in Southern Illinois adopted a similar ordinance whether it had a massage parlor or not.

The parlor owners fought the ordinance in the courts and were able to stay in business legally for about another year, until they had used up their legal options. They then played hide and seek, setting up businesses in rural trailer parks. One massage parlor, the Executive Club, continued to operate out of a trailer court near the Southern Illinois Airport until May 1982, when it was raided at the behest of a Jackson County sheriff candidate trying to make headlines.

1975

Another group attempting to get a referendum on the ballot did not fare as well as the Citizens For Decency. The group was the National Organization for the Reform of Marijuana Laws. In March the city council turned down NORML's 1,000-signature petition requesting an advisory referendum on whether the city should use its home rule power to "decriminalize" the possession of less than 30 grams of marijuana from a misdemeanor to a city ordinance violation, punishable by a $25 fine. The council had little desire to legalize pot, and even less to have a "reeferendum" on the same city election ballot as the mayor and two council seats. A pot referendum might have done what all the radicals, riots and rallies had failed to do -- get SIU students to vote. (For all the interest in politics on campus, with the exception of Susan Mitchell, who helped start the Food Co-Op and Shawnee Solar Project and served on the council from 1979 to 1981, community activists were never successful, nor even tried very hard, to use "student power" to take over city government by legitimate means.)

During the summer Carbondale made the network news again when SIU physiology professor Harris Rubin received $60,000 from the National Institute of Drug Abuse to pay male volunteers to get stoned and watch dirty movies while having their "sexual response" measured. Rubin explained males were used because their sexual response was easier to measure than females'. The experiment was a follow up to an earlier study in which Dr. Rubin had measured erections in drunken males. But the Carbondale Citizens For Decency couldn't see the purity of his research, and

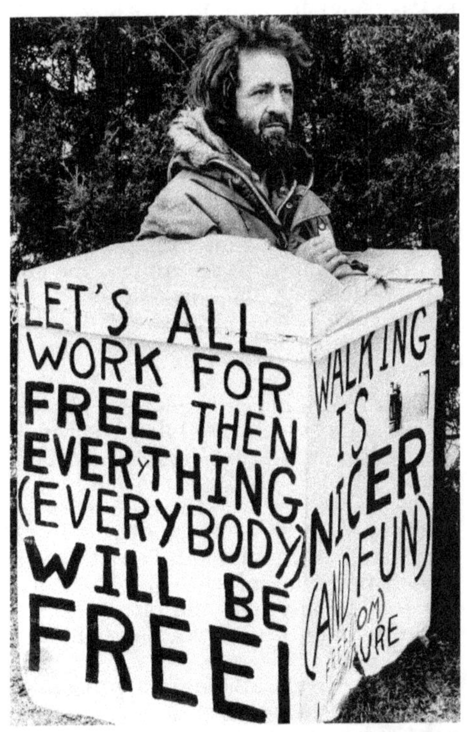

neither could the U.S. Congress, which cut off funding before a single "sex-pot" party could be held.

In August, a 42-year-old former factory worker and mental patient pedalled into town and began passing out literature promoting a moneyless society. Mike "Freedom Man" Belchak soon became as much a part of the strip's landscape as the Dairy Queen. He was rarely without a leaflet and a smile, and one of his favorite attention-getting ploys was to wear a dollar bill dangling from a wire hanger perched on his head.

Belchak was a harmless enough soul, but Carbondale police just couldn't seem to leave him alone. They gave him numerous tickets for traffic violations on his bicycle, and then confiscated the bike when anarchist Freedom Man wouldn't pay for a $1 license plate. They kicked him out of the abandoned trailer he had been squatting in on the south edge of the strip, and several weeks later took him to jail for trespassing when he returned to the trailer. Although Police Chief Kennedy described Belchak as "comic relief," his officers had charged Freedom Man with nine petty offenses by March 1976.

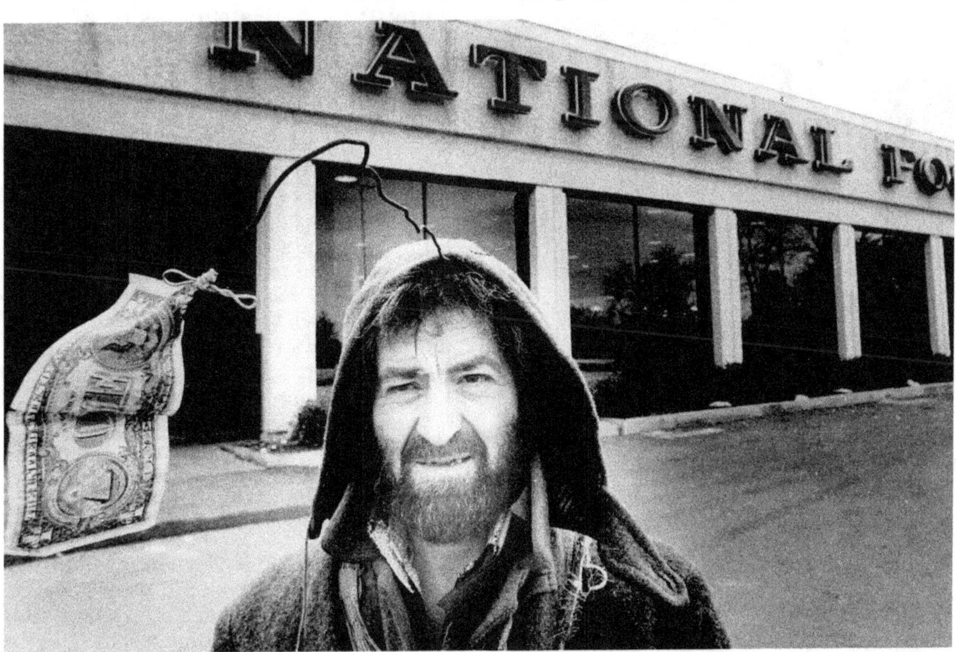

Mike Freedom Man Belchak used a variety of props to espouse his anarchistic philosophy, including painted cardboard boxes and a dollar bill hanging like a carrot in front of his face.   *--Ron Bath--*

Two days before America's bicentennial, when Belchak had prophecized money would become obsolete (and just two days after vandals had dumped honey all over the abandoned house he had been living in), an embittered Belchak paid the $1 to get his bicycle back from the police and left town. He returned for a short visit in 1978 and was greeted with a hero's welcome. In August 1980, Freedom Man was killed by a hit-and-run driver while riding his bicycle on a Michigan highway.

Belchak was but one of countless "characters" who drifted into town, graced the strip for a time, and faded away. To a great extent the street people and the strip fed off each other: Carbondale's loose atmosphere was conducive to the survival of eccentrics, vagrants and spare change artists, and their presence only added to the strip's mystique.

Local musicians had a similar relationship with the strip. Whether it was a bar owner in quest of patrons, a radical trying to attract a crowd, or the police trying to find a diversion to "cool out" the students, they all called on the

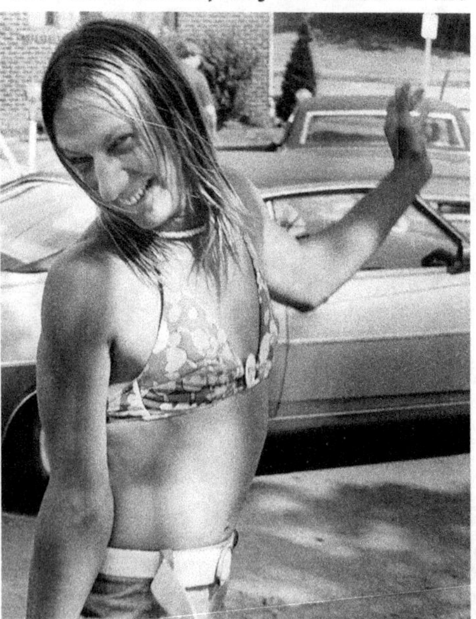

Another street character, transvestite Joe Scorpio, who claimed he had better luck picking up women when dressed like this. --Ron Bath--

bands, which usually produced the desired results, and some mighty fine-to-extraordinary music to boot.

Carbondale's music scene has been largely overshadowed by the riots and street parties, but it has been one of the strip's more redeeming qualities. Carbondale musicians surfaced and disappeared with the regularity of street people, and the names of the bands changed as often as the radical groups on campus. But one thread that runs about as true as any in the raveled Carbondale music scene is the career of "Robbie Rocker" himself, Robbie Stokes.

There were other early Southern Illinois "rock stars" such as John Nearman, Buddy Rogers, Danny Cagle, Kevin Cox, Gus Pappelis, Jon Taylor, Mike Potter, Radar Hurst, Brad Davis, Paul Fredricks, Larry "Big Twist" Nolan, Chuck Cochran, Pete Special and Terry Ogolini, who achieved prominence and longevity, but Robbie may hold the record for the sheer number of different bands he has played in.

Stokes first strummed onto the Carbondale music scene in 1963 as the pint-sized high school sophomore guitarist for the Satellites, a rock 'n' roll band that also included John Nearman, Bob Crain and Gary King. In 1964 Stokes joined the Viscounts, which played British invasion and surf music. While still in high school he joined an acid rock band, Om, with Brett Champlin, Bob Lawton, Steve Sweigart and Bucky Harmon. In July 1968, Om changed its name to Devil's Kitchen and headed west to seek fame and fortune in Haight-Ashbury. The band found neither, but did get to tour with such music heavyweights as the Grateful Dead and Allman Brothers, and play in the Filmore West. Devil's Kitchen held its own in San Francisco, and in May 1970 it was on the verge of signing a record contract with a major recording company. But the road and the drugs had taken their toll, and the group disbanded.

Robbie returned to Carbondale and was soon playing with a new group called Coal Kitchen, which was a "coalition" of several bands -- Robbie from Devil's Kitchen; Carla Peyton and Andre Massotti from Coal Dust (Coal Dust's

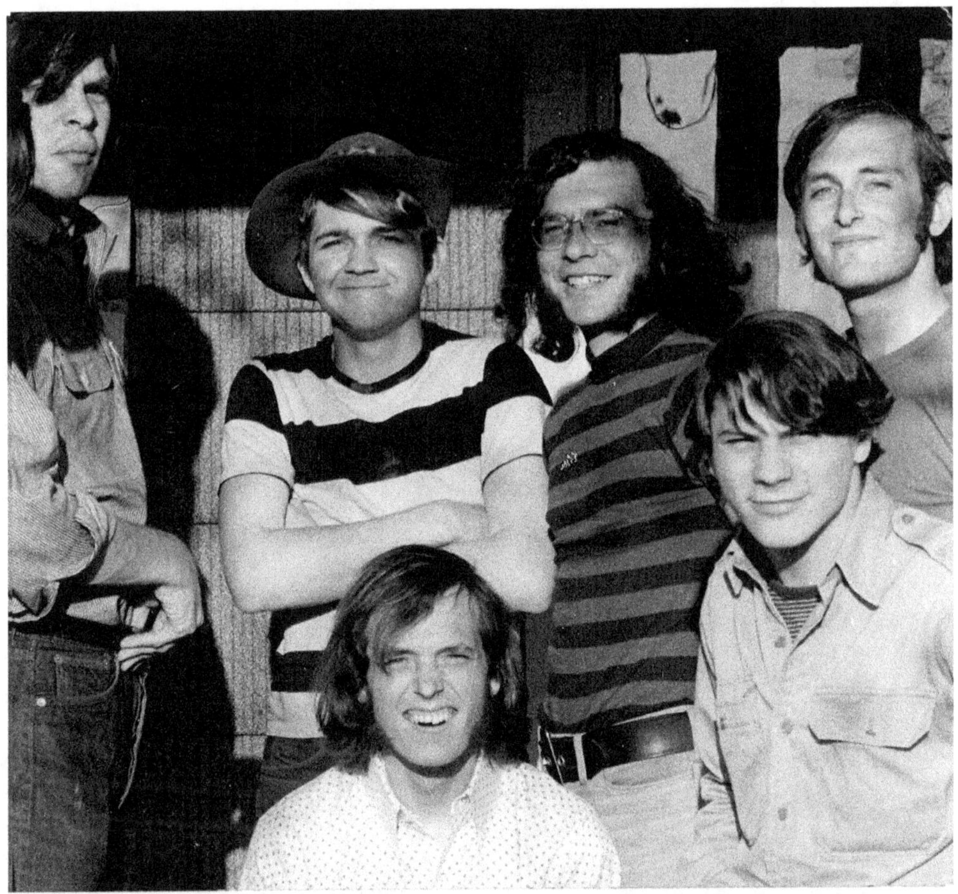

Devil's Kitchen: (from left) Bob Laughton, bass; Robbie Stokes, lead guitar; Steve Sweigart, percussion; Karl R. and Bucky Harmon, roadies; Brett Champlin, rhythm.   *--Yolan Presley--*

other member, James Meredith, became a booking agent); and Kevin Cox, Bob Pina and Randle Bradle from Zoo (Zoo's other members, Terry Mueller and Bill Carter, now own Golden Frets music shop). Coal Kitchen was Carbondale's premier band until 1972 when it relocated in Champaign, went "commercial" and recorded several albums. Stokes left the band in 1971 to try to pick up where he had left off in San Francisco. Things didn't work out, and in 1973 he returned to Carbondale and began playing in Rolls Hardley with Pina, Bradle and Joe Krzyiak.

The mid-1970s were the golden age of the Carbondale music scene. In addition to Rolls Hardley, which played high-powered rock 'n' roll and jazz, there was also a country swing band, the Dixie Diesels; a black rhythm and blues band, Big Twist and the Mellow Fellows; a white rhythm and blues band, the Skid City Blues Band; a jazz quartet, Mercy; and folksingers Shawn Colvin and Jim Bruno.

So far, the music of the '80s has been a murky mix of new wave and punk, reggae, rockabilly and '60s nostalgia. More recent quality bands include Vision, Riff Raff, Doctor Bombay, the Gus Pappelis Jazz Band, David and the Happenings, Katie and the Smokers, the Boppin '88s, the Thugs and Entropic.

Some of Southern Illinois' music makers, such as the Egyptian Combo, Coal Kitchen, Dixie Diesels and Big

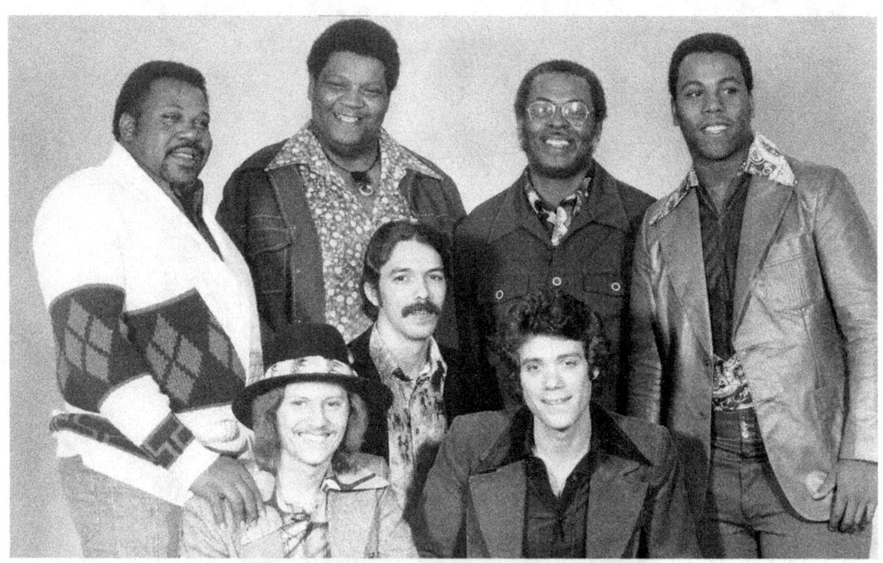

Big Twist and the Mellow Fellows (above, from left): Denny Best, Pete Special, Terry Ogolini, Larry Williams, Larry "Big Twist" Nolan, Ronnie West, Sr., Ronnie "Tango" West in 1976.
--*Shawnee Talent*--

Dixie Diesels (left): Bob Valentine, Brad Davis, Shawn Colvin, Willie Wainright, Mike Potter, Charlie Morrill, Ralph "Radar" Hurst in 1976.
--*nonSequitur*--

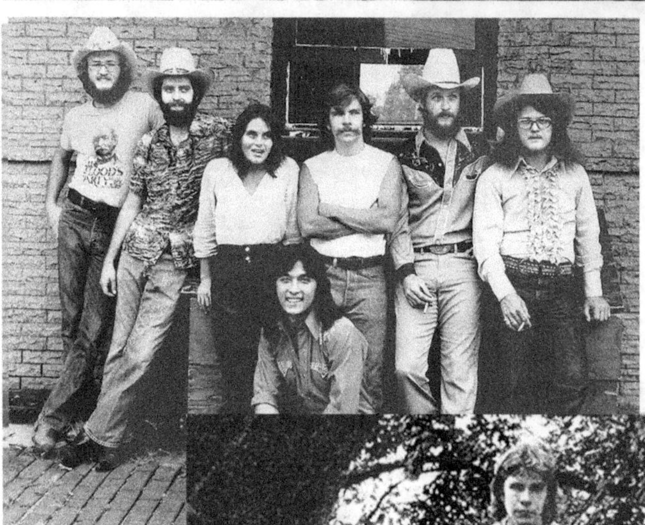

Pontiac Jones
Terry Ogolini,
Paul Fredricks,
Mike Potter,
Pete Special,
Rusty Ward,
Dean Milano,
in 1971.
--*Paul Fredricks*--

Twist, made records or found success in larger cities. Others, such as John Nearman, Tom Hood and Herb Krause, are dead. And some, such as Rockin' Robbie, just keep on keeping on.

Street takeovers were no longer making headlines in 1975, but they had become larger and more frequent than ever. In the early '70s the street parties occurred mostly in the block between Merlin's and P.K.'s at the north edge of the strip. But after Holden Hospital closed in 1971, the city tried to disperse the crowds south, toward the campus, by issuing liquor licenses to Das Fass, Jim's Pub and The American Tap, which were near College Street. The city also allowed beer and wine to be sold at Gatsby's and Quatro's, another block closer to campus at Freeman Street. Instead of dispersing the crowds, however, the new bars only expanded them, and by 1975 the street closings had crept south from Elm to College Street.

City officials were fed up with the strip, but divided on what should be done about it. Mayor Eckert and Police Chief Kennedy wanted to alleviate crowd problems by having more bars in other parts of town and extending the drinking hour to 6 a.m. City Manager Carroll Fry took the opposite view, opposing any more expansion of the strip either physically or temporally. The council -- Archie Jones, Helen Westberg, former police chief Joe Dakin and soon-to-be-mayor Hans Fischer -- were ambivalent.

More and more the council was becoming sympathetic to Fry's philosophy that the strip was the problem rather than the solution to controlling SIU's volatile students, and the turning point may have come at an informal council meeting Oct. 27, 1975, the Monday between Homecoming and Halloween weekends. The city had allowed the bars to remain open until 6 a.m. for Homecoming, and Eckert had proposed weekend bar hours of 6 a.m. for Halloween and on an experimental basis every weekend for the next six months. Chief Kennedy endorsed the idea saying by the time the bars closed the kids would be too wasted to want to take over the street.

But Fry noted the bars had been open until 6 a.m. for Homecoming and the street had been closed anyway. Dakin, Westberg and Fischer sided with Fry, and the bars continued to close at 2 a.m.

So did the streets.

1976

When students returned from their Christmas vacations in January, they were confronted with a radical change in the strip -- Merlin's had gone disco (see "Carbondale After Dark II"). The bandstand had been replaced by a garish dance floor, and records had replaced live music.

The gala grand opening of the disco was marred by an embarrassing incident on the dance floor. A couple of males who were dancing together were escorted off by a couple of Merlin's orange-vested bouncers, who made a policy that same-sex couples couldn't disco. The dancers filed a sex discrimination complaint with the city liquor commission, which almost held a public hearing.

Soon, other bars were converting their operations to discos, and SIU students started getting into the disco mentality -- buying first-hand clothes and holding hands when they danced. A small "disco sucks" faction boycotted bars that had stopped providing live music, but young attractive coeds in particular were attracted to the disco scene, and that was all that mattered. Disco thrived for about four dismal years.

The city council continued to nudge the strip south, voting one month to deny a liquor license for a proposed bar at 118 S. Illinois because the location was north of Walnut Street (even though the city had no ordinance prohibiting bars in that area) and voting another month to issue a full liquor license to Gatsby's, a beer-and-wine-only bar in the Campus Shopping Center south of College Street (even though the city had a beer-and-wine-only policy for that area). The council also rejected another attempt to lengthen the drinking hours, this time to 4 a.m.

One person who did not waver in his views on what should be done about the strip was City Manager Fry, and he laid out his plans in an article by Jim Santori for the March 1976 issue of *nonSequitur*. Fry proposed a massive downtown "redevelopment" project using millions of dollars in federal money to wipe out small businesses and hippy houses and replace them with a federal building and other sterile edifices more suitable for the hanging out of pigeons. Many of the changes Fry predicted in 1976 have since come to fruition. A federal office building was erected just off the strip at Cherry Street, and the new train station opened in 1981. In spite of some recent legal setbacks, the convention center-parking lot project was still alive as this book went to press, as was the $100 million dollar railroad relocation project.

Over the summer of '76 the city was confronted with another kind of "strip" problem -- nude swimming at the new city reservoir, Cedar Lake. The new lake was clean, scenic and virtually unsupervised, and it rapidly became a favorite party spot, rivaling the Crab Orchard spillway, Little Grassy, Devil's Kitchen and the Perry County stripmine pits. But some of the people living near Cedar Lake didn't appreciate naked hippies sauntering across their lawns and they complained to the city. Soon skinnydipping and practically everything else that was fun was prohibited, and swimming was restricted to a small weedy area enclosed by a yellow rope. Then the city decided to construct a beach and boat ramp, which required dropping the level of the lake 12 feet, leaving a swamp-like perimeter. It took more than three years for the lake to fill up again, and most of the swimmers abandoned the area for more pleasant settings such as the Kinkaid Lake spillway.

1977

Trial and error continued to be the city's approach to regulating the strip, issuing more liquor licenses south of College Street, and denying a license for a proposed bar on Hospital Drive, in the middle of the unofficial liquor zone and half a block off Illinois Avenue itself.

The council decided to allow a liquor license for Crazy Horse pool hall, next door to Gatsby's, in spite of a warning from Police Chief Kennedy that it would be more difficult to reroute traffic if street takeovers occurred south of College Street. The liquor license for Crazy Horse did not result in street takeovers, but several months later, after the issuance of a license to Silverball (now Great Escape) across the street from the pool hall, the police barricades sometimes had to be moved as far south as Mill Street. Too late the council learned that it was bars across the street from each other rather than clusters of bars on the same side of the street that precipitated street takeovers.

The proposed bar the council denied a

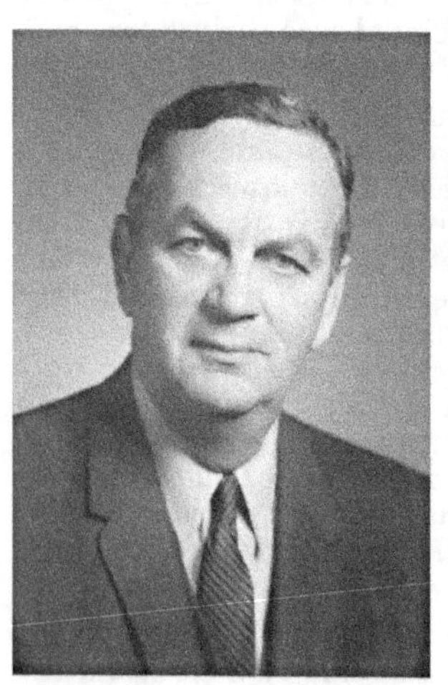

Former Mayor David Keene

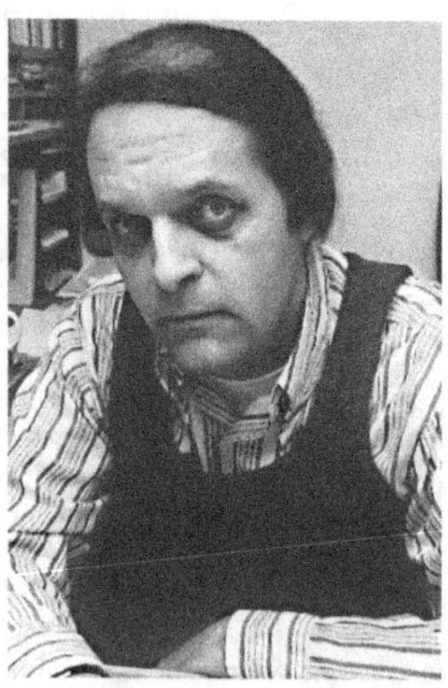

Mayor Hans Fischer

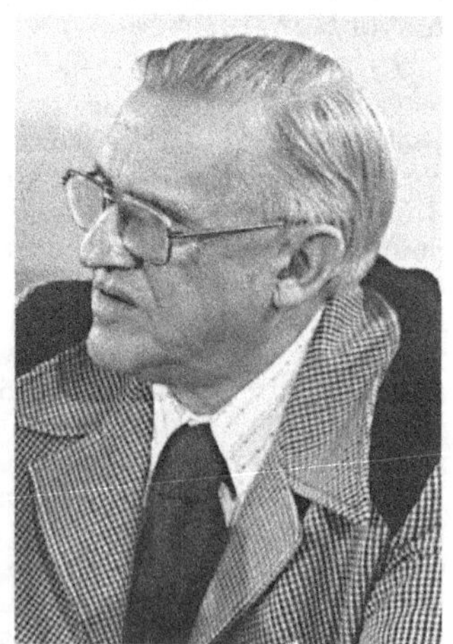

City Manager Carroll Fry

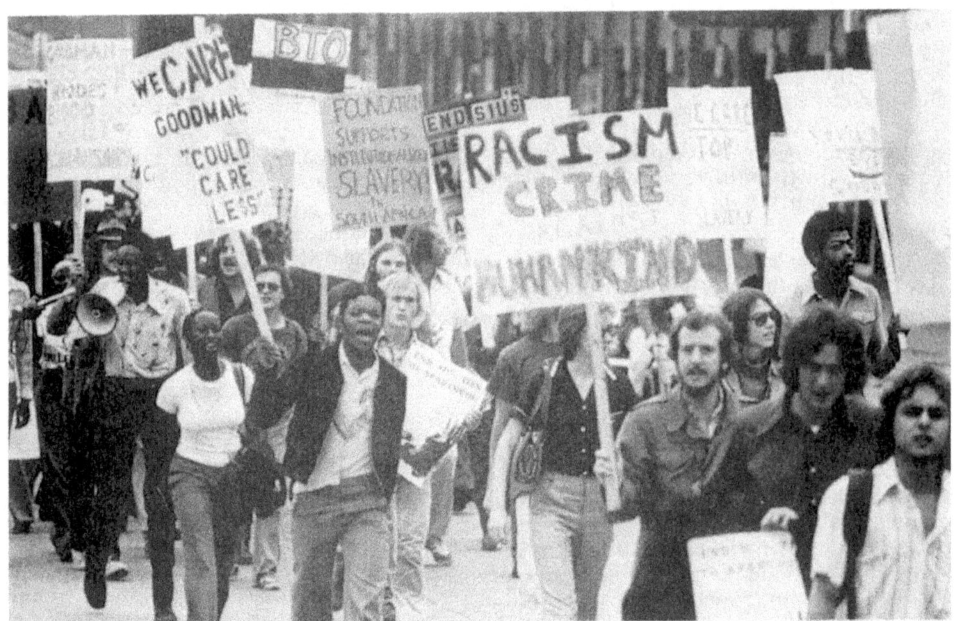

In June 1977 students protested SIU's $1 million investment in corporations doing business in South Africa.
--Andy Piper--

license to would not have aggravated street problems and probably would have eased them, because it was not to be on South Illinois Avenue. Several partners wanted to take two old houses near the bank parking lot and Hospital Drive and convert them into a rustic restaurant and lounge called Bogart's. Another old house on the strip had been made into Das Fass, one of the more stylish bars downtown, but when the city council considered the request in May, Councilman Fischer said he didn't think old frame houses should be renovated for public use. (Ironically, Fischer's son was the manager at Das Fass.)

City Manager Fry commented, "My vision of the downtown, if I can have one, does not include this type of building."

(Perhaps a clue to Fry's vision can be deduced from later developments: A year later the same investors were granted a license for a bar on South Illinois Avenue across the street from the bank parking lot. Only instead of using old houses, the owners erected a pole barn and appropriately named it Hangar 9.)

Over the summer there were a couple of political protests downtown. In June the *Daily Egyptian* reported the SIU Foundation owned more than $1 million of stock in corporations that did business in South Africa, and a group calling itself the Coalition Against Racial Exploitation (CARE) staged a small but vocal protest, including a march downtown. Women libbers picketed Das Fass in July when the bar held a wet T-shirt contest offering $100 to the female with the most winsome bosoms.

The weekend before Halloween, about 6,000 people, many of them in costumes and from out of town, closed South Illinois Avenue from College to Walnut. The city had not granted an extension of the 2 a.m. drinking hour, but Saturday night the bars stayed open an hour later because of a time change from Daylight Saving Time. When the bars emptied, a bonfire was lit in the street, rocks and bottles were thrown, and a few people took off their clothes. There was some property damage, 10 arrests and a lot of trash left behind. So much, in fact, that men with shovels had to clear a path before garbage and street cleaning trucks could enter the area.

Several weeks later the council again wrestled with the problem of street parties. The new police chief, Ed Hogan, said police would no longer tolerate drinking on the sidewalks and in the street, although to avoid confrontations they would continue to reroute traffic rather than clash with partiers. Councilman Fischer suggested closing the bars when the crowds became ugly, but Mayor Eckert said that would be unfair to the bar owners.

City Manager Fry suggested firemen "lay down a column of water" on unruly crowds.

1978

Despite the bravado of city officials, the '78 Halloween street party was as large as any in the strip's history (estimates range from 10,000 to 15,000 people), and a truly unique celebration as well. The weekend before Halloween was Homecoming, and seemingly oblivious to the consequences, the city council once again granted permission for the bars to stay open until 6 a.m. If the extended bar hours and the momentum of the party from the previous years weren't enough, Bob Dylan was in town to do the Saturday night Homecoming concert.

Whatever the reason, by 10 p.m. Friday South Illinois Avenue between College and Walnut had been transformed into Bourbon Street at Mardi Gras. There was the usual sloppiness -- vandalism, trash fires, horny aggression, overdosing and arrests -- but the number and quality of the costumes turned the party into a happening. There were coneheads, Wild and Crazy Guys, transvestites, hermaphrodites, sex organs, animals, monsters political figures, flashers and an occasional streaker.

The sound of that party was also impressive. From blocks away could be heard an eerie metallic clunking roar, made by thousands of feet kicking, crushing and walking over thousands of beer cans and wine bottles. Police confiscated toy weapons and arrested about a hundred vandals and fighters, but they made little effort to stop partiers from drinking and smoking in the street, or entering bars that already had more than the allowable number of patrons according to the fire safety code.

A week later Police Chief Hogan suggested turning the unsanctioned street party into an official festival, by combining Homecoming activities with a Saturday night street party until 6 a.m. and allowing drinking in the street. The city and university did adopt many of Hogan's suggestions and co-sponsored "Carnivale '79" the next year. But as will be seen shortly, the city had a more final solution in store for the Halloween party and the strip itself.

There was one organized demonstration of note in 1978, although it was only marginally political. In May about a dozen Yippies and perhaps 500 other people, some wearing paper bags, gathered at the free forum area in front of the SIU administration building, and as SIU security policy watched from the sidelines, they lit up joints and got stoned. The act was a bit more defiant than usual because it occurred in the midst of the Paraquat scare, in which it was alleged drug agents were spraying Mexican pot fields with poison. After getting a good buzz going, the group held a nostalgic march through downtown Carbondale in mellow protest against marijuana laws.

Also in May, the city council flirted with enacting an obscenity ordinance to set community standards defining pornography and outlawing "public actions intended to arouse prurient interest." City Attorney John Womick tried to follow the council's wishes, but confessed "I tried to prepare an ordinance which prohibited everything it should, but it was too obscene to print."

The hubbub had arisen over the reappearance of topless go go girls who were performing at the Plaza Lounge and Buffalo Bob's (now Mundo's). In December the council did enact an ordinance specifically banning "topless and/or bottomless" dancing. Six months later a young Carbondale cop busted the topless dancers at the Plaza, a courageous act considering the Plaza happened to be a popular cop bar.

1979

Preparations for Carnivale '79 got under way during the summer, with businessmen and students working with city and university officials to provide a festive but less chaotic Halloween party than the year before. The city got permission from the Illinois Department of Transportation to close U.S. 51 between College and Walnut Saturday from dusk to 4 a.m., and the bar hour was extended until 4 a.m. (Partiers got an extra hour because of another coincidental time change from Daylight Saving Time). Student government promised booths and vendors for the street carnival, and student party monitors or "Halloween helpers" to aid the police. Bar owners agreed to enforce the occupancy limits and help keep glass off the streets.

But when Halloween weekend rolled around, things didn't go quite as planned. The party was scheduled for Saturday, but by 10 p.m. Friday, partiers had closed the street. And on Saturday night, after police placed barricades at College, students surged into the street near Freeman, forcing the police to move the barricades south to Mill Street. Little attempt was made to keep the bars from becoming overcrowded or bottles and glass from accumulating in the street. On Saturday the carnival booths were set up, but they were dwarfed by the crowd and had little impact. The "Halloween helpers" never materialized, and with all the elaborate preparations, no one had thought to provide porto-potties, so the pungent odor of 90 proof urine was everywhere.

Chief Hogan had been the first to suggest an official festival after the '78 party, and after the '79 party he was the first to declare the experiment a smashing failure. In a report to the city council a week later, he said the party had outgrown the space and resources to accommodate it and that "street closings of this type should be stopped."

Hogan estimated the crowd at close to 15,000 people, which he said was 20 percent more than the year before, and he noted the glass and trash problem was as bad as ever. In addition to safety problems posed by broken glass in the street, and the potentially catastrophic consequences of a fire occurring in an overcrowded bar, Hogan noted 16 freight trains passed near the party scene over the weekend. (Hogan's fears of a train

accident came true in 1981 when a partier was severely injured trying to hop a freight train Saturday afternoon of Halloween weekend.)

Some city officials suggested closing the bars early as one way to end the party, and others urged moving the festivities somewhere besides downtown. City Manager Fry recommended a city-owned farm near a sewage treatment plant on old Illinois 13 east: "If the liquor stores close up here at 8 p.m. and you serve beer out there, you might get some of them to stagger out there," he commented.

Party-pooping talk from the city was not the only signal the strip's nights were numbered. Over the summer one of its anchors, Merlin's bar, closed. Its closing had little to do with the strip (it was widely rumored owner Bill Hitchcock had gambling debts) and the bar reopened as T.J. McFly's several months later. But the strip without Merlin's is like a *Playboy* without a centerfold.

Another indicator was a half-hearted street takeover the first weekend of fall semester, Aug. 25, 1979, when a small crowd of about 150 people briefly closed Illinois Avenue between College and Cherry (see "The Last Street Takeover").

The occurrence was not technically the last street takeover, as there continued to be street parties on Halloween weekend, but there was not another spontaneous street takeover until nearly three years later, in May of 1982.

In November of 1979, SIU's students proved political protests don't have to be anti-American to be ugly. The disruptions were a spontaneous expression of nationalistic anger over the taking of the American hostages in Iran. But they were also a thinly veiled expression of the long-festering racism against the many foreign students at SIU.

Partly to increase enrollment and partly to fulfill Delyte Morris' dream of making SIU an internationally ac-claimed institution, over the years the university had established missions and exchange programs with more than 70 other countries. One result was a large enclave of several thousand foreign students in Southern Illinois. The foreign influence added a cosmopolitan flavor to Carbondale, but some of the foreigners were "uppity," staging protests against American imperialism and, heaven forbid, dating white women.

In the early and mid-'70s the pro-Palestinian and anti-Shah rallies were received with sympathetic if lukewarm support by SIU's white radicals. But when about 50 of SIU's 150 Iranian students held an ill-advised send-home-the-Shah protest in front of the Student Center Nov. 8, less than a week after the hostages were taken, they were harassed by about 30 white SIU students waving Old Glory and chanting "go home."

The next day about 400 placard-toting students calling themselves Americans for America held a noisy three-hour protest on the campus that included a semi-mock hostage-taking of 20 Iranian students who happened to be eating lunch in the Student Center cafeteria. That night carloads of soccer-player types cruised city streets harassing pedestrians who looked un-American, while on the strip drunken bullyboys draped themselves in the American flag and stalked "doon coons" between stanzas of "America the Beautiful."

Conspicuously absent from downtown that weekend were SIU's 3,500 Persian, Palestinian, Arab, Oriental, Malaysian, African and South American students.

1980

As the '70s turned into the '80s, the strip was beginning to die. And when the state raised the drinking age back to 21 in January 1980, downtown suddenly got deader. The strip was an eyesore, but at least it had centralized some of the drinking and partying away from residential neighborhoods. After the drinking age was upped, there was a sudden increase in "keggers" -- large and noisy house, yard and/or block parties in residential areas or Giant City State Park, where the libations were dispensed out of a barrel or truck, a hat was passed to cover expenses, and nobody checked I.D.s. Police began raiding the parties, there was resistance, and mostly exaggerated tales of police brutality began to circulate.

Another popular alternative to the strip became the Carbondale Park District summer series of Thursday night Sunset Concerts, held throughout the city, including in front of Shryock Auditorium on campus and Turley Park on the west side. The music ranged from hard rock to chamber music, and the bluegrass concerts were especially well attended by students and townspeople alike. There was lots of drinking, a moderate amount of smoking, and some rowdiness (and one stabbing in 1981 at a concert held at Attucks Park on the east side), but the mix of students, families, babies and senior citizens resulted in generally mellow crowds.

Carbondale briefly got a real live jazz club when three local jazz musicians, Joe Liberto, Buddy Rogers and Russell Branch, bought the gay bar below ABC Liquor, the Washington Street Underground, and turned it into the Cypress Jazz Lounge. The bar was cool, but it never got hot, and folded after a year.

Although the bar crowds had dwindled, the infrastructure was still in place, as evidenced by an SIU research project that concluded Carbondale had more taverns per capita than DeKalb, Bloomington, Peoria, Champaign and Chicago. As Halloween neared, the city council pondered various options for ending the celebration. It finally settled on "containment rather than confrontation," meaning the city would continue to close the street instead of fight the partiers. But the so-called Halloween Ordinance also included short and long-term policies geared to phase out the party -- and the strip -- entirely. Its most far-reaching provision prohibited new bars on the strip or the reopening of existing bars after they went out of business. The ordinance also banned the sale of beer, wine and pints of hard liquor in bottles the week of Halloween; ended the practice of extending bar hours or closing the street for special events; reordered the police to enforce the drinking age and occupancy limits; and requested SIU not to schedule any major events such as Homecoming or Bob Dylan concerts for Halloween weekend.

The ordinance did not dull 1980's Halloween party, however, as once again 10,000 to 15,000 revelers closed the street about 9 p.m. Friday, Oct. 31. The presence of an NBC camera crew perched atop the Dairy Queen ensured a spirited celebration, and the bottle ban had a dramatically positive effect on the trash problem.

But Saturday night, which was the night after Halloween, there were about 7,000 people in hangovers, not costumes, and the party got sloppy and sublime. Once again the city declined to provide public bathroom facilities, with the predictable results.

In the year's most significant protest, about 250 people, most of them females, gathered shortly before Halloween at Mill and Illinois for a seminar called "Take Back the Night" to discuss sexual harassment and rape. Since the liberation of coeds from curfew hours in the early '70s, rape and other sex crimes had increased. Speakers at the seminar offered various solutions including drop-dead looks, deflating one-liners and self-defense. One speaker said you don't have to hate men to be a feminist, "but it helps."

If manhating is helpful to the feminist movement, then the strip should get an award for its contributions to women's liberation. It would be hard for any self-respecting female to not resent men if she spent any time there. But to conclude that men cruised the strip for sex while women were there for other reasons would be simplistic. Sex has always been a prime motivator of males and females alike who are drawn downtown at night -- the CBers hadn't tagged Carbondale "beaver city" for nothing. The problem was one of sophistication. There was plenty of sex to be had, but all too few people seemed to know how to go about it. Instead of glib come-ons, males often resorted to lewd comments; instead of tender affection there was drunken fondling; and instead of artful kiss-offs there was often a mindless flirtaciousness that only aggravated the situation.

SIU's bounty of young, attractive and sexually active females also attracted an unfortunate number of bona fide sociopaths whose violent acts, window peeping and dirty phone calling further damaged relations between the sexes. City and university officials installed a few street lights, sometimes funded a small transit system for women, and erected signs warning women not to walk along the "Ho Chi Minh Trail" between Brush Towers and the campus, but law enforcement agencies have not had much success in preventing crimes against women or apprehending the offenders. Nor have the males ever shown much inclination to police, or at least restrain, themselves. There have been a couple of male consciousness raising seminars, but most turned out to be fronts for gay lib.

1981

Two attractive young women, Joan Wetherall and Susan Schumake, made unasked-for headlines in 1981 by becoming victims in unsolved sex-related murders. The police took a lot of heat for not solving those and several other murders that year, and Carbondale got the greased pole again in a sensationalized account of the Wetherall murder on the front page of the *Chicago Tribune*.

The murders did create some tension, but nothing like the Atlanta child killings that year, and in general, Carbondale and the strip had become more sedate. The economy and a more "serious" or "materialistic" student population were given as explanations for the shrinking crowds downtown. Whatever the reason, there was a definite recession on the strip. Bars began closing on Sundays and Mondays, and they hired bands less often. For some reason Thursday became the most crowded bar night. Fridays were usually disappointing and Saturdays downright dismal.

To beef up business, the bars dropped their already low cover charges (the patrons complained anyway about having to pay $1 to see a band which they couldn't have gotten close to in Chicago for less than $3), offered two-for-one drink specials and raffles. Perhaps T.J. McFly's went the furthest with its "contests," which included beer guzzling, balloon busting, body taping, passionate kissing, and that all-time favorite, goldfish swallowing. Another godsend to the bar owners was the blooming video game craze.

After the disco and urban cowboy fads of the late '70s, the two discernible youth trends of the '80s became the alligatored inanity of prep and the rainbow-haired regalia of punk. Seemingly antithetical of each other, preppies and punkers shared an attitude of aloof passé-ivity.

In June the city council showed it meant to live up to its promise of reducing the number of bars on the strip by voting unanimously to deny a request to reopen a downtown bar, Das Fass, which had closed three years earlier. Mayor Fischer explained his vote saying, "Over the years I have seen the demise of that area as a commercial area, except as a strip to serve liquor."

The owner of the bar, SIU women's gymnastics coach Herb Vogel, appealed the decision to the Illinois Liquor Commission, so far to no avail.

Later in the year, however, the council did allow a bar just off the strip at 213 E. Main to reopen. The location had long been a liquor outlet, first for adults, as the Flamingo Lounge and Rumpus Room, and later for students, as Bonapart's Retreat and Second Chance. In 1981 it became The Bar, which turned out to be for gays.

Carbondale has always had an ample gay population, but except for the bathroom walls at Morris Library they have usually kept a low profile. There were, however, always one or two bars that got a reputation for being gay bars, with or without the blessing of the bar owners. In the mid '70s it was the Washington Street Underground below ABC Liquor, and later the New Yorker at 501 E. Walnut. The Gay People's Union also held well-attended dances at the New Life Center at Grand and Illinois. Other significant gay "events" include a nationally award-winning play by homosexual playwright, Lane Bateman, Lying in State, produced by the Southern Players in 1974, and an appearance in 1975 by gay sailor Leonard Matlovich.

Not content to strangle the strip slowly with its new liquor license policy, the city put into high gear its downtown redevelopment plans, concocting a Rube Goldberg financing scheme to fund construction of a convention center and parking lot complex. The 10-story, 230-room hotel would include meeting rooms, a restaurant/lounge and probably an emporium. Although it would ultimately be owned by a private corporation headed by Carbondale Holiday Inn owner Stan Hoye, it would be financed with $10.5 million in city-sponsored industrial revenue bonds and a $2 million federal HUD grant. To make way for the hotel, every building on the block bounded by Illinois Avenue, Monroe Street, University Avenue and Walnut Street would be knocked down, including the Fettish head shop, the Walnut Street Baptist Church, and the Southern Barbecue restaurant.

The three-tiered, 350-space, $4.25 million municipal parking lot a block south would wipe out another block of businesses between Elm and Walnut, including a book store, bicycle shop, gem shop, pizza restaurant, Indian clothing shop, Christian Science Reading Room, Carbondale Community Center and P.K.'s bar. Although the first level of the parking lot and the lobby of the hotel are expected to contain shops, it is unlikely they will include the hippy hangouts like head shops and biker bars. In fact, the closest thing to a strip in the two blocks to be transformed by the project would be the sirloins served at the hotel restaurant.

Adding insult to injury, strip-goers have been asked to help pay for the parking lot in the form of a 1 percent tax on food and drinks. Ironically, of all the groups to be displaced by the projects, the one that put up the most vocal opposition was the Walnut Street Baptist Church.

At the same time the city was approving the amusement tax, it turned thumbs down on a 3 percent usage tax on electricity to pay for a proposed Municipal Solar Utility that would "retrofit" homes with energy saving devices and develop alternative energy sources (the council did approve a scaled-down energy conservation project, sans tax). The MSU -- and the tax -- were the brainchild of the Shawnee Solar Project, a non-profit energy conservation group made up of futurists and long-time Carbondale political activists. Rather than pass hats at rock concerts or push drugs, Carbondale's radicals have learned the delicate art of grantsmanship -- forming non-profit corporations, legal aid societies or social service agencies, and securing government grants.

Speaking of drugs, usage patterns had changed again, as evidenced by some Southern Illinois Enforcement Group busts netting astronomical quantities of cocaine. In the 1980s there are still some psychedelics and pharmaceutical speed available in Carbondale, but cocaine and "lookalike" speed caffeine pills are more prevalent. Quaaludes and angel dust have also gone out of vogue; heroin use is less than ever, and even marijuana consumption has fallen off. Only alcohol consumption seems to have held steady.

In the late '60s most of the pot came from Mexico and had names like Michoacan and Acapulco Gold. In the early '70s there was a lot of excellent Jamaican Ganj around, and some potent weed from Southeast Asia. In the mid-'70s the best smoke in town came from Colombia and bore little resemblance to today's commercial 'Bo except for the multitude of seeds. Lately a new product has entered the market, sinsemilla, a scientifically homegrown virgin female strain of hemp, much of it grown locally, which rivals the best pot of the past, but costs in excess of $100 an ounce.

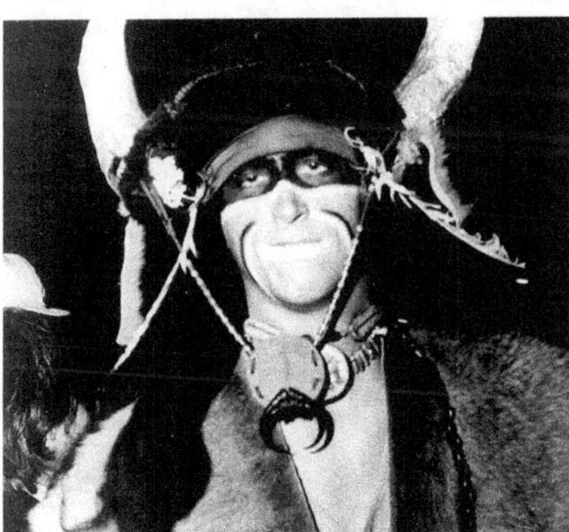

Halloween 1981   *--Kurt Prell--*

Halloween was once again attended by 10,000 to 15,000 partiers in '81, but only about half of them were costumed. Twenty-four were arrested and 85 required medical treatment, including one man who fell off a roof and another who fell under a train.

The weekend was punctuated by a lot of large and rowdy house parties in residential neighborhoods, and the next month the council enacted a noise ordinance that gave police the authority to raid loud parties without neighbors having to swear out a complaint and face retaliation. The ordinance also prohibited hosts from accepting donations to pay for the booze.

1982

One day before his 75th birthday, April 12, 1982, Delyte Wesley Morris died at the Union County Nursing Home in Anna. In the later years of his life, Morris suffered from Alzheimer's syndrome, a degenerative brain disease marked by progressive senility. In Morris' case, senility may have been a relatively merciful way to spend the twilight of his life. After all he had done for the university between 1948 and 1970, in the end he was demonized by his students and victimized by his political friends. And in spite of his monumental accomplishments, the university had more of a reputation than ever.

As a party school.

But Morris might have been pleased had he been able to attend the SIU Spring Fest that occurred just a couple of weeks after he died. It was an enjoyable and well-attended celebration of life held at the Old Main quad. Except for the faint odor of marijuana and punkers on rollerskates, the event was reminiscent of the traditional spring carnivals held on the campus in the 1950s and '60s. There were fireworks, food, fun and games, roller dancing, kite flying, fencing, roving clowns, carny booths, arts and crafts, rhythm and blues, a car sledge slam, lots of beer coolers, and a bad film festival featuring, who else, the Three Stooges. Maybe next year they'll bring back the carnival rides.

If Morris would have been pleased, city officials must have been dancing for joy at the sight of 5,000 young people drawn to an event on the campus instead of the strip. The main thing that has always kept the campus from becoming a strip is that the sale of alcohol was never allowed there. For many years state law was the reason. In the mid-'70s, after the law was diluted and other universities began allowing liquor, there were several attempts to sell alcohol at special events, football games and the Student Center canteen. When the university finally took the big step and served mixed drinks at the Pink Cotillion hospital auxiliary ball in the Student Center in 1980, *Southern Illinoisan* reporter Tom Woolf pointed out that Carbondale did not have the authority to grant SIU permission to serve liquor because SIU had never been annexed to Carbondale. SIU is in Carbondale Township, and Carbondale Township is dry.

But given the worsening financial condition of education in general, it's not hard to imagine SIU coming to view the sale of liquor in the same way the city did a decade before -- as a quick way to whip up some revenues. After all, everyone has been drinking on campus for years. In the dorms, at tailgate parties in the parking lot of McAndrew Stadium, on the hill at baseball games and in the bleachers at Arena rock concerts and basketball games. If the university was getting a percentage on all of that alcohol consumption, it could pay for a lot of sabbaticals.

Current SIU President Albert Somit has made overtures of reviving Morris' goal of involving the university in community service. And Somit has also acknowledged that one aspect of commuity service is taking more responsibility for the impact of partying students on the surrounding area. But it is unlikely SIU will ever do anything to allow a strip to evolve at the Student Center, Brush Towers, Old Main quad or anywhere else on the campus, no matter how lucrative the short-term financial benefits might be.

For no apparent reason, in the spring of '82 the city moved toward passage of an ordinance that would regulate the few existing Carbondale head shops out of business. Among other things, the proposed ordinance would require the purchasers of hash pipes, hookas, stash containers and roach clips to sign their names in a ledger.

The city council also denied a liquor license renewal to The Bar, an increasingly popular hangout for gays and other trendy types at 213 E. Main St. The city cited various improprieties, the most serious of which was an alleged rape or sexual assault in an alleged unisex restroom. The majority of the violations,

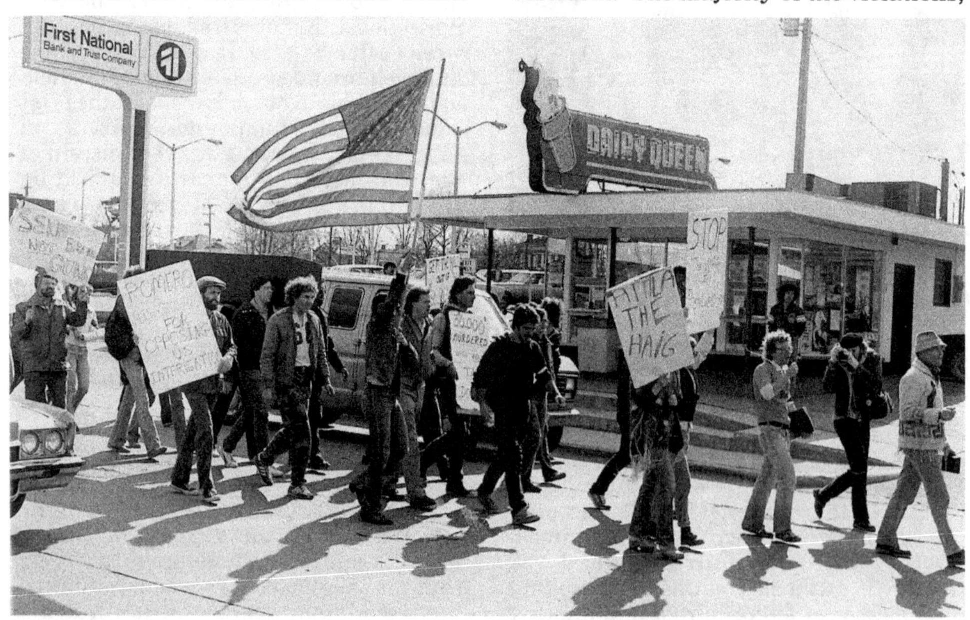

"Attila the Haig" was among those blamed for U.S. involvement in El Salvador during a small demonstration in the spring of 1982.
--Deb Browne--

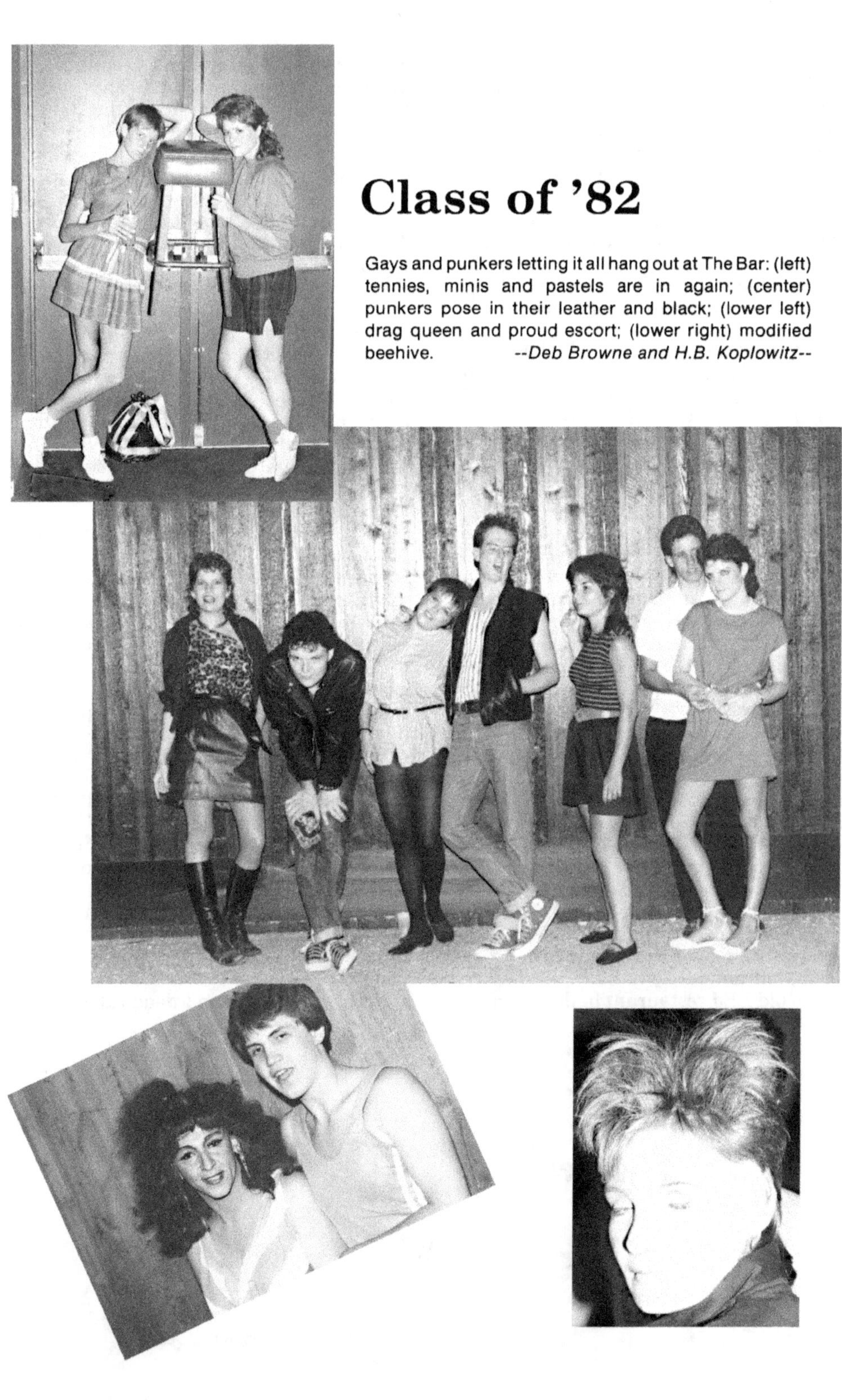

Class of '82

Gays and punkers letting it all hang out at The Bar: (left) tennies, minis and pastels are in again; (center) punkers pose in their leather and black; (lower left) drag queen and proud escort; (lower right) modified beehive. *--Deb Browne and H.B. Koplowitz--*

such as under-age and after-hour drinking, were not uncommon complaints at the other downtown bars, and the gay and punk communities viewed the city's action as discrimination. The Bar was allowed to remain open while its owner appealed the decision to the Illinois Liquor Commission, and the appeal was still pending as this book went to press.

Another bar, Mr. B's, on the levee, was denied a liquor license renewal and closed after it was raided in a major drug bust.

In the first six months of 1982 there were some feeble signs that students were becoming politically aware again. A group called Coalition for Change organized a week of activities opposing U.S. involvement in El Salvador, and other groups protested nuclear weapons, infanticide, and tuition increases.

During the week of El Salvador activities, one speaker exhorted a crowd by saying, "If you've ever wanted to live in the '60s, here's your chance." Indeed, the group took to the streets and held a march down Illinois Avenue. But the small march, led by a police car, closed only one lane of traffic and turned off at Cherry Street.

Another throwback to an earlier Carbondale occurred the Thursday and Friday night before spring graduation, May 13 and 14, when students participated in spontaneous street takeovers at 2 a.m. on South Illinois Avenue between College and Cherry. Whether the protests and street takeovers were a last hurrah of a dying era, or the birth of something new, only time will tell, but there were also several other signs that the strip might be down, but not out.

The old LBJ restaurant building on the levee reopened as Tres Hombres, a Mexican restaurant and bar, John Dough's, a 24-hour doughnut shop, opened on the strip, and bikers and punkers began migrating to The Club. But the most significant factor that contributed to the preservation of the strip came from a most unlikely source -- Jackson County Circuit Judge Richard E. Richman.

In the city's haste to redevelop downtown into a tourist and convention center, it filed "quick take" imminent domain lawsuits against property owners who had refused to sell their land to the city. In a decision that stunned most everyone (except some at the Walnut Street Baptist Church who claimed divine intervention), Judge Richman ruled the city's imminent domain ordinance was unconstitutional.

City officials squealed foul and lamented that the aborting of the convention center project would set back downtown revitalization 10 years. Indeed, without its so-called anchor for a new downtown, the city would have difficulty attracting others to invest in its grand masterplan, property values would remain low and bluebloods would stay away.

But the possible cancellation of the convention center could also be viewed in another way: Sparing the small storefronts and keeping the property values low enables the small shops, unpretentious bars and student hangouts to survive. Instead of becoming the turf of outside interests and large corporations, downtown may yet remain the domain of independent entrepreneurs and young people.

Maybe the strip ain't dead after all.

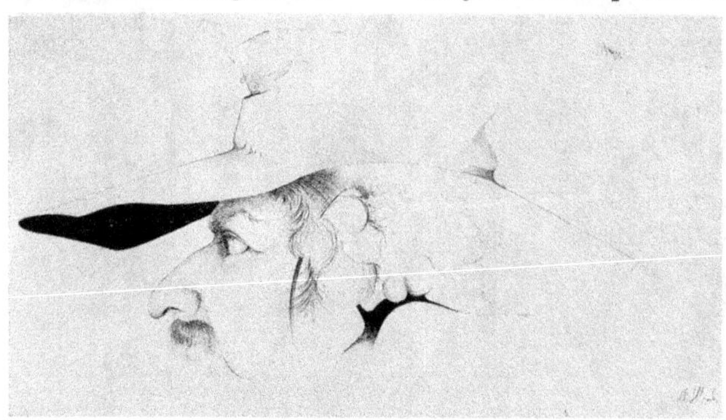

--Anteater by Dan Wood--

Carbondale After Dark I

"Carbondale After Dark" first appeared in Scum, *one of four mimeographed "underground" newspapers published during the summer of 1967. Each of the newspapers had a different name -- The Germ, Scum, The Bod and The Observer. The staff and facilities were the remnants of the* Tower Times, *the University High School student newspaper. U-School was a "laboratory" nursery-through-high school where experimental teaching methods were tested on the child prodigies of the SIU faculty and others fleeing the public schools. It all took place under the ivory clocktower of Pulliam Hall on the spacious SIU campus.*

When I was a 16-year-old sophomore, SIU decided to close U-School and phase its students into the public schools. Needless to say, there was a certain dip in "school spirit" among students, teachers and administrators alike, creating an atmosphere of cynicism and permissiveness that allowed something like Scum *to be published. In addition to satire, the newspapers had articles on drugs, Marxism, Greenwich Village and sex. The editor was a most remarkable young man named Jerry Magnus.*

Although the first street disturbances were occurring and drugs were beginning to trickle onto the campus, in 1967 Carbondale was still considered a sleepy little college town, the home of the Salukis and a nutty professor named Buckminster Fuller. There were few bars, and the strip, such as it was, was Freeman Street, a one-block alley between Illinois and University avenues. Much has changed in Carbondale since 1967, but some things . . .

Are you one of those unenlightened

Carbondale transplants who is always complaining, "Oh golly gee, there's never anything to do in this boring old town. Now back in Chicago (or San Francisco, New York, Los Angeles, or Boulder, depending on where you're from or whom you wish to impress), there's always something to do and never a dull moment."

Indeed, a typical summer afternoon in Carbondale can be the pits. But when the sun goes down (it goes down a bit late because folks around Carbondale are on Daylight Saving Time so the farmers can finish their chores) the pulse of the town quickens and all the excitement lying dormant during the day comes out. And if you follow the following instructions, you can hit most of the hotspots in one memorable evening.

Start your big night precisely at sundown, at the corner of Oakland and Mill streets. With celestial splendor, as if the hand of God had suddenly swooped down for just an instant, the streetlights will simultaneously flicker on all the way down both streets. Some people will spend the entire evening just watching moths trace trails around those shining spheres, but there's so much more to see and you must move on.

Proceed east on Mill Street until you come to University Avenue, angle left past "the island," and then enter the very heart of this titillating city of nightlife. Stop briefly at a hangout at 701 S. University called Moo 'n' Cackle (now B. and A. Travel Service). The significance of "The Moo" is neither its anemic hamburgers nor its grainy malts but the fact that it is an excuse for there to be a Moo 'n' Cackle parking lot. The hangouts ringing the lot -- the Moo, Tiffaney III, Spudnut's, Crazy Horse and Dunk 'n' Dip

-- each has its own specialized clientele. The lot in between serves as neutral turf for the various in-crowds who migrate back and forth.

But before grazing in the Moo parking lot, you should masticate on pizza at one of the town's three pseudo-Italian restaurants:

Pizza King, which recently moved from a drafty frame house at Mill and Illinois to 308 S. Illinois, is a no frills (and in 1967 no alcohol) eatery with red and white checkered tablecloths, candles poking out of wax-covered wine bottles, and wood partitions breaking up the room so no one can see who's making out with whom. At Italian Village, south of the levee on Washington Street, plastic vines and

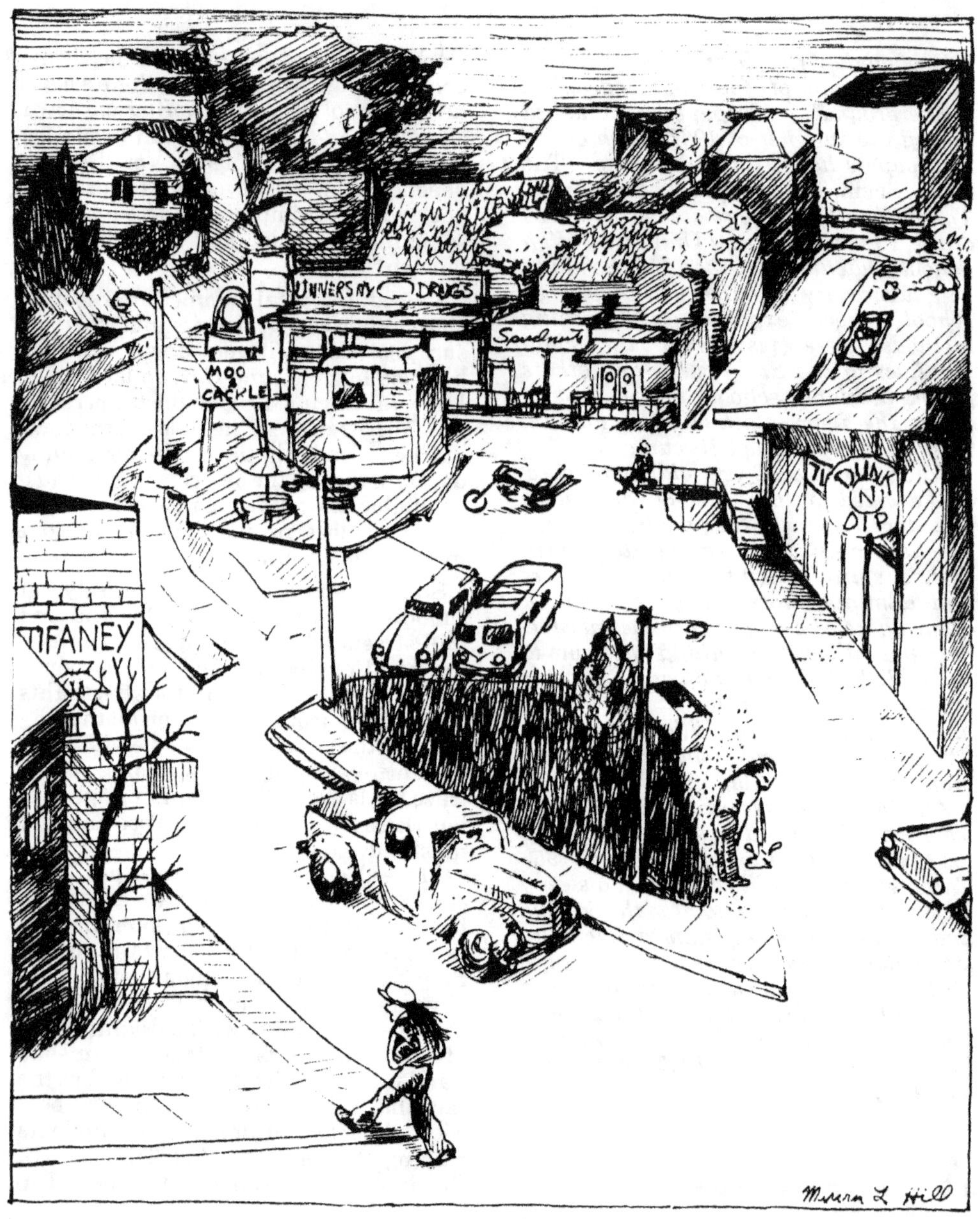

Chianti bottles dangle from the ceiling while a barbituated organist plays medleys of daytime soap opera themes. Over at Jim's Pizza Palace, at College and Illinois (Jim's Pub) the atmosphere is more cerebral. Bearded men with thick accents move chess pieces stained with tomato sauce, oblivious to the banter of the high school boys trying to impress their cigarette-smoking dates.

After dining you should visit the fabulous SIU campus where you can play "dodge the rapist" at Campus Lake, or mingle with the foreign students in the television room at the Student Center. But don't get sucked in by Rawhide. Soon it will be time to do some serious cruising, or, as they call it in Carbondale, "scooping the loop."

There are three ways to scoop the loop, depending on your age and mode of transportation. Twenty-one-year-olds can get looped at the bars on the levee or the out-of-town roadhouses like the Bird Cage, the Road Runner or Midlands. If you have a car and are in high school, scooping the loop means visits to various parking lots, starting with McDonald's on the west side (where Turley Park is now), and then to the Moo, the Dairy Queen, Italian Village (watch out for those speed bumps), then back to McDonald's again. But the most common form of scooping the loop, and the one that requires neither adulthood nor an automobile, is ambling across the Moo parking lot on foot and putting in appearances at the various hangouts along the rim.

At the Moo you can join the high school kids and frat brothers who sit at the umbrellaed metal tables and throw french fries at pedestrians.

Crazy Horse (Gatsby's) is a below-street-level pool hall where all sorts of unsavory characters will accost you and try to induce you to "shoot some pool" with them. Do not do it. Remember, you are looking for the real action, not some easy money. Feed some nickels to the decrepit pinball machines and then leave.

Tiffaney III, on the island, is where you can spy on the radicals planning the revolution or the budding liberals having their racial flings.

Spudnut's, a 24-hour doughnut shop in the Campus Shopping Center (now Quatro's), is where the late-night speed freaks, test crammers and beatniks loiter.

And for bohemians who find even Spudnut's *passe,* there is the less-peopled Dunk 'n' Dip ice cream and coffee shop next to 710 Book Store. The patrons there like to sit in wrought iron chairs, order banana splits and then make *avant-garde* sculptures out of the leftover food and styrofoam cups.

At the stroke of midnight it is time to return to the Moo 'n' Cackle parking lot. All of the wild characters who have been to the private parties and drinking orgies on country roads will have gravitated there in search of late-night thrills. But you have to be careful whom you talk to now. There are real drunks and fake drunks. Some just come to watch the real drunks get sick in the lot. You can spend the rest of the night vainly chasing "snatch," in the language of the natives, or else staying on the sidelines and watching the seasoned veterans make asses out of themselves.

At long last, after what has surely been the most memorable night of your life (if you have followed these instructions), the dawn begins to break, and the fabulous nightlife vanishes underground for another day. But you still have the most eerie, the most exciting, the ultimate ecstatic wonderful climactic event yet to witness. Hurry or you'll miss it. Hurry down to East Main Street.

Somewhere in the night you hear a great door being opened, and to the ear it sounds like the great gate of Troy itself. Diesel engines clear their throats, and oversized wheels rumble on the pavement. As the fantastic white contraptions lumber past you in solemn but awesome array, your breath will be taken away by the inspiring street cleaning machines, intent on their noble but futile mission of removing all the bottles, butts, vomit and vermin left behind by the evening's madness.

1970

Seven Days In May

In May of 1970 I was 2,000 miles away from Carbondale, trying to be a Yippie in Los Angeles, where the protests were relatively mild. Ironically, my parents, who wanted nothing to do with riots but happened to own Kay's dress shop on Illinois Avenue, were exposed to tear gas before I was. So the following account is not firsthand. It was compiled from Southern Illinoisan *and* Daily Egyptian *newspaper clippings, materials from the SIU Morris Library Special Collections, and interviews with officials, towns-people, professors, and former students. It was first published in the May 1977* nonSequitur *and an abridged version was in the* Southern Illinoisan *May 4, 1980.*

Few events in Carbondale's history have had as profound an impact as the riots. It could be argued they caused city and university officials to stop taking students for granted. Indeed, the university dropped the last of its in loco parentis *policies and allowed a non-voting student on the Board of Trustees; and the city began holding free concerts in the streets and handing out liquor licenses like they were lollipops. But it also could be argued that most of those changes were in the works before student protests erupted into violence.*

The riots undoubtedly crystallized the growing backlash from townspeople against not only the students at SIU but also the entire "hippy" anti-war movement. They crippled downtown, both physically and psychologically, as a business center and created a stigma of decadence and radicalism that persists to this day.

SIU students still like to play in the street on Friday nights. But most of them take the loose atmosphere for granted and few are aware of how Carbondale gained its dubious reputation.

On a warm spring night in May 1970, a crowd consisting largely of SIU students protesting the Vietnam War and the deaths of four people at Kent State University went on a rampage through downtown Carbondale. In a few short minutes, 78 businesses were trashed and an estimated $100,000 damage done to property owned not by the military or some multi-national corporation, but by townspeople, Carbondale residents, whose responsibility for the things the rioters were protesting was tenuous at best.

The next day martial law was declared. Sales of gasoline, alcohol and firearms were prohibited, as were public gatherings, and a sundown-to-sunrise curfew was put into effect. The hundreds of soldiers and police sent to restore order subjected innocent students and townspeople to tear gas and violence, keeping the tensions high. The disruptions continued for several more days, resulting in the closing of SIU-C before the end of the semester.

Then-State's Attorney Richard Richman (now chief judge of the circuit court in Jackson County) summed up the situation as "a fascist police state brought on by students who act like a bunch of Hitler youth, and the over-reaction from police officers."

The streets are quiet now, although the memories remain for the townspeople, teachers, police and former students who lived through the eruptions. A lot of people would rather not be reminded about what happened in Carbondale in

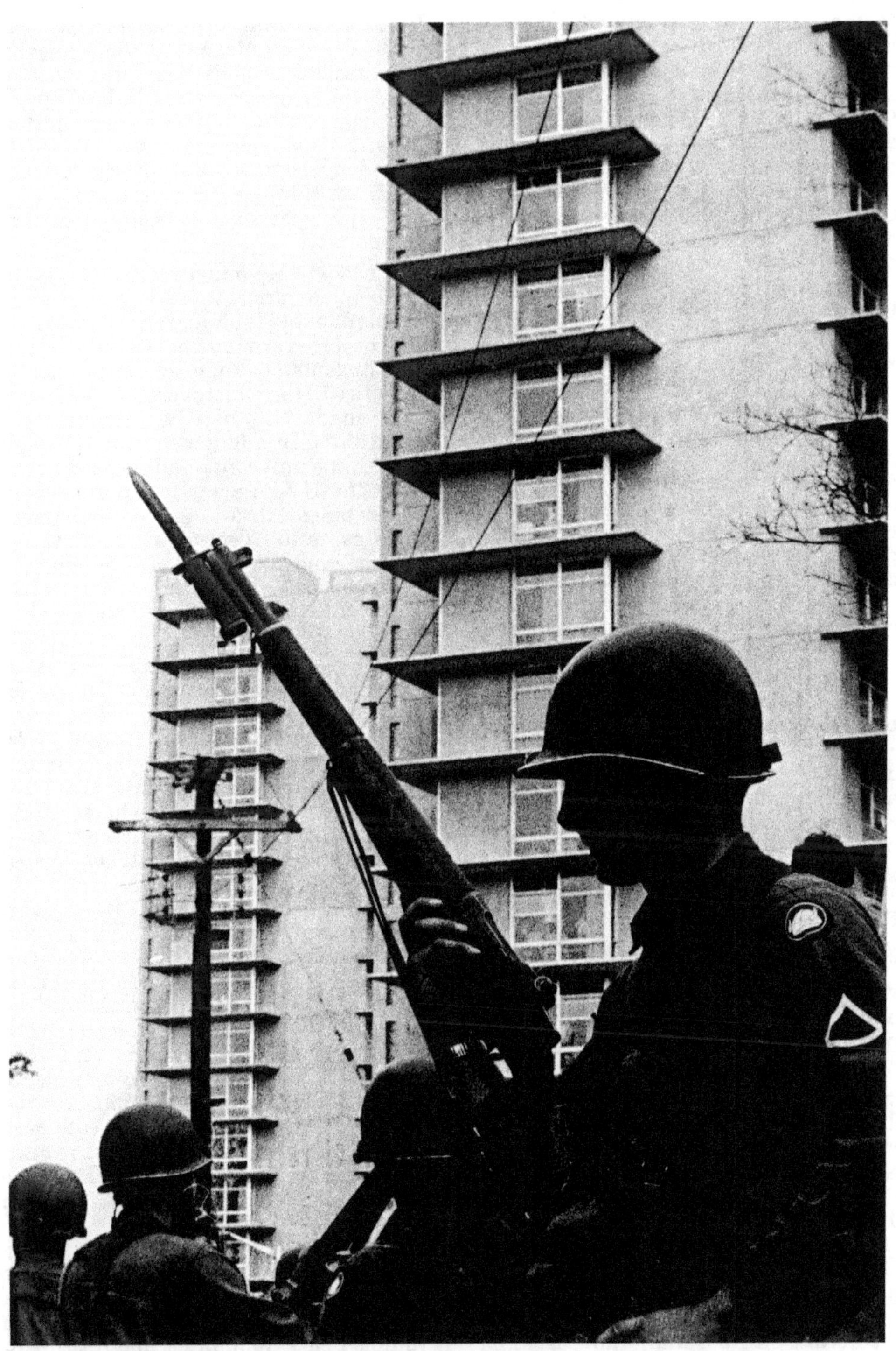

The Illinois National Guard was called onto the SIU campus in May 1970. *--Southern Illinoisan--*

May of 1970. But how and why a large, volatile crowd of concerned citizens, curious observers, cops, street people, students and teachers could suddenly be transformed into a panicking, violent, nihilistic mob, is perhaps something we'd better not forget.

The fuse of the riots that shook Carbondale in 1970 was lit nearly a decade before in the libertine communes of Haight-Ashbury and Greenwich Village, the student power movements at Berkeley and Columbia, and the freedom riders in the South. Eventually the various political, social and cultural movements came together over the issue of the war in Southeast Asia.

The resulting movement, the anti-war movement, composed of groups as diverse as the Black Panthers and the Quakers, was in many ways a unique phenomenon. Under the umbrella of a mutual cause, people with radically different backgrounds began to communicate. The outcome was a cultural explosion, a renaissance, as everyone exchanged roles. Whites smoked pot and blacks organized political parties. The alliance was never very organized, but it sure was big -- and threatening.

What began as passive resistance and civil disobedience became more militant as the war droned on and popular resistance to it increased. And as one president after another invested his political capital in the rice paddies of Vietnam, the government's response to the peace movement also became more militant. So when the '60s turned into the '70s, and the revolution had worked its way inland to Kent, Ohio, Jackson, Miss. and Carbondale, the struggle had lost much of its glamour. But it had become more intense.

Perhaps the first documented instance of civil protest in Carbondale was in the early 1950s when then-SIU student Dick Gregory desegregated the Varsity Theater by refusing to sit in the balcony. In 1964 the SIU chapter of Stokely Carmichael's Student Nonviolent Coordinating Committee (SNCC, pronounced "snick") picketed the Family Fun restaurant on East Main (now JR's) for refusing to hire blacks; and in 1966 the first of several anti-war groups, the Radical Action Movement (RAM) began draft resistance activities. The largest of the local anti-war groups, Bill Moffett's Southern Illinois Peace Committee, began mobilizing marches on SIU President Delyte Morris' house as early as 1967; but through 1969 these groups did not enjoy wide support from the student community.

In fact, the major disturbances in Carbondale prior to 1970 had been a couple of panty raids and street takeovers that occurred around final exam time. But as students became more politically sensitized, they discovered local issues that made the national issues more immediate. In addition to the draft and ROTC, the university had gotten a grant from the U.S. Agency for International Development to set up a "Vietnamese Studies and Technical Assistance Center" and the SIU Board of Trustees was about to build a new house for President Morris for $1 million.

The "revolution" officially came to Carbondale, at least symbolically, on June 8, 1969, when SIU's oldest, most revered building, Old Main, was destroyed by fire. To this day it is not known whether the fire was set deliberately, and if so, by whom. At the time, however, many believed the burning of Old Main was politically motivated arson.

Unlike today, in 1970 SIU student government was active, radical and relatively influential. Though its official powers were less than today's Undergraduate Student Organization, it aggressively pursued its goals with university administrators and city officials. Under student body presidents Ray Lenzi and Dwight Campbell in the late '60s, student government was actively involved in issues that ranged from eliminating women's hours in the dorms to establishing a rat control program on the northeast side. Furthermore, student government was recognizing and appropriating money to leftist organizations such as Students for a Democratic Society and the Southern Illinois Peace Committee; and to bring in speakers such as Abbie Hoffman, who came to SIU Jan. 18, 1970.

The faculty was also relatively active in politics, as teachers like C. Harvey Gardner and Doug Allen spent as much time on soap boxes as they did behind lecturns. (The firing of 104 teachers several years later, under David Derge's administration, put an abrupt end to the faculty's flirtation with politics. Since the purge its major preoccupation has been unionizing.)

In January, February and April there were mounting protests over ROTC and the Vietnamese Studies Center (for image reasons the center had dropped "Technical Assistance" from its title). Windows were broken and arrests made. Interest in the April student government election was running high, as seven candidates representing a spectrum of views were vying for president. The black-controlled Unity Party's candidate was Ellis John May III, who advocated student power and community development. Another candidate was Tom Busch, who since has steadily climbed the ladder as an SIU administrator. His party, the Action Party, was as radical as Unity in its politics but more moderate in its tactics. There was also the conservative Majority Party candidate Mike Ellis, who called for the administration to deal harshly with those who attempted to disrupt classes; and a return-to-normalcy Student Party candidate, Tom Scherschell, who represented the views of SIU's not-so-silent majority, the Greeks and Thompson Point.

Another candidate, David Kite, ran on the Apathy Party ticket. Kite claimed he should be declared the winner if less than half the students voted, and vowed to disband student government if elected. At one of the heated debates between the candidates, someone asked Kite why he was running for office if he was so apathetic. Kite answered that he was a "quasi-militant-apathist," which cracked up the audience and candidates alike.

The campaign climaxed with an election-eve firebombing of one candidate's driveway by members of his own party in an effort to discredit the rival radical party. In the end the radicals split their votes and the Greeks re-established their traditional control over student government with 28 percent of the vote.

The election occurred April 29, and when the campus radicals found themselves about to be shut out of university politics, there was an increasing pressure to take to the streets. Then, Friday May 1, President Richard Nixon announced the escalation of the Vietnam War and the Cambodian "incursion." At 10 p.m. that evening a restless and angry crowd of about 150 people formed on Freeman Street between Illinois and University avenues. The street was taken over, a trash fire was started and wine bottles and marijuana began to circulate. Bricks were thrown at police who came to investigate. Suddenly several columns of Illinois State Police marched onto the scene, cut off escape routes, and physically broke up the crowd. Sixteen people were arrested.

As luck would have it, the next day was a city-council-proclaimed All America Day in Carbondale. Several civic-minded groups, including the student council at Carbondale Community High School, had organized a "support America" parade to express their patriotism and counteract the anti-war demonstrations. It was a tense day, as the conservatives paraded in the streets and the radicals scowled from the sidelines, but no incidents were reported.

Things seemed to be quieting down on Sunday, but by Monday evening May 4, "The Kent State Massacre" had electrified campuses across the country. That night an emergency meeting of the SIU student government was held, and with 400 students looking on it voted unanimously to join a national student strike in which every university in the country was to be shut down. The boycott of classes was to start at noon Wednesday and last indefinitely. (When the Mississippi highway patrol snuffed six brothers at Jackson State May 6, the SIU Black Student Council voted to join the strike.)

Tuesday at noon a crowd estimated at 2,000 gathered in front of Morris Library to discuss Cambodia and Kent State and what action to take. Opinions ranged from peaceful protest to armed revolution. The student strike was scheduled to go into effect the next day, and in an attempt to appear sympathetic, school administrators announced a three-day mourning period that would include suspension of classes on Thursday and a memorial service in the SIU Arena.

At noon Wednesday, another rally was held in front of the library, and methods of extending the class boycott past Thursday were discussed. Deciding not to wait until Thursday, the crowd moved through nearby Lawson Hall and the Wham Building, disrupting classes and urging students to join the strike. Then someone pulled a fire alarm and classes had to be dismissed. The growing crowd surged toward Woody Hall, which housed administration offices and the Vietnamese Studies Center. Some people threw rocks and broke windows. A few people entered the building and vandalized it. By 2 p.m. all Carbondale police had been put on duty and state police assistance had been requested.

About 1,500 protesters then moved to Wheeler Hall, where ROTC was located. Using bricks from the remains of Old Main they broke windows and attempted to occupy the building, which was protected by SIU security police. On the order of Chancellor Robert MacVicar, the police were withdrawn and the students continued to occupy Wheeler and Woody Hall. At 4:30 p.m. Jackson County Sheriff Ray Dillinger asked Gov. Richard Ogilvie to send in the National Guard.

Inside Wheeler, students ransacked the ROTC offices while others drew up a long list of demands that included abolishing the Viet Studies Center and ROTC, amnesty for those arrested during the demonstrations, the disarming of police, a statement from the administration condemning the Cambodian invasion, and removal of the Old Main cannon. At 6 p.m. about 1,000 protesters marched through downtown Carbondale and back to Woody Hall, where several hundred people were still inside. Finally, the police cleared the two buildings, incurring several injuries in the process. The crowd formed again downtown, and about 1,000 people clustered in the vicinity of Freeman Street and University Avenue, uncertain of what action to take next.

It was a standoff between police and demonstrators until midnight, when a simple gesture by a local businessman averted what might have turned into a messy encounter. Where tear gas and riot clubs had failed to disperse the crowd, and as state police were preparing to charge the protesters again, Lou Cerutti, then operator of Papa Caesar's restaurant, began to dispense free coffee and soda to the demonstrators and police. Tempers cooled and the crowd quieted.

When several students tried to repay Cerutti for the free drinks, he suggested they donate the money to a bail fund. Commented Cerutti: "If we saved one head from being busted, it was worth every damn penny." The crowd disbanded peacefully.

By Thursday, May 7, the day of the worst rioting, $13,000 damage had already been done to university buildings, scores of people had been arrested, more than 30 police had been injured, and 89 state police and 600 National Guardsmen

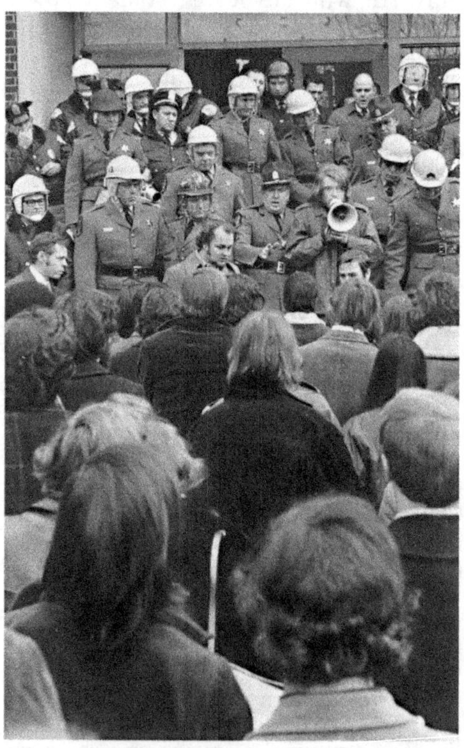

Police negotiate with protesters in front of Woody Hall during Wednesday's demonstrations.

--*Southern Illinoisan*--

were stationed in Carbondale. The evening began peacefully, as another rally, attended by 2,000 people, was held in front of Morris Library. By 9 p.m. several thousand demonstrators, students, spectators and street people had gathered at the intersection of Main Street and Illinois Avenue, blocking highway traffic. The crowd sat down at the intersection and vowed to stay there until the next morning when they planned to continue boycotting classes.

After officials conferred, they decided to avoid a confrontation by rerouting traffic and allowing the protesters to remain. The police announced the protesters could stay as long as they did not block the railroad tracks. There were some speeches, some singing, marijuana was smoked and wine and beer appeared.

Observers remember the crowd at this point as being low-key, somewhat festive but benign. The nominal leaders of the rally were stationed at the north end of the crowd, which stretched south along Illinois Avenue from Main Street. One block north of the intersection, at Jackson Street, 40 state troopers were poised. A contingent of National Guardsmen was waiting nearby. Monitors wandered through the crowd, telling people to stay calm, remain seated, and that everything would be all right.

Then, about 10 p.m., about 150 militants and street people broke away, and in defiance of the police order, blocked the railroad tracks at Main Street. Mayor David Keene used a bullhorn to ask the group to get off the tracks, as that was a violation of federal law. Protest leaders also unsuccessfully tried to persuade the group to vacate the tracks.

It was at this point that the authorities decided to disperse the entire crowd "in a southeasterly direction" with the use of tear gas. Suddenly the night sky was lit up with the eerie flares of tear gas canisters shot into the crowd from grenade-type launchers by the state police two blocks away.

The protesters were taken completely by surprise. Most were unaware of the group that had blocked the tracks, had not heard the mayor's appeals, and were under the impression that authorities had agreed to let them stay in the street through the night. Their initial reaction was fear, anger and betrayal. When the tear gas bombs began exploding, the crowd panicked. The group that had been blocking the tracks charged south down Washington Street, away from the troopers and guard, which began to advance. The main crowd, which had

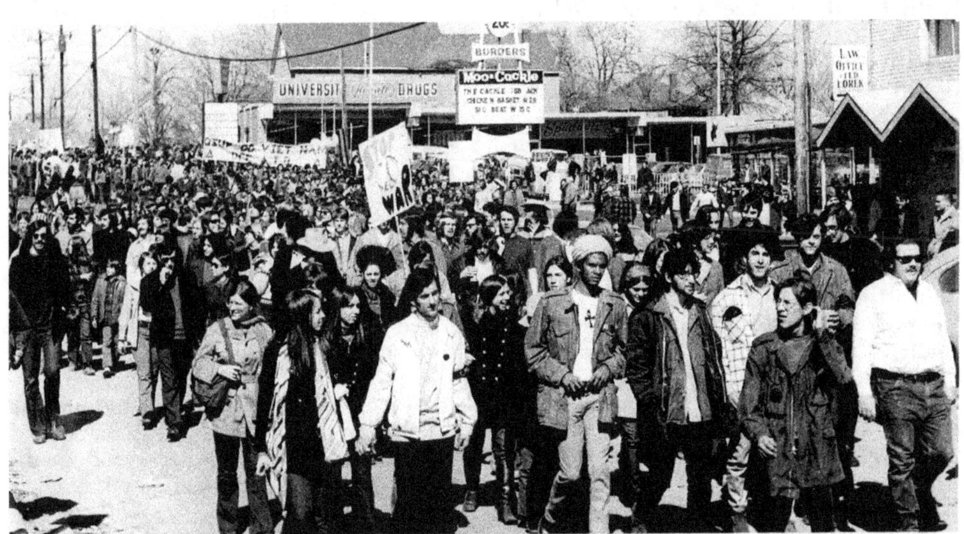

The Wednesday march through downtown as protesters passed the Campus Shopping Center and "the island" on University Avenue.

--Southern Illinoisan--

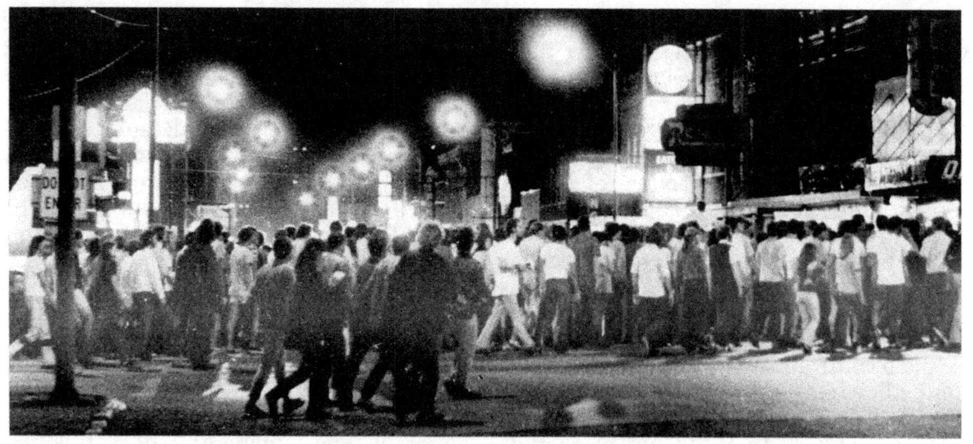

Thursday night demonstrators blocked the intersection at Main Street and Illinois Avenue . . .

become an enraged mob, retreated south down Illinois Avenue. In the midst of the chaos, some people began breaking windows. In less than a half-hour, an estimated $100,000 damage was done to 78 businesses by rock throwers and spontaneous looters.

A disciplined line of National Guardsmen drove the rioters south. But the mob reformed near the Lutheran Center, at Freeman and University, and when the soldiers got to the area they were showered with a hailstorm of rocks and bottles. Observers saw several guardsmen fall under the barrage, but the soldiers did not break ranks. Several soldiers fired tear gas toward the crowd, but the rioters refused to disperse and continued to pelt the guard with debris.

Then, at the height of the violence, someone lit some firecrackers, which sounded like gunfire as they exploded. The fireworks scared the demonstrators as much as the guardsmen, as they realized the soldiers might think the sounds were coming from a sniper and return the fire.

Two trucks were dispatched to save the soldiers, but as they approached the men they were bombarded by more stones. The drivers, who were young and not used to such situations, panicked and turned down a side street before they were able to reach their comrades. Then, the rest of the 600 National Guardsmen mustered in front of Woody Hall and marched in formation up University Avenue. The crowd was intimidated by the number of soldiers and began melting away. The soldiers marched up the street until they reached the trapped soldiers and then marched back to Woody Hall. Sporadic incidents, including police gassing of student dormitories, went on into the night, but the major violence of the evening was over.

At 2 a.m. Friday morning, Mayor Keene declared a state of emergency. Sale of firearms, package liquor and gasoline in containers was prohibited. The city was put under a sundown-to-sunrise curfew and police were instructed to disperse groups over 10 in number.

By the time the gas had cleared, 70 people had been arrested, 60 injured and emotions were running high. Nevertheless, Dean of Students Wilbur Moulton announced classes would be held as usual.

Friday dawned with yet another rally in front of Morris Library. While a police helicopter ("whirleypig") hovered overhead, about 100 students discussed nonviolent demonstration tactics. When the crowd swelled to about 400 people, police and soldiers moved in and the crowd dispersed.

An evening rally had been planned at Brush Towers, but in another display of force, National Guardsmen stood shoulder to shoulder in a line that stretched from Illinois Avenue to Wall Street, cutting off the students from the downtown area.

The students were relatively subdued

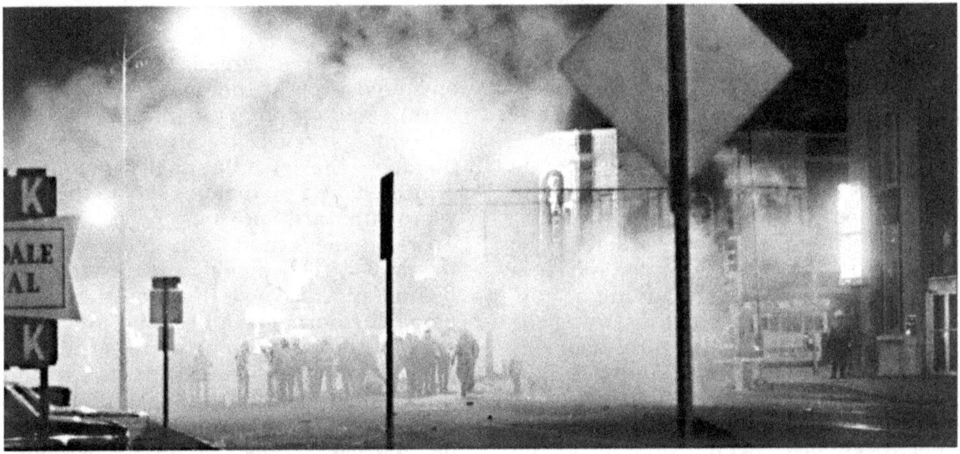

. . . and were tear gassed by police.   *--Southern Illinoisan--*

on Saturday, but the police, and especially the out-of-town police, were not. Using the curfew and order to disperse as an excuse, they retaliated against the abuse they had suffered over the past several days. They radicalized more than a few innocent bystanders with indiscriminate gassings, clubbings and arrests. Several dormitories were gassed, as were several downtown businesses where fleeing students sought refuge.

Much of the police retribution was more or less spontaneous, but one incident in particular was not. At 9:30 p.m. Saturday, six police units in state police uniforms, wearing gas masks but not wearing badges or name plates, raided a house at 508 Bridge St. Ross Scalise, who today is a medical student in Texas, remembers the raid vividly. He was inside the house at the time. Scalise, then a sophomore at SIU, said the house was rented by a group known as the Radical Youth Movement, a splinter group of Students for a Democratic Society. RYM published the *Big Muddy Gazette*, a local underground newspaper. Scalise said the group was a "political collective" composed of "serious radicals" who thought rioting was "stupid."

The group of about 15 individuals was sitting at home, obeying the curfew, watching television, Scalise said, when tear gas canisters smashed through every window in the house. Terrified and suffocating, the group members walked out of the front door, hands held high or helping others who were about to faint. They were clubbed and beaten anyway, according to Scalise. He said police entered the house, without a search warrant, and trashed and looted it. The 15 SDSers were arrested for unlawful assembly, but the charges were dropped. Scalise said that when he returned to the house after getting out on bail, he counted 27 tear gas canisters.

Virgil Trummer, then assistant SIU security director (now director) said his recollection of the incident was that "we had gotten information which led us to believe there were meetings being held there (508 N. Bridge St.) for the leaders of the riots. We had also heard that bombs were being manufactured in the basement of the house. I think the police had reason to go in and search."

Over the weekend, Chancellor MacVicar organized a new group known as the "Peace Volunteers." The purpose of the group, made up of faculty and students, was to guard campus buildings in lieu of a continued National Guard presence. Professors who served with the group remember spending the night in campus buildings, waiting to be bombed or whatever, as a terrifying departure from their normal academic duties.

On Monday the madness continued. Groups of more than four people would form, police would gas and charge, and everyone would run. Pete Mueller, a cartoonist now living in Madison, Wis., was a freshman at the time. Mueller's memories of Monday sound like a bad dream: He went to a late afternoon class at Lawson Hall, but was lured outside by the pungent odor of tear gas. He ran over to Woody Hall where there was a crowd, only to be gassed by a squad of state police. He sought cover in the Home Ec building, but the police gassed inside the building. Next he ran east, across the tracks, to the Newman Center, where a group of 200 people were having a "rap-in" and trying to figure out just what the hell was going on. A history professor was trying to deliver a speech about how America should heal its wounds, but he was being interrupted by tear-gassed student refugees seeking sanctuary, and rumors were spreading that the police were about to storm the building.

"If we all stay calm and remain quiet, we won't be gassed," Mueller remembered the professor saying. At just that moment, the door flew open, but it was just more refugees, the stench of tear gas trailing ominously behind them.

After the rap-in, it was nearly 6 p.m. and time for Pete to make it back to his dorm room before the curfew. But at Brush Towers dormitories, the battle was still being waged. Vietnam, neo-colonialism, the military industrial complex and all the rest of the rhetoric had been completely overshadowed by the more immediate issues of police violence and martial law. The students were protesting the sundown curfew by defying it, which gave the police more excuses to fire tear gas.

There was a squad of state police clustered around the doorway of Pete's dorm, and some students stood just beyond its reach taunting the police. Suddenly the police charged, the students scattered, and an escape route to the door was temporarily open.

Pete made a mad dash and got inside the lobby. The doors were then bolted behind him because the protesters were using the dorms as an escape, and some were throwing trash and fireworks from the windows. Pete walked up to the second floor, totally exhausted and nauseated from the gas. At the second floor landing he paused to look out the window, thankful to be inside. Bam, a tear gas canister crashed through the glass and landed beside him. The last thing he remembered was dragging himself up to the seventh floor where he passed out.

The history professor who spoke at the Newman Center, Donald Detwiler, has other memories of the day. He had been at the noon rally at the library. "There was an incredible aimlessness in the crowd," he said. "They were looking for direction. It was a very volatile situation. I guess I was there like everyone else, just not wanting to miss anything. They were responsible kids, upset over an undeclared war and the killings at Kent State."

Detwiler's remarks to the students at the Newman Center were later published

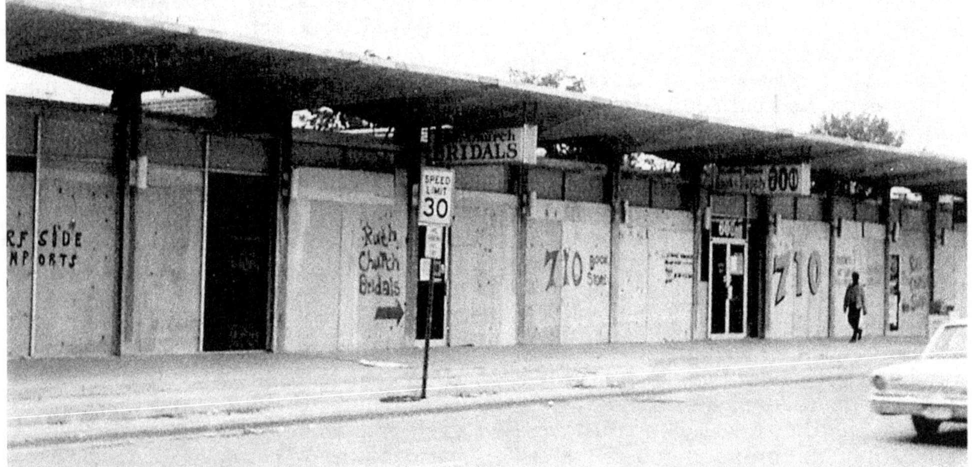

Plywood City: The Southgate Shopping Center . . .

in the *Southern Illinoisan*. In part, he told the students: "Anyone who opposed violence in Vietnam, Cambodia or Kent State only demeans his cause by practicing violence himself. This is the one kind of action awaited and, unfortunately, provoked by the authorities to justify their forceful and sometimes crushing reaction. Frenzied mob anarchism, far from being merely an ignoble form of hysterical self-indulgence, thus strengthens the hand of those it is supposed to weaken, provoking the very repression it protests."

Tuesday, May 12, the state police and National Guard were withdrawn and President Morris attempted to get things back to normal. Early in the day he announced that "under no circumstances would the school be closed." The afternoon was calm, but by 6 p.m. about 1,000 people had gathered in front of the library. An hour later the crowd had grown to 2,500 in defiance of martial law. After several speeches, it was decided to stage a march. The group, with William "Anteater" George and several other motorcycle gang members at its head, marched down Grand Street to Brush Towers to pick up more people, who came flocking like moths to a light. By the time the crowd had marched up Wall Street, down Main Street past City Hall, and then down Illinois Avenue past the boarded-up storefronts, it had grown to an estimated 5,000 people.

The marchers came to a halt on the lawn in front of President Morris' home and office, where the north end of Faner Hall is now. Windows were broken and several people entered the office, but Morris did not appear. Chancellor MacVicar did, however, and said Morris was going to call an emergency session of the Board of Trustees the following morning to discuss student demands. When the students responded with "close it now," MacVicar said he would ask Morris to hold the board meeting that night. "It is, in my opinion, no longer possible for this university to operate on a normal schedule," he said.

At 11:30 p.m., MacVicar announced that after he had conferred with Morris and Gov. Richard Ogilvie, it had been decided to close the school "indefinitely."

The announcement was greeted with wild cheering and shouts of "peace." The crowd then moved downtown, not to demonstrate, but to celebrate the closing of the school. There was little police could do as 5,000 people blocked the street, opened bottles of liquor and consumed drugs in the open.

At 12:30 a.m. Mayor Keene closed the bars, calling the downtown scene "one of the most disgraceful orgies imaginable. If these are our children, God help us." At 2 a.m. he attempted to recall the National Guard, saying "they have taken the campus, we can't just let them take the town."

By 4 a.m. the partiers had cleaned up their own mess and gone home. The Guard stayed in town until the weekend, when the dorms closed. There would be further disruptions in coming years, but the worst was over.

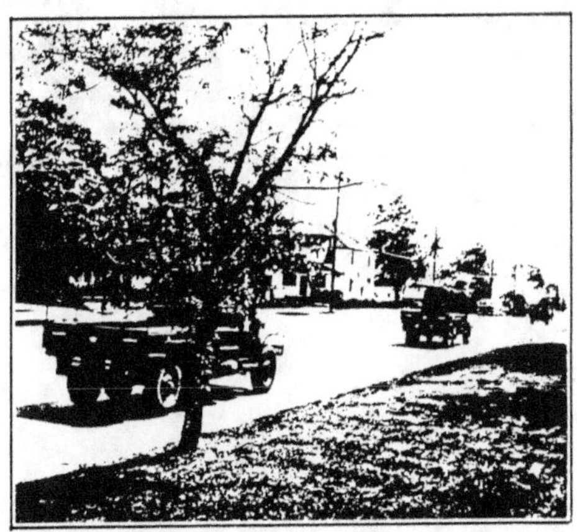

. . . Guard jeeps on city streets . . .

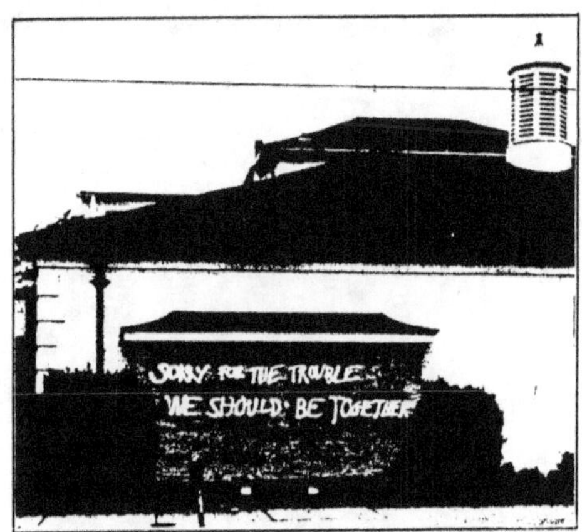

. . .apologetic graffiti.   *--John A. Miller--*

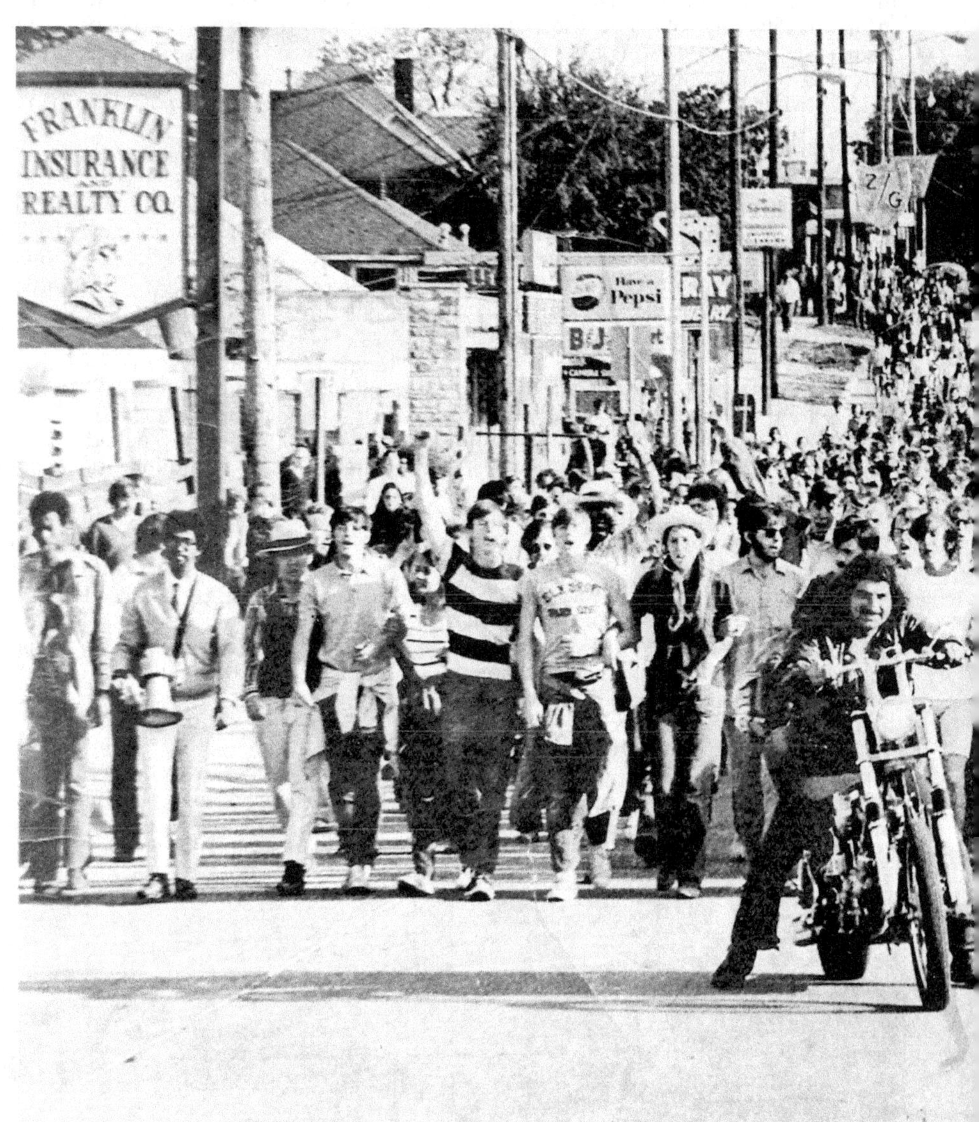
FRANKLIN
INSURANCE
AND
REALTY CO.
Have a
Pepsi
B/J
Z
G

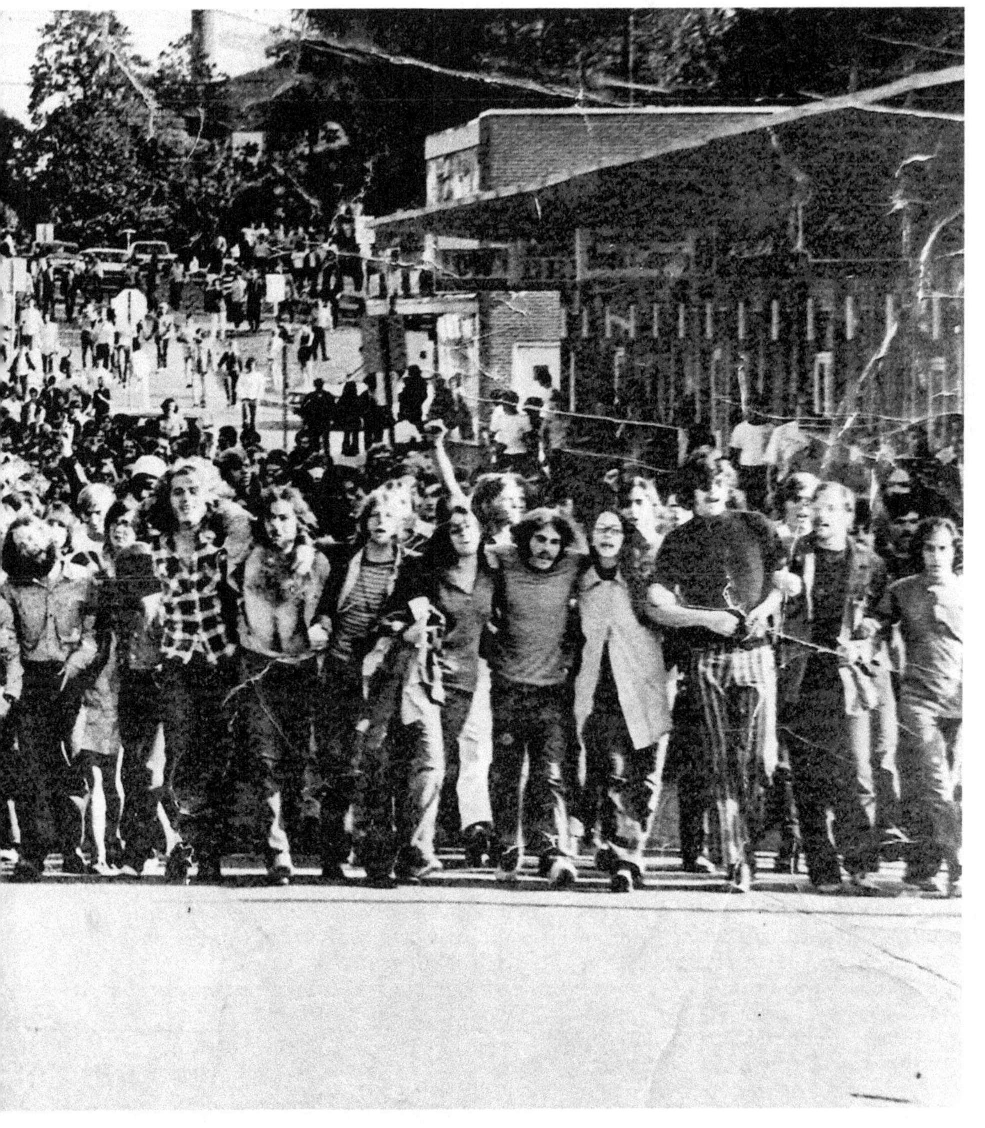

This classic photo was taken by Ralph R. Kylloe, Jr. at Illinois Avenue and Mill Street during the Wednesday, May 6 1970, march through downtown Carbondale. William "Anteater" George led the parade on his Harley, while Bill Moffett (far left) directed the marchers with a bull horn. It was first published in the *Daily Egyptian*.

Wonder Boy

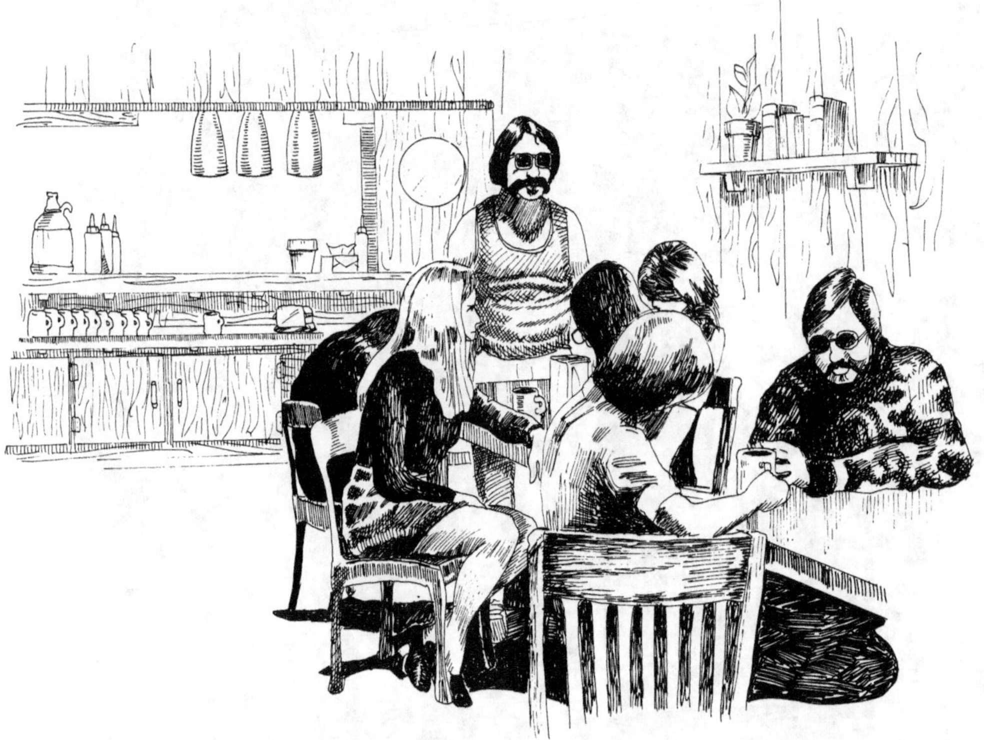

"Wonder Boy" (originally titled "Mitchell Hedrick Goes to Miami") is loosely based on people and events in 1971 Carbondale. The scene of much of the action is the old Papa Caesar's Restaurant in the Campus Shopping Center on Freeman Street, although I used the name of another hangout, Moo 'n' Cackle, for poetic purposes: It is much easier to call the people in this story Moo 'n' Cacklers than Papa Caesareans. For the May 1976 non-Sequitur the locale was updated to a more current hangout, Southern Barbecue, with illustrations by Tom Minton. The present version uses Minton's Southern Barbecue illustration but has the scene switched back to the Papa Caesar's of 1971. At that time, downtown was starting to become more of a strip. After the 1970 riots the last of the townspeople vanished from downtown, and the number of bars was increasing, although the cafe scene was still popular, too. There was a young man from Carbondale who tried to become a delegate to the 1972 Democratic National Convention, but he never made it to Miami.

In Paris it might have been called a bistro, and Hemingway might have hung out there. In London it might have been a pub and Sam Johnson. Even in New York City it could have passed as the Pump Room and maybe Ed McMahon or somebody.

But it wasn't. It was Carbondale,

Illinois, and it was called Moo 'n' Cackle, a hangout for pubescent high school hippies from Carbondale Community High School and their college-aged equivalents at SIU. Frustrated artists, speeding test crammers, derelicts, pushers, pushovers, paranoids and an occasional wayward bad-ass biker.

Suspend the festivities of Moo 'n' Cackle and consider Mitchell Hedrick, veteran Carbondale scene-maker of four years. During his years in Carbondale High School, Mitch had spent a lot of time following people around. He had run for student council several times but always lost. He had marched for community civil rights groups but never got into the steering committee meetings. He provided the transportation, money for booze and cigarettes, and when his parents were away, he provided the place -- he even did impressions of John Wayne and Gregory Peck -- but he just never quite got there socially.

But Mitch wasn't a complete schmuck. His act was as legitimate as anyone else's. And internally, through the maze of his neurosis, he was a thinking individual, trying to find the light at the outer edges of his illusionment. Oh, sure, he was trying to be cool because he thought he could get attention that way, but he also envisioned a morality of cool where everyone could win and nobody had to lose. He thought everyone ought to be that way.

In college it seemed as if his luck was changing. A new environment, new people, a clean start. He ran for SIU Student Senate unopposed and was elected off-campus representative. He started making it with some women, wearing bubble sunglasses and walking with a characteristic strut.

Eighteen-year-old college freshman Mitchell Hedrick is standing in front of Moo 'n' Cackle. It's a Thursday afternoon in August 1971. He is armed with a clip board, petition and ink pens, and he's bristling with the fervor of opening night. Mitchell Hedrick is about to make a stab at the big time:

Take a nervous gulp of air and enter. Look around furtively and take in the who's who, make sure no pimpy friends are in the area, spot homely big-legged philosophy majoress coffee-and-text-booking it alone in a booth at the rear. Swoop.

"Um ... excuse me, my name is Mitchell Hedrick and I'm trying ... I'm running for the Democratic National Convention as a Muskie delegate. Uh, are you a registered voter?"

Homely philosophy majoress glumly sizes up the eager beaver invader of her booth. Trying to figure out what's happening. Is this cat for real or is this a line? If it's a line should she go along with him or inject some hostile vibes of a deflationary nature? And if he's for real should she sign his lousy petition? Looks at Mitchell somewhat sarcastically. "Are you for real?"

Mitchell, feeling foot in the doorishly, thrusts the official-looking petition at her. "Yeah, here, look ... I mean, um, uh, yeah, who're ya gonna vote for?"

Philosophy majoress inspects petition, starts reading the small print, gets eye fatigue after about five words, considers Mitchell's last sentence fragment. "Oh, I don't know, McCarthy I guess, if he were offered, no offense."

Choosing one of his memorized responses he counters, "Yeah, but McCarthy isn't even going to be on the ballot for the primary and Muskie is. So if we're going to get our people into the convention we're gonna hafta get there as undercover agents, ya dig?"

Majoress considers this last bit of romantic logic. "Yeah, sure, why not ... "

Mitchell Hedrick makin' the scene. He's discussin' current events with the Poly Sci majors and wowin' the women with his wrap-around sunglasses. He's got the romantics, the what-do-the-elite-really-do - between-meetings - in - a - Miami-hotel room, the gee-wouldn't-the-kids-be-impressed, he's even gathering a modest following of too-young-to-vote-yet-still-concerned citizens.

Whether they are for Muskie or against him, skeptical or indifferent, envious, radical, reactionary, redneck, Black Muslim commie dope addicts, whether they are registered to vote or not, they sign his petition. Send some local stock to Miami Beach. Maybe he'll change the world, come home hail the conquering hero. Maybe he'll get to be a deciding vote on something. Maybe he'll get interviewed on network TV and be so nervous he lets loose an improvisational fart. So they sign Mitchell Hedrick's petition.

And then something weird and wonderful happens. Mitch gets his signatures together and files his petitions first. And it turns out that since he got his petitions in before anyone else his name will be placed at the top of the ballot. And it also turns out that when most people vote in primaries they don't know who the delegates are so they "X" down the list under their candidate as many times as they are allowed. From the top down.

Street corner socialite about to make good. He's getting approached on the streets by cool lookin' dudes he never had the guts to bum a smoke from and they turn out to be from the Peace and Freedom Party and they're sweetrappin him and turning him on. And tellin' him about the party: "Hey man wanna come to a party?"

The primary comes and Mitchell Hedrick makes the cut. And everybody is loving the winner. Cranky existentialists who never could stand his absurd optimism are gesturing their pipes at him, heavy hippies who used to cringe at his polyester complexion sandwiched in a plasticine leather jacket ensemble are buying him coffee and his old school chums are bygoning the bygones.

And Mitchell Hedrick? What's Mitchell Hedrick think of all the halibut? For a while he's thinkin' he's made it. That he's the cream of the Moo crop. But then it occurs to him that becoming the Boy Wonder of Moo Town wasn't that hard. Damnit! It wasn't even real. He hadn't turned anyone on. No one was saved. He fooled them. And even worse, he didn't contribute a whole lot towards their delusion. No dragons were slain, no emancipation proclamations had been issued, no battle scars or changes in everyday existence. All he did was gather signatures and file forms. So he beat their game. The thought fills him with joy. But it also fills him with anguish. There must be more to cool than this. With cool you oughta be able to stop the war in Vietnam, find out who shot JFK, something . . .

He turns bitter toward his new-found identity and his new-found friends. It was all too easy. And insignificant. And empty. One night, after having sat three hours at the same booth going over seven dozen variations of the same argumentative lines with a random sampling of Moo 'n' Cacklers, it occurs to him that he has been putting them on. A thought that has occurred to him before, usually filling him with a sense of smugness, of having everything under control. But this time it freezes his index finger at mid-point. For he suddenly realizes that the dragon remains to be slain. So far it's been a game, armchair quarterbacking. But in Miami, in Miami, that's where he is to confront the reality. That is where he must raise his sword on high, destroying once and for all the bullshit of smoke-filled back room political morality and replacing it with a return to the good old days of grassroot democracy where everyone has a share of the say.

His rap changes. A new burst of energy. He begins coming on real mysterious, man on a missionish, cloudy premonitions on this year we're gonna have the riot on the convention floor, and this is gonna be the year no one is elected president. Step aside boys, a man is tryin' to be born.

Surreal flashes of poignant convention sidelights. Old ladies fanning wrinkled breasts, three convention days of grasshoppers and stingers, belching and tugging at sweaty crotches, endless verbiage pursuing a pre-ordained conclusion, cigars and party horns and balloons and cheerleaders.

A procession of irritating mannerisms, chin pulling hand gesturing foot tapping finger drumming tongue to moustache massaging, bugger eating men in VFW hats. Active sweaty speakers, passive whiney speakers, compromising let's-keep-the-party-together speakers, totally incoherent speakers.

And in another corner we find a modest cluster of left leaning uncertainties, and some others. A caucus consisting of undercover socialists, undercover Muskie persuasionists, four undercover cops, seventeen reporters, several populist liberals advocating a sit-down strike in that fine old civil rights tradition, one long-haired Yippie full of guerilla-raid notions consisting of pulling plugs and

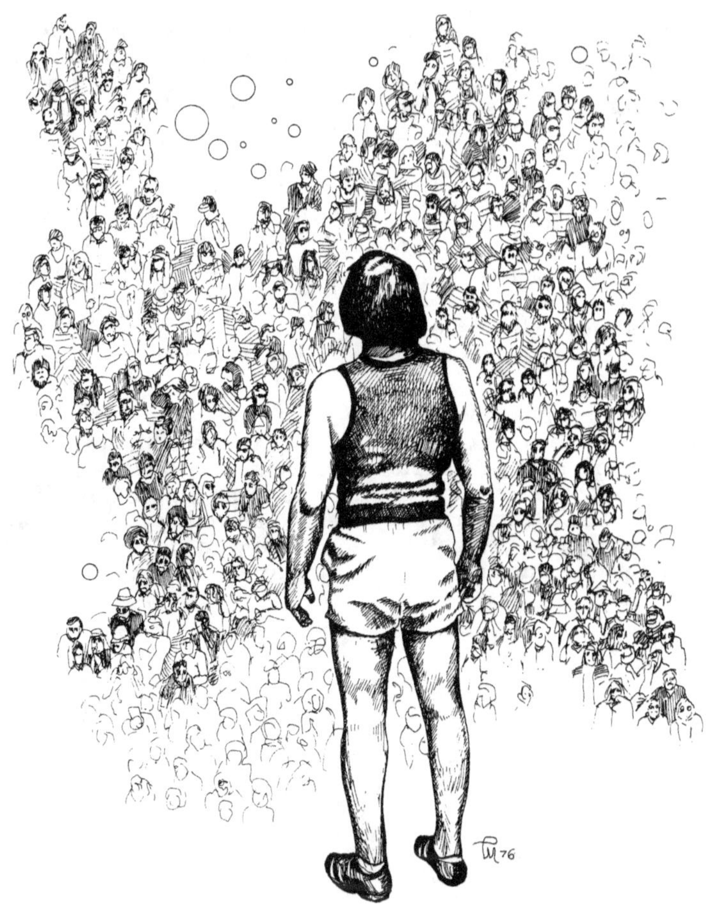

cutting wires, and Mitchell Hedrick, full of tactics for getting some word in edgewise before the meeting is adjourned.

Recommence the festivities at Moo 'n' Cackledom as once more Mitchell Hedrick makes the scene. Only this time he is welcomed as a returning warrior, standing ovation thrown in, a montage of hands beckoning him to have a seat at their table, let us be the first to hear tales of the big city.

Mitch almost turns tail and runs. Almost starts bawling. But blinking back the tears of confession, he peers hesitantly out at the sea of hands, hoping to find one that is graceful and feminine, or appetizing in some other way. For though Mitchell Hedrick would prefer never to return to the Moo, in some perverse-bordering-on-nostalgic way, he feels that he must. For Mitch has a message, brought all the way from Miami Beach, to the kind folks of Moo Town. A message about the future of his generation.

His eyes take in the room slowly, his new Peace and Freedom buddies yelling at him from a booth along the wall to his right, some high school girls jiggling and giggling from a table in the center, another table of high school jocks, some Jesus People smiling snidely, even a table of nodding junkies wanly waving plastic coffee spoons as a sign of recognition.

Mitchell Hedrick, feeling trapped in the center ring of a Barnum and Bailey production, takes several uncommitted steps in no particular direction, suddenly spots a group of his old school chums clustered at a table near the jukebox. Makes his way in their direction, avoiding the snags of peripheral well-wishers. Someone offers him a seat, and he collapses.

He suffers through the first volley of hey mans and how ya doins and whats happenin' babies. Slowly they close in on him with well how was its and how'd it goes. The room is shifting chairs and craning necks to catch glancephrases. A crowd of people has gathered and they're all trying to find a piece of his back to lay a slap on.

For several gruesome moments Mitch is having claustrophobic gags, but as he stares out at the pile of smiling faces, he forgets the burden that he bears; it's good to be back home, and he's laughing and getting high on how they're all lighting up when he mentions their names.

A voice asks about the riot. Mitch's head jerks around at the sound. "Riot? Riot?! The whole thing was a riot. The whole thing. This whole thing. One bigass riot. What good is havin' a riot in the middle of a riot?"

There is something in the way that he says it that causes the crowd to pause an instant before passing it off as flippant Yippie humor, and some are already laughing less heartedly and beginning to rub sides of noses with index fingers.

"Did you vote for Muskie?" someone asks.

"Nah. Are you kidding?" he sneers.

"What about McGovern?" asks a pre-convention conquestess.

"It doesn't make any difference who I ended up voting for," said Mitch.

"Well who *did* you vote for?"

"Harold Stassen."

Carbondale
After Dark II

"Carbondale After Dark II," with photos by John Barry, was first published in the April 1976 nonSequitur. Between 1967 and 1976 a war had ended, a business district had eroded and a subculture had evaporated. But the most profound change in Carbondale was the sudden proliferation of bars under the administrations of mayors David Keene and Neal Eckert.

There were a number of factors at work in the decision to liberalize the city's liquor policies. One was a new mayor's desire to do away with the monopolistic practices of the past. Another was the state's lowering of the drinking age to 19 and the reasonable enough rationale that as long as thousands of college students were trashing downtown, the merchants might as well make some money off them.

It was the bars that completed downtown's transformation into the strip, but the alcohol and atmosphere the bars served also hastened the area's demise as a hotbed of radicalism and underground culture. More than ever, it was just a place to get drunk and party. By our nation's bicentennial, the bar scene was solidly entrenched, and city officials have been trying to untrench it ever since.

You are coming from Chicago, on your way to New Orleans where you'll hop a banana boat to Colombia. But you got a late start, the sun's going down, and your Alfa Romeo could use a quart of oil. You decide to pull off I-57 and get an early start in the morning. But your body is still buzzing from the road, and as you try to unwind with the Magic Fingers in your motel room, you begin to feel that familiar urge for a woman, a bottle, and struttin'

the stuff in the electric night.

So you put on your leather and denim, your cowboy hat and high-heeled sneakers, and you think you're ready for anything.

But are you ready for Carbondale after dark?

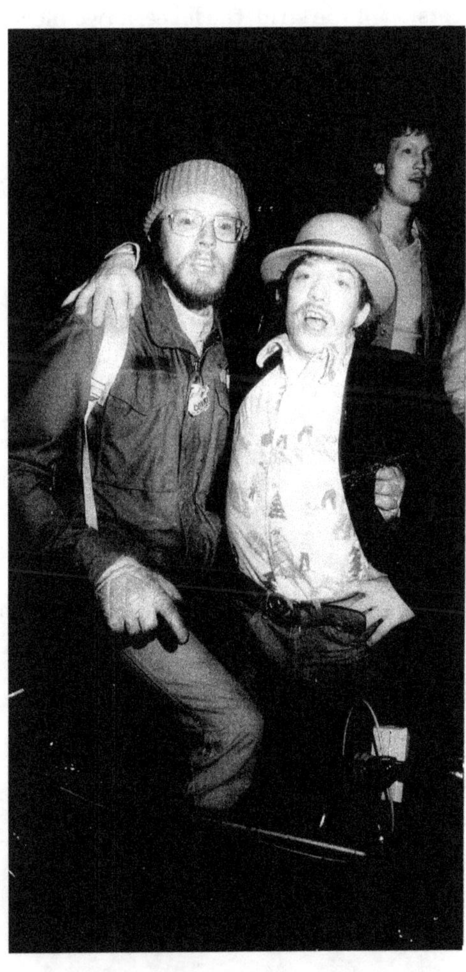

You used to live in C'dale, and you remember SIU as a party school. An oasis of decadence in the midst of the Bible Belt. In the late '60s and early '70s, Carbondale was very much a part of the cultural and political upheavals. It was then that downtown made the transition from a marketplace for townspeople to an annex of the university and a rest and recreation area for every derelict, wino and biker between here and Champaign.

As your Alfa purrs into town, you pass several motels with connecting lounges. The Plaza and Bleu Flambe have topless dancers, but you barely ease off the gas as you approach Wall Street. You've got bigger fish to fry. Your first stop is at the I.C. tracks where a slow freight train gives you a chance to look up Washington Street to your right to the black folks' version of the strip, the levee, a two-block expanse of crap games, winos and cheap tricks. At the south edge of the levee, below ABC Liquor Store, is the Washington Street Underground, where the gay crowd hangs out.

Finally the train passes, you hang a Louie at University, then scoop the loop twice before coasting into a parking space across from Quatro's Pizza in the Campus Shopping Center on Freeman Street. The parking lot that runs between Quatro's and 710 Book Store used to be the old strip back when LSD was king. Quatro's was Spudnut's, a 24-hour doughnut shop, Truck On In was Papa Caesar's restaurant (now Quartertime Junction, a pinball arcade), and Coal Kitchen would play for free in the lot.

But when the students began to feel their oats (or more accurately, their barley), the non-alcoholic sitdown joints went out, and the bar scene which became the party scene which became the boogie scene which became the glitter scene which is becoming the disco scene (which has since gone through an urban cowboy, punk and prep scene) took over. You saunter up Freeman Street to Illinois Avenue where the south end of the strip officially begins with Gatsby's.

Gatsby's

Gatsby's is a bar full of contrasts and contradictions, but presently it is one of the most popular bars in C'dale for the many who are looking for an alternative to the madness just up the street. It's surprising Gatsby's is as popular as it is. It's licensed to sell beer and wine only, and the music is a double anachronism -- live and acoustic. The decor of Gatsby's takes one back to the age of flappers, Model Ts and honky tonk pianos. You snake your way to the bar and order a Lowenbrau from their fine selection of imported beer. You could easily kill an hour loading up on free popcorn, but after a set you head up the street.

Jim's Pub

Much of the strip has changed, but one place has remained almost the same. The only thing new at Jim's Pub on the southeast corner of Illinois and College, is that backgammon has replaced chess as the house game. (After 1976 Jim's remodeled and took out its pizza ovens.) Jim's is the only bar on the strip where people go out just for dialogue, or where dialogue is feasible. "Wheelies" (people in wheelchairs) prefer the Pub. Whether it's atmosphere or accessibility, Jim's, along with PK's and Merlin's, are most often frequented by the disabled. You hazard a pit-stop and are saddened to discover they painted over the graffiti again.

Das Fass

Das Fass (north of Jim's, now closed) is the strip's version of a swinging singles bar. The decor looks like a cross between a German ski lodge and an Escher painting. The resident band at Das Fass is the Scheisshaus Five Minus One (tr: just as it sounds). The Scheisshaus is actually a combo of extremely capable musicians, including jazz keyboardist Gus Pappelis, who for reasons of poverty and lack of appreciation have been reduced to playing oom pah music. Oom pah music is a polka rendering of most any song under the sun (and some that never see the light of day), accompanied by scores of foot-stomping, wet-mouthed, slurring patrons.

Whereas the ambience of the upstairs is ribald, the downstairs of Das Fass is quiet

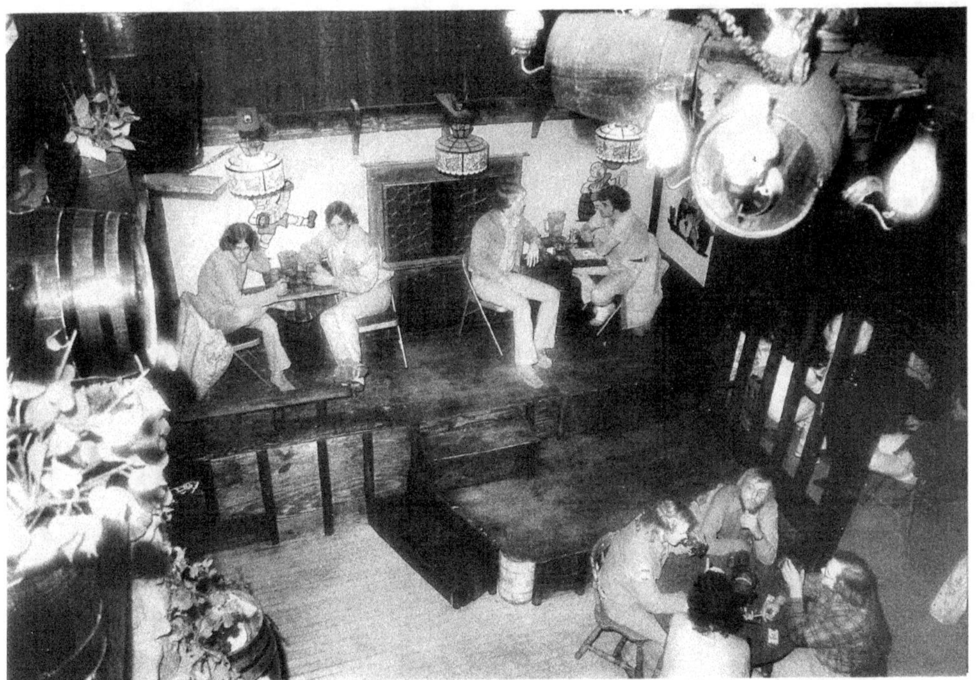

The interior of Das Fass

and intimate. The patrons recline on low slung couches and listen to romantic melodies while they ply each other with liquor and negotiate where they'll be eating breakfast. You consume a beer and hot pretzel, then move on.

As you stroll up Illinois Avenue, you brush shoulders with the multitudes that reside in the towers or the point. You go into a reverie as you pass the First National Bank parking lot next to Dairy Queen. A hospital and old folks home with lush green lawn and ancient oak trees once stood on that site. Back in the '60s, street people turned the lawn into a Carbondale version of People's Park -- playing music, smoking dope and watching the sky turn paisley. But to the residents of Carbondale and patients of Holden Hospital, the students looked less like people than a kind of bird in an Alfred Hitchcock movie. After the riots in 1970 a chain link fence was erected around the lawn, and soon after the "park" was replaced by a parking lot.

Upper Room

You see some friendly faces clustered around a guitarist as you approach a place called the Upper Room. It doesn't take you long to realize that these are Jesus people. Nice folks, but you pay your respects and find an exit. You pass Shad's, which means hot dogs, and then you are there. At the essence of The Strip. The melting pot of all the diverse elements that are pursuing their fantasies in the frantic madness of downtown. Merlin's, PK's, and the street between, squalid as they might be, are unquestionably the gestalt of what the downtown scene has become.

Downtown is glitter, glamour, struttin' and shovin', it's clingers and pinchers and yick yaks and prick teasers, it's horny and violent and passing out, it's loud music and heavy drinking, blowing off steam, falling in love and acting obscene.

Merlin's

Merlin's (once Golden Gauntlet, now

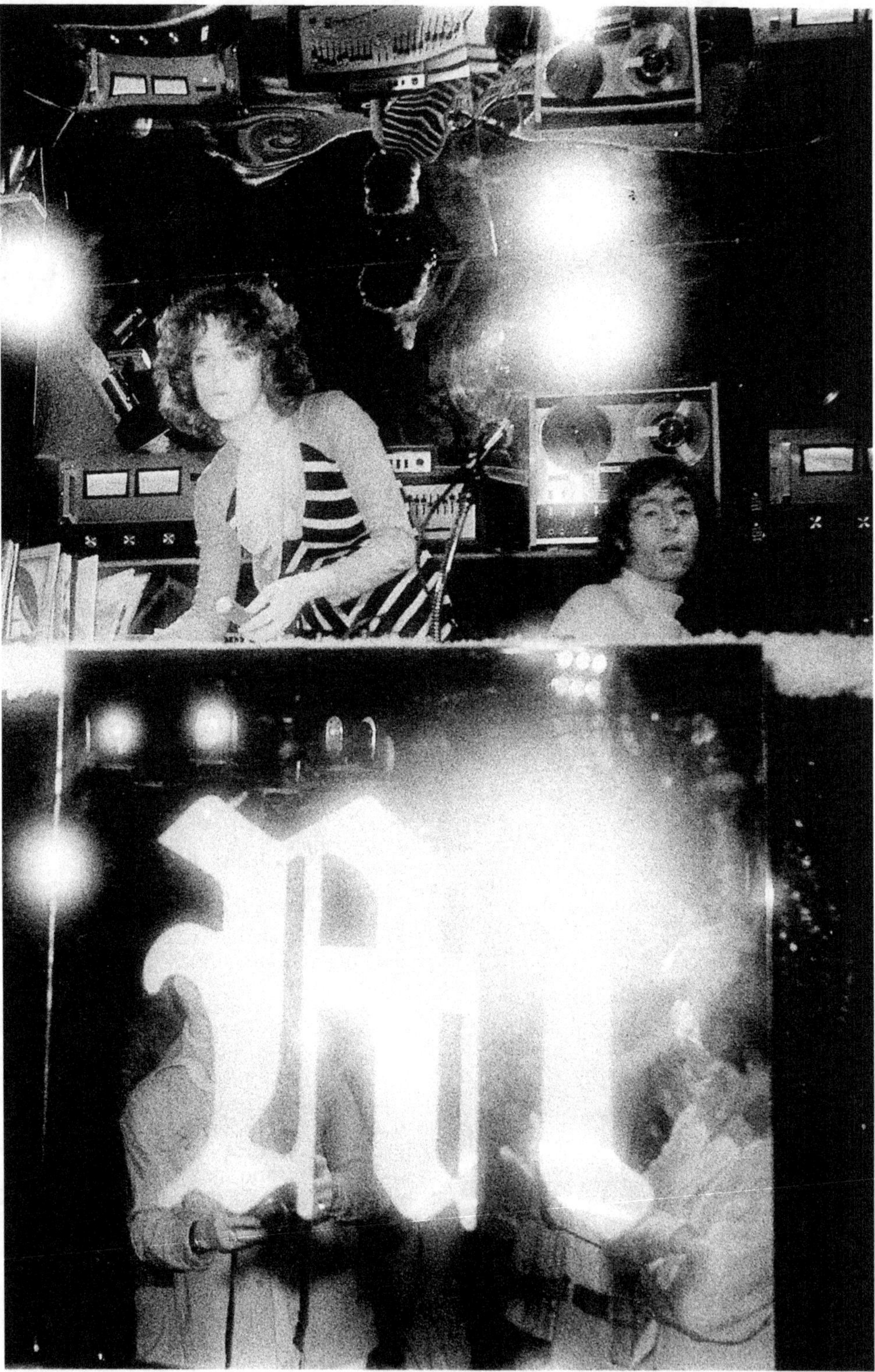

T.J. McFly's) on the southeast corner of Walnut and Illinois, still has the most ritualistic door check of any of the bars. First the IDs, then the limp wrist, then smeared ink on your arm. There is no cover charge for the front bar, and several nights out of the week there's live music that ranges from sweet soul to country boogie, frantic jazz and hard rock. The bar is rectangular, and dimly lit booths line the walls. You circle the bar once, looking for your spot, but nothing feels comfortable. So you assume a poetic stance by the cigarette machine at the "hot corner."

The hot corner is where all the guys who don't want anyone to know they're looking for chicks end up standing. Someone has foam on his mouth and he's not holding a beer so you decide to ooze around the corner and check out the middle bar.

The middle bar has changed. There are mobs of people brushing against each other, and at the entrance to the big bar is what appears to be a ticket booth for a cinema. Only instead of a marquee, an ominous hi-fi speaker looms above the booth. Like the others, you hesitate to go inside, but inevitably you're drawn to the ticket window. One of Merlin's many yellow-jacketed bouncers stamps your hand again, and you head down a furry orange tunnel. You nod to a knight in full armor, turn another corner, then find yourself in psychedelaramaland.

To your right, where the band used to be, is an elaborate dance floor. And to the left is a high platform where a woman in black leotards and earphones that look like Mickey Mouse ears is doing the grind, occasionally shouting something into a mike like, "let's boogie," twisting another dial, and the electronic crowd goes wild.

The dance floor is a thing of beauty. Triple leveled, the first two tiers are made out of naughty mirrors, and the top level is plexiglass over banks of flashing lights. Flanking the dance floor on two sides are walls with more colored lights that flash in funky patterns with every flick of the deejay's finger. The rest of the room is broken up into various environments; tables and chairs on stair-stepped patios, island bars to lean on; most everything but a waterbed.

You crush your cigarette out on the orange fireproof rug and mutter to yourself that it's too plush to last. The kids will tear it to pieces inside of a month. You don't want to like the disco. It's gaudy, pretentious and kitsch. It takes the magic relationship between performer and audience and throws it out the window. Instead, it exalts the technician, the engineer, the artificial sound and

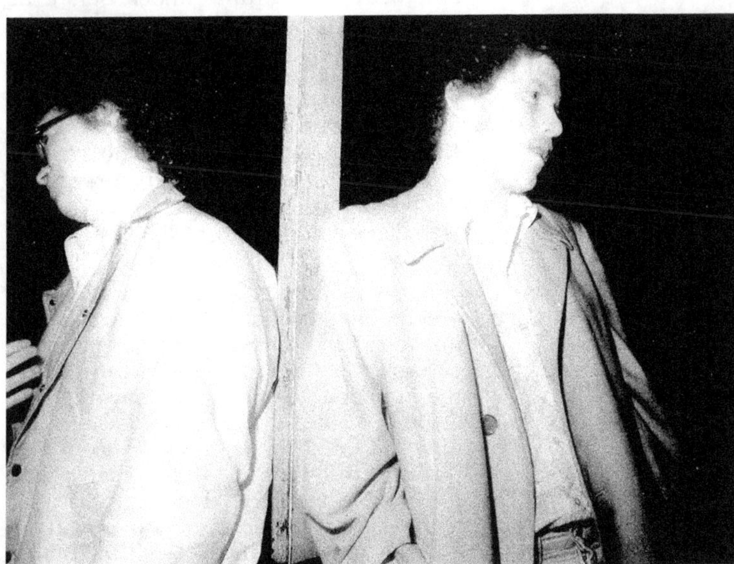

Two views of Merlin's: The disco deejay and the hot corner.

light show.

Even so, vulgar, garish and ostentatious, the room is an architectural masterpiece and an acid head's haven. Dancing on the $20,000 dance floor, surrounded by flashing lights and flailing limbs is like a total body massage. And you never have to worry about finding a dance partner just in time for the song to end and the band to go on break. The old ballroom was never much of a place to cruise, but the new layout allows you to lose yourself in the crowd and wander around almost as if you're in a medieval garden. Another positive aspect of Merlin's disco is the wide assortment of races and nationalities that mingle. Merlin's is one of the most integrated bars in town and the male-to-female ratio is also the best.

By now you've gotten pretty loaded and you're feeling pretty loose. You elbow your way through the crowd, step over a fallen downer freak, cop a caress from an inebriated sophomore, stare down a thug who wants to get laid or beat somebody up, a guy asks for the time then kisses your hand, you look away from an interracial couple who are looking at you looking at them, wink at a couple of dingaling freshwomen who are giving everyone the slip, dodge some dancers, then step outside and cross the street.

Pizza King

If Merlin's is the heart of downtown, then PK's is its guts. PK's is definitely hard-core, and not for the fainthearted. If you enter PK's expect to be mauled, stepped on and checked out as if you were a slab of meat. It also helps to be aggressive or patient because it usually takes a long time to get served. It's worth it, though. At 35 cents a beer and 65 cents a speedrail, PK's is the cheapest bar in town.

The attractively rugged owner of PK's is Gwen Hunt. More accessible and congenial than the other bar owners, on a busy night Gwen is sure to be behind the counter keeping the customers satisfied. Since PK's got its liquor license, it's been a hangout for bikers and junkies. Before the city began towing vehicles off the strip, there was sure to be four or five Harleys parked out front. The new bikers seem younger and are increasing in number, as are rumbles in the alley outside. Despite the many hard-nosed people who frequent PK's, there are surprisingly few fights inside. Those that do occur are quickly ended, either by the bartenders or the police.

You ease into a space along the bar, order a shot of whiskey, which is delivered in a plastic cup, and stare at a painting across from you that conveys far more of the atmosphere of PK's than words ever could. You hand the bartender a dollar and tell him to keep the change. He pockets the money and rings a bell attached to the light. Heads turn because the bell is rung so seldom. It's an oddity of Carbondale nightlife that so little tipping is done.

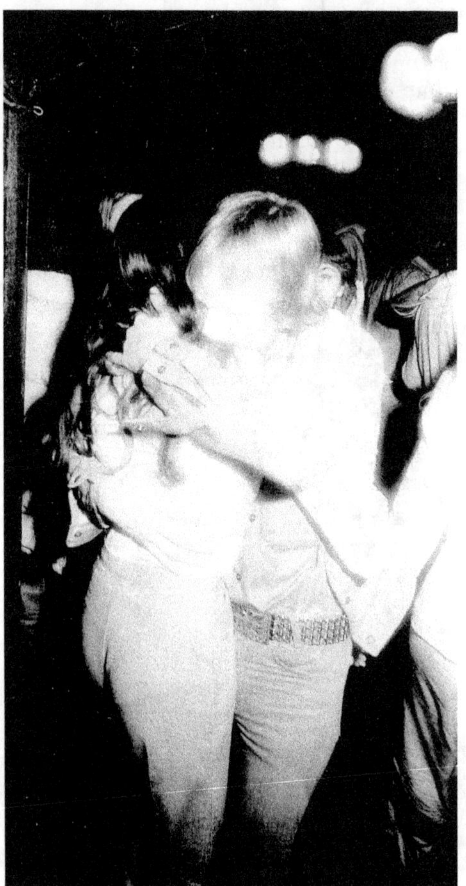

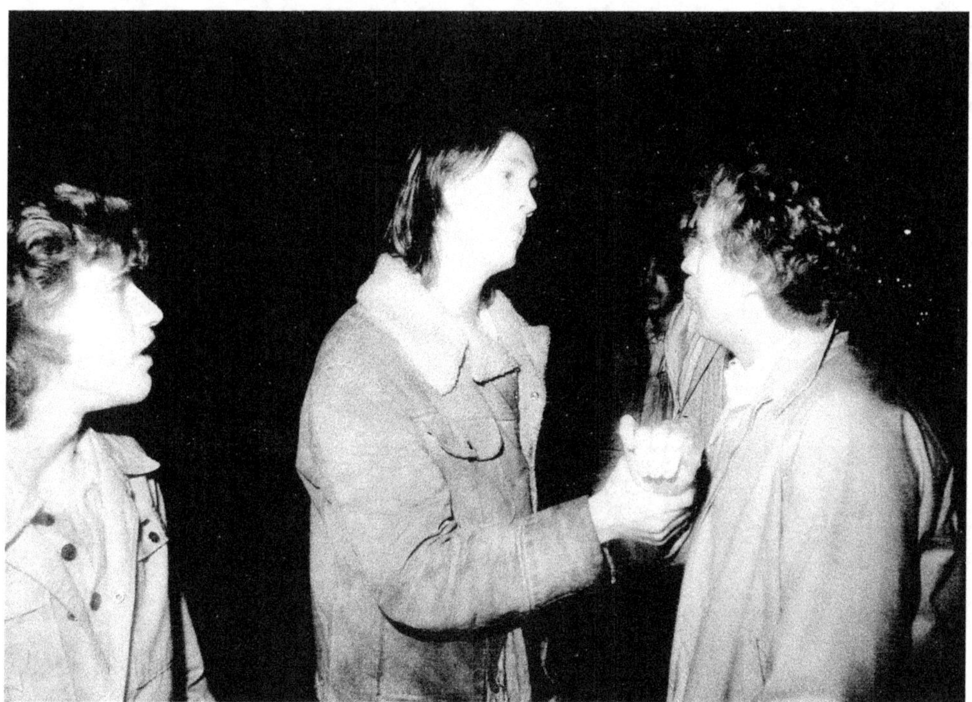

An unshaded lightbulb at the bar is turned on, signifying last call for drinks. You head toward the exit, as hundreds of people from every other bar in town simultaneously hit the street.

If Merlin's is the heart of downtown, and if PK's is its guts, then the street between has got to be its asshole.

The Street

By the time you reach the cool night air the festivities already have begun. Somebody in a black leather jacket has just whacked somebody else across the head with a crutch. The man is bleeding from the forehead, yet he continues grappling with his attacker. Several punches are thrown, then they wrestle each other to the ground and roll around in the garbage along the gutter. The crowd oohs and aahs but keeps its distance. Someone comes forward to break the combatants apart, but another attacker in a leather jacket leaps through the air and slugs him from behind. Several friends of the would-be referee rush to his defense and before more

leather jackets can enter the fray, they whisk him away.

Meanwhile, more and more drunken children are wandering into the street to play in the traffic. The object of their game is to stop the cars and get the police to reroute the traffic to another street. Several cars slow down and their fenders and windows are pummeled and kicked. Another car doesn't slow, and people dive out of its way. Several beer glasses are hurled at it as it continues up the street.

One particularly obnoxious partier has gotten a car with out-of-state plates to stop. An enraged black woman gets out of the car and advances toward him. He stays just out of her reach and trades insults. She finally gets back inside the car and turns down Elm Street. The crowd cheers. Another absurd victory for insanity.

As you gaze at the rapidly deteriorating situation, a rational explanation eludes you. Where else do they engage in such senseless escapades, except perhaps the running of the bulls at the festival of San Fermin in Pamploma, Spain? And what other than a Freudian explanation can be used to distill a meaning out of the chaos before you? You remember back to the '60s when thousands of students took to the streets to protest the war and other crimes against humanity. Then, too, the rallying cry was "No business as usual. The streets belong to the people!" Riots were always ugly, but they symbolized the frustrations of people of conscience who had tried all legitimate means of airing their grievances and still found the government unresponsive.

The mob on Illinois Avenue has all of the ugliness of a political demonstration, but it lacks any semblance of justification. It is senseless, violent and utterly without content.

You decide to call it a night and head back to your car. All around you people are staggering, throwing up and engaging in exhibitionist forms of lovemaking. You are pleasantly surprised to see that nobody took out his sexual frustrations on your Alfa, and you smile to the frosted blond beside you as you gun the engine to life.

On the way out of town you stop at the Clark Station for gas. "Wasn't that Charlie Pickle?" you ask, as you pull away from the pump. "Wow. Just what is this town coming to, anyway?"

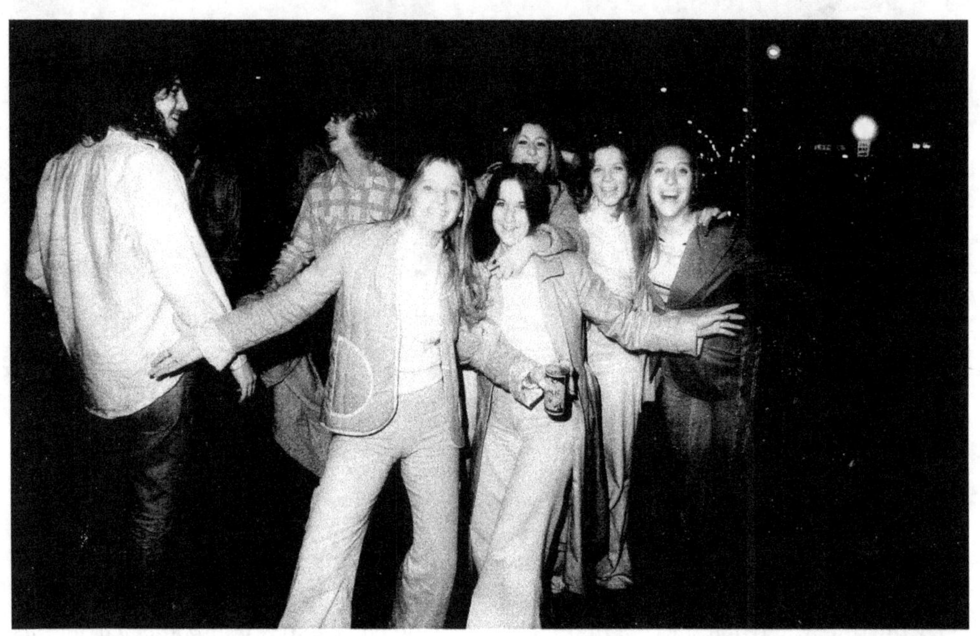

--photos by John Barry--

The Last Street Takeover

Although the Aug. 25, 1979, street takeover was not technically the last of its kind in the strip's history, it did mark the end of the era of frequent street parties. There have been street closings at Halloween in the 1980s, but except for two nights of small street parties during spring graduation week in 1982, there have been no other street parties this decade. The last street takeover was a fitting requiem because it was tied to no special event -- a ritual without meaning, a form without function. In 1966 a surprise panty raid along a sidestreet had been termed a "riot" by city officials, but by the late 1970s the police had become so accustomed to street closings they had stationed portable barricades near the intersection of College Street and Illinois Avenue so they wouldn't have to hunt some down every time the kids went wild. And except for my column, which ran in the Southern Illinoisan *several days after the event, the closing of a federal highway in the middle of the business district by hundreds of drunken revelers did not get a mention in the newspaper.*

"**A**ll right, everybody into the street," cried several alcohol-primed members of the crowd. It was about midnight, Saturday, Aug. 25, 1979, the first weekend of the fall term for some 20,000 SIU students. About 50 people began ambling across Illinois Avenue in Carbondale -- The Strip -- between The American Tap and Jim's Pub. As they waded into the street, several hundred bystanders began to howl "hoo-eey" like a tornado siren.

A dozen uniformed Carbondale police hustled the encroachers back onto the sidewalk, using verbal threats and assertive arm motions, but not their billy clubs or fists. The restraint exhibited by the police was matched by taunts from the crowd.

An expressionless and slightly irritated Ed Hogan watched from the curb near Jim's, biting on a toothpick. The Carbondale police chief had dealt with crowds on Illinois Avenue before, and he stood in the midst of this one, gauging its size and potential for violence.

Hogan, the city council, civic leaders and the majority of city residents would like to put a stop to the street takeovers. He hoped a show of force by the police would be enough to avoid this one, but the strategy did not seem to be working. The uniformed police were becoming verbal targets for agitators and they were keeping the crowd on edge. On the crowded sidewalk people milled around, psyching themselves up for another invasion of the street.

Late-night street takeovers in Carbondale have become a bizarre tradition. They have their roots in, and vaguely resemble, the political demonstrations of the late '60s and early '70s. But last weekend's "demonstration" seemed pointless. When asked, several in the crowd said they wanted to take over the street because, "it's there," "the sidewalk is crowded," "to socialize," and -- my favorite -- "why not?"

The "hoo-eey" brought back 10-year-old memories of the Indian war whoops protesters used to yell before confronting riot-gear-equipped police when protesting the Vietnam War and other emotional social issues. So when the crowd began to chant, "The streets belong to the people," I didn't know whether to laugh or cry.

Handling the kind of mob that gathers on Illinois Avenue is a tricky affair. Under Hogan, Carbondale police cajole and threaten, but seldom arrest or manhandle individuals. When they see open cans of beer, they pour them out, giving the offenders only a warning. And for the most part they take the verbal abuse good-naturedly. Some might criticize the police for being too soft, but one wrong move, one inciting incident, could turn the scene from one of childish shenanigans into violence.

Once again, the crowd, which had grown, began to holler, and more people meandered onto the pavement. Hogan could see the police would either have to let the crowd have the street or use force to clear it. A squad car, its lights flashing, appeared at the intersection of College Street and Illinois Avenue, and a patrolman began to direct traffic down a side street. It is hard to imagine the police in Chicago, Philadelphia or a lot of other places making that decision.

And yet, surrendering the street to the relatively small crowd seemed to pacify it. There was hardly even a roar of victory as the crowd realized it had triumphed. One could feel the tension leave the air, and the people, now not so tightly packed as they had been on the sidewalk, became more relaxed and wandered aimlessly around, enjoying the cool night air and each other's company.

In some ways the strip serves a constructive, or at least cathartic, function. It provides a reasonably harmless outlet for the frustrations, violence and lust many strip-goers feel, and it contains the craziness away from residential neighborhoods. Maybe SIU isn't in the Big 10 and maybe the guy grabbing antennas off of cars isn't going to pass his English exam tomorrow, but on the strip he can stop traffic, bait cops, rebel against authority and be victorious at something.

On the other hand, Carbondale's finest aren't being paid to baby-sit college students, and the physical location of the strip -- a federal highway in the middle of the business district -- has lost any political meaning it once had.

Police Chief Hogan stood near the squad car, his hard features, silver hair and canary-colored T-shirt making him stand out from the shorter and younger crowd. When he sensed the crowd's resolve had weakened and its numbers had dwindled sufficiently, he ordered the police to clear the street again. A patrolman drove the squad car through the thinning crowd, and traffic started flowing behind it. And, as one philosopher once sang, "nothing was revealed."

Beyond Edge City

The strip is dead. Comatose. As if they'd sprayed vaporized Quaalude out of Army Hueys from one end of Illinois Avenue to the other. As if they'd drafted all the 18-to-20 year olds, bombed all the buildings, and dug a trench through the center of town for good measure.

Bars and young people still dominate the landscape. But the strip bears little resemblance to that same stretch of pavement 10 or 15 years ago. It's not just the old hangouts -- the Spudnut's, Merlin's and Holden Hospital lawns -- that have disappeared, but also the energy, madness and magic. The mobs, street parties and riots. The mad scientists, mystics, radicals, freaks and hippies.

Oh sure, there is still an occasional pair of brooding eyes amongst the red and glassied ones. And brooding eyes were never a common commodity in the best of times. Certainly the hippies, Yippies and acidheads of yesteryear provided no less material for the satirist than the bent-eared urban cowboys and mohawked punkers of today. But as absurd and insane as the '60s were, folks were experimenting with what Ken Kesey called "Edge City." They were investigating the "beyonds" of sanity, society and morality -- burning draft cards, living in communes and freaking out on drugs.

Today, a protest is what happens when Pac Man is out of order, and communal living is what they do at Thompson Point dorms. And people don't "freak out" anymore. They "get buzzed" or "toot snow."

What killed the strip? Certainly the city administration has done its best to "redevelop" downtown by banning new bars, turning hangouts into parking lots and uprooting businesses (after uprooting the trees). The increase in the drinking age and drop in SIU's enrollment have also had an impact, as has a recession and an end to an endless war.

But in some ways the strip -- and the forces that created it -- were on a course of unplanned obsolescence from the beginning. Acid trips, experimental lifestyles and flower power couldn't last forever. And by being so far out, so radical and so outrageous, the hippies of the '60s left their successors with few options for acting out their own rebellious tendencies.

All the causes had been fought, all the sexual variations had been tried, all the dreams had been dreamt. How could anyone be "different" today? About all that was left was terminal cynicism. Everything had been tried, ergo, everything was passe.

Fuck art let's dance.

I don't know whether I'm getting old or what. At least I could fathom the peace-love patter of the hippy generation. But what is one to make of a subculture like punk where everyone dresses like Robert DeNiro in "Taxi Driver" and acts like they are on the set of "Clockwork Orange"?

Then again, as I gaze at the college sophomore posing at The Great Escape, slightly uneasy beneath his shaved scalp, horn-rimmed glasses and bowling shirt, I can't say I'm not reminded a bit of my ponytailed self a decade ago. Perhaps I am being sentimental and biased. Was everyone in 1969 engaged in some glorious mission, or weren't most of them just getting stoned and getting into mischief, the same as today?

Of course they were. Hanging out

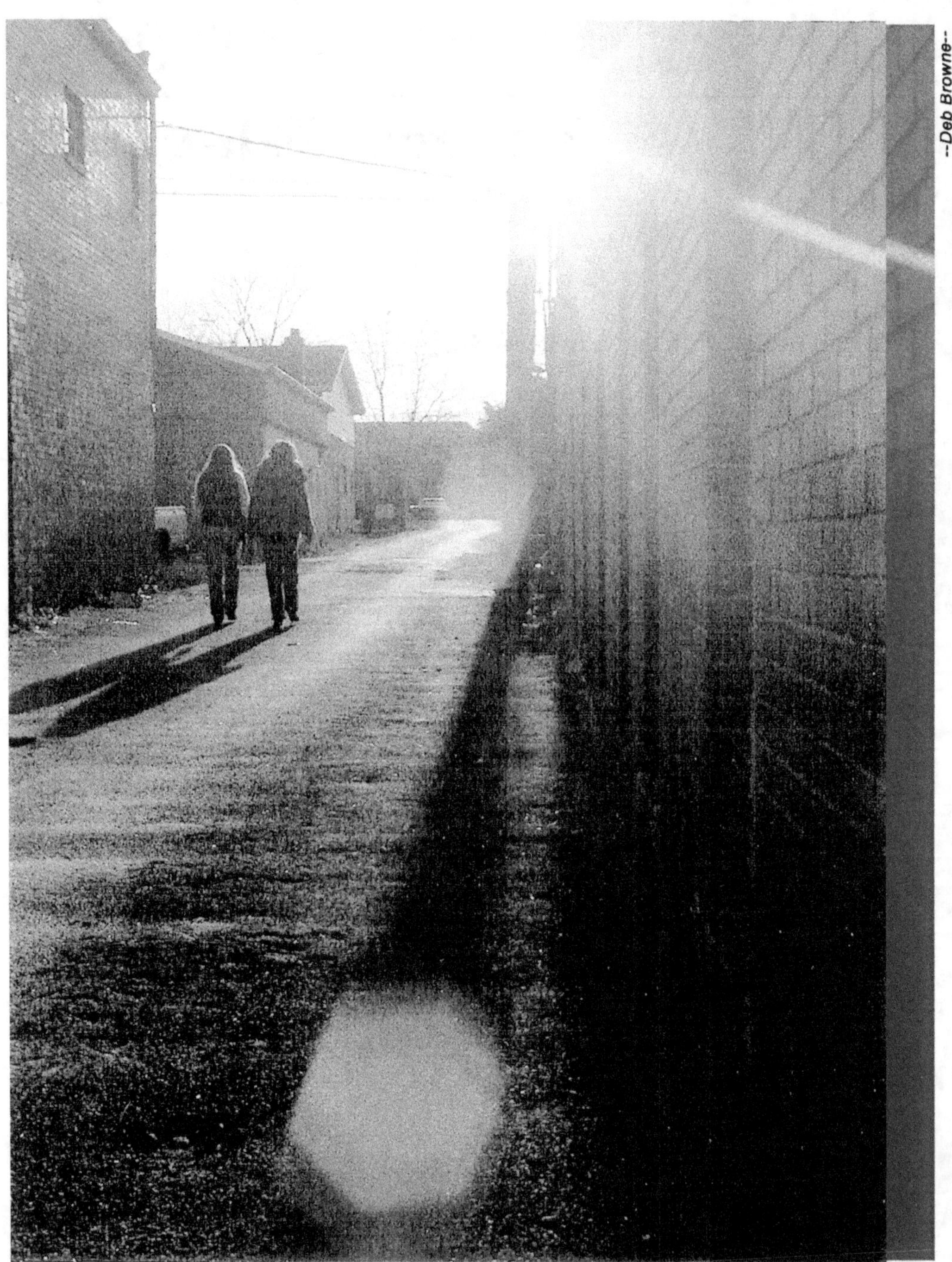

means goofing off and that's what the strip has always been all about. If you had something important to do, you'd go somewhere else to do it.

It's just that waiting for Godot had more piquancy a decade ago, before everyone figured out he wasn't going to show up.

Pontifications

Part 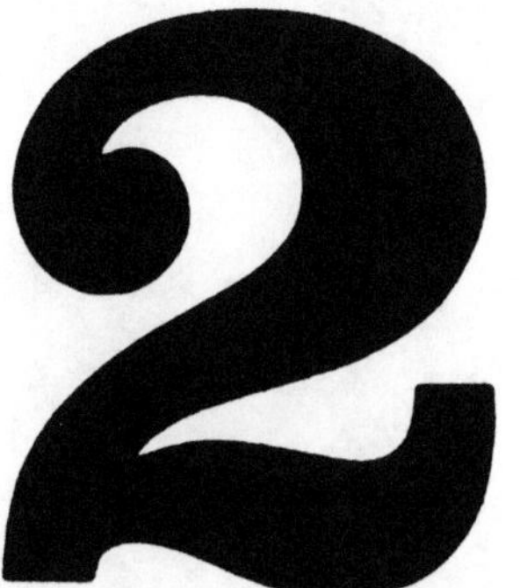

Kent State: Who Fired the First Shot?

"Kent State" and "Come Together For the Hell of It" were published on May 25, 1971, in a mimeographed leaflet called Spare Change. *("Kent State" was reprinted in the May 1975 issue of* nonSequitur.*) It was my first professional writing job. I hawked the leaflets on the street for spare change. I think I made $3.23.*

As Woodstock in 1968 signified the peaking of the hippy phenomenon, in 1970 Kent State marked the beginning of the end of the anti-war movement. The realization that Amerika would send soldiers onto college campuses to murder the children of the middle class before it would change its insane course in Southeast Asia was a sobering thought to even the most idealistic activist. And to someone like myself, whose faith in utopian visions was lukewarm at best, Kent State called for an immediate re-examination of "the movement" and my participation in it. Kent State, and especially what followed -- a wave of government repression and no apparent change in the war -- seemed to confirm what the militants had been saying all along: Non-violent protest didn't work. To end the war, the peaceniks would have to go to war themselves. But a lot of us middle class pacifist types weren't up to shooting at people, even Spiro Agnew.

There was a final burst of angry rioting during the national student strike that followed Kent State, but then the people went their various ways. Some turned to Weatherman violence, some to religion and some to communes in the wilderness. It wasn't the cause we lost faith in. It was the method.

A word of warning on "Come Together." This story contains explicit language, and if you start to read it, as a courtesy to the author, please plow through to the end, lest you be left with the wrong impression . . .

The Kent State Massacre of May 4, 1970, has undergone as much analysis as a rocket launch. Everyone from the FBI to James Michener has issued his conclusions. Yet one bit of information still is not known. Namely, who fired the first shot?

Assuming the order to fire was not given and that no guardsman felt his life to be in dire jeopardy (an assumption, like most assumptions, unprovable, but one not contradictory to any information up to now), the man who fired the first shot becomes the crux of the matter. If he had not fired, no one would have fired and no one would have died. The reason he fired is the reason for four deaths. Without the knowledge of who fired the first shot and why, all of the investigations and analyses, no matter how thorough or bigwordy, are no more than vague speculations into the unknown.

I submit that no one fired the first shot.

Imagine an Italian movie with Gina Lollobrigida as a housewife and Anthony Quinn as the milkman. They are in her kitchen arguing over the price of curds. She is bellowing curses in Italian and he is stamping his feet. They come closer, stare heatedly into each others' eyes, and suddenly she slaps him across the face. Not to be defaced by Gina Lollobrigida, Anthony pinches her nose. They violently shake each other, and all of a sudden there they are on the floor, passionately making love.

Consider the drama of sneezing, excretion, orgasm, or any of the bodily functions. Or the phenomenon of spontaneous combustion or nuclear fission. What is common to all of the examples is that the action, whether it be particles accumulating in the nose or electrons bombarding a uranium atom, reaches a point, a peak, a threshold, where a cosmic snap occurs as stored up potential energy suddenly becomes kinetic.

Could that same process have been in effect at Kent State that fateful afternoon? No one would deny there was a high degree of tension in everyone on campus that day, which is slyly similar to saying there was a tense feeling in the air. The tension mounted as curses, tear gas and stones were hurled. The crowd would be parted by soldiers pointing bayonettes one moment, the next moment the soldiers would be forced to retreat as they found themselves flanked on three sides.

Just as a cloud can store up only so much electricity before lightning occurs, the air at Kent State could stand just so much tension before it released a thunderbolt of kinetic energy, an explosion, a report, a spark, that ignited soldiers to wantonly ejaculate bullets into a crowd of people standing 100 yards away. The cause of the tragedy of Kent State, then, is overly energized air.

There are those, of course, who will say "slyly similar" is not a logical connective equivalent to equivalent, that my poetic license should be revoked, that if trees fall in the forest without someone there to hear them they make no sound. In short, they don't care what I say, they know it must have been a human being that fired the first inciting shot. The Red Sea didn't part, the Jews just knew where the rocks were. It is for their benefit that I manifest Ohio National Guardsman Abner Doubleday.

Abner joined the guard to get out of going to Vietnam. The guard was really a nice place to be as far as he was concerned. He had to drill several weeks out of the year, and the rest of the time he could go out drinking with Billy and Bob or take Gloria to the drive-in. But all of a sudden his unit was activated to go on some campus and dodge rocks. As Abner ate a breakfast of two hamburgers, potato chips, pork and beans and a Coke on the morning of the massacre, all he could think of was, by God, if those damn hippies riot, I won't get to see Gloria until Monday.

On the campus that day, Abner was subjected to the same pressures as everyone else, plus one. The plus one pressure was located somewhere in his intestines, and as Abner released the pressure in his intestines, his finger accidentally pressed the trigger. What was the reason for the extra pressure? Beans! It was the beans that gave Abner the gas to shoot first.

In the final analysis -- that is, in trying to ensure that another Kent State never occurs -- whether one believes the cause was overly energized air or an overly gassed Abner Doubleday, the conclusions are the same. One cannot legislate away overly gassed Abner Doubledays any better than one can outlaw thunderstorms. If the beans hadn't gotten to Abner, the Coca Cola would have.

Anti-riot laws, new weaponry and activating more National Guard units are just more beans. The laws are more excuses for confrontations, new weapons are provocative, and the more law enforcers there are, the higher the probability of there being another gaseous Abner Doubleday.

Like it or not, nothing can be done to eradicate overly energized air. Nature (as humans) follows a cycle of building things up to a peak and then exploding and starting over. Once seen in this light, one is not freed from the cycle. But one does have a choice of how to sublimate that excess energy. And some ways of releasing tension are more satisfying than others.

Like Gina Lollobrigida.

Come Together For the Hell Of It

A nation is a unified collection of people. Nations are made, not born. But clear thinking people aren't going to come together for the hell of it. They need a reason. Well, there are all kinds of reasons for getting together, but most nationalistic tendencies can be classified into one of two categories: People either unite because they like each other's company or to defend themselves against a common enemy.

Take, for example, Nazi Germany. The Germans united for two reasons. First of all, they liked each other's company. Hell, why shouldn't they? They were nothing less than Supermen. Pure white, blond hair, blue-eyed Aryan scene and all that. Secondly, they had to protect themselves from corrosive subversive elements that were threatening to pollute the all-Aryan gene pool. Kikes. Jews are an inferior breed of people. They have crass gauche disgusting hygenic social habits. You can smell one a mile away. And the males have overdeveloped penises. If a Jew entered an Aryan girl he would enlarge her vagina amid much suffering and pain and make her unsuitable for normal sexual relations with Aryan men. For the safety of the citizenry, then, they must be isolated, concentrated, eliminated.

Take, for another example, 19th and 20th Century America. There were two reasons for Americans to come together. First of all, they liked each other. Hell, why shouldn't they? They were nothing less than Americans. White Anglo-Saxon Protestant hard-working, humble, down-home folk scene and all that.

Secondly, they had to protect themselves from corrosive subversive elements of the local out group that were threatening to pollute the all-American gene pool. Niggers. Negroes are an inferior race of property. They are lazy, stupid, ugly, scary and Christ, I mean, they are black, you know. You can spot a spade a mile away. And the males, they have overdeveloped penises. All a nigger wants is a piece of honkey ass, and then she's no good for anything but maybe to copulate with horses. So for the good of God's chosen ones, don't let our children be exposed to those Black Devils in our schools, buses, restaurants, neighborhoods, or baseball teams. Hey, I got a great idea, let's all go get drunk and tar and feather one of em!

In the 1950s Americans found more reasons to come together. First of all, they liked each other. Hell, why shouldn't they? They were the No. 1 everything in the world. And there's nothing like being a No. 1. Secondly, they had to unite to protect themselves from the local No. 2s, the dirty Commies, who happen to be everywhere -- in the arts, in Hollywood, in the State Department, in Jews slipping across the Indo-China borders, South America, Cuba, homosexuals, you never can tell, your very own daughter may be messing around with one of em. For Communists, you see, don't necessarily have big noses or black skin. They can look like anything. So let's employ an army of people to spy and tape record and photograph...hey Dagwood, be the first on your block to turn in a Red. Good for business, ya know.

In a present tense, consider 1971 America. First of all, Americans like each other. Hell, why shouldn't we? We're still numero uno. We've put men on the moon. We are slowly but surely getting out of Vietnam, with honor. Schools, neighborhoods, and professions are slowly but for surely being integrated. The pollution problem is being worked out and new

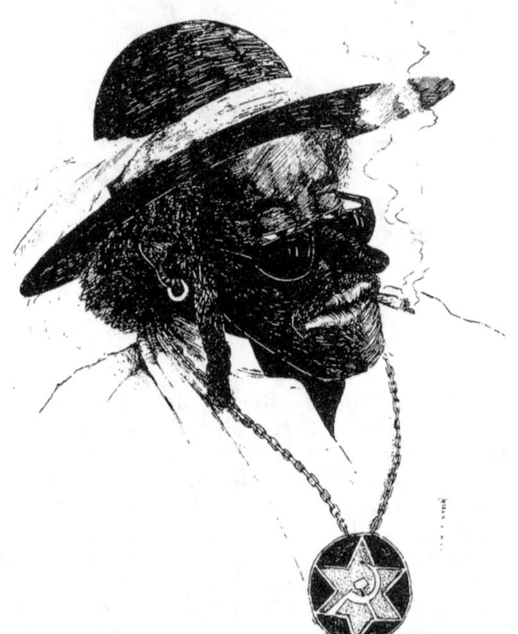

solutions and legislation are progressing every day. And movies are better than ever. If ever a flower were destined for eternal life, it must be our own US of A. I love you fellow righteous God-fearing Americans.

Secondly, we have to protect ourselves from the enemy: Hippy dope addicts. Once inseminated by a socially taboo drug, an individual is transformed into an inferior sub-human niggercommiekike. His nature generally degenerates. He doesn't like war or Merle Haggard and he doesn't take baths, cut his hair, wear shoes, or change his clothes. Kin smellum fum a mile away. It degenerates until the fellow doesn't appear human at all. Why, they even get on them drugs like LSD and do things like strip off all their clothes and perform all sorts of obscene masturbation fantasies. Yuk. How disgusting! They are lazy, stupid, ugly, scary; they steal cheat lie forge fred hide and deal.

God damn the pusherman. Don't let him hold a government job, play baseball, cut records or appear on TV shows. Build special "processing centers" for them. Put them in prison. Draft them. Murder them. Keep the race pure. Hi yo, Silver, away!

Humor me one more example. Consider Woodstock Nation, 1971. First of all, we Woodstockers like each other. Hell, why shouldn't we? We have scraped the plastic off of ourselves, been baptized and annointed with pure natural organic psilocybin. We have become the keepers of the flame, the chosen people, the superman star baby, the liberators, everything you say we are plus one more right on. And we are No. 1 because we are the people, and that's just about everyone.

Except for you straight repressive imperialistic racist male chauvinistic capitalistic pigs. You know, you can feel a honkey's vibes a mile away. They always look uptight, you know, they're stupid, ugly, scary, Buddha, and all those obnoxious underarm and mouth and hair preservatives they pour all over themselves. The males have little itty bitty penises that couldn't do more than your pinky finger, and their women just lay there. They marry as virgins and for the rest of their lives act out humiliating fantasies of sexual inadequacy. And the dirty old men are always trying to rape our women -- all those rednecks want is a piece of that "free love" ass.

So, to defend ourselves from the local out group we will sky-jack, kidnap, riot, loot, burn, bomb, subvert, revolt, kill our mothers and fathers, and live in $700-a-week apartments. Happily ever after.

Those Wacky D.E. Columns

In 1976 I wrote about a dozen columns for the Daily Egyptian. *It was the first time my writings were widely exposed to the public, and they generated a lot of interest. One anonymous letter-writer may have summed up the feelings of many when, after my first column, on meditation, he or she said I wrote like* "Howard Cosell cut off at the knees." *The columns were bright and brash, but they sometimes lacked logic, and I have taken the liberty of tidying them up a bit. Nevertheless, no Koplowitz anthology would be complete without at least some of them, kind of like putting out an album without including the hit 45.*

Disco Discrimination

A couple of unisexers were bumped off the dance floor last Friday night at Merlin's disco. It must have been an absurd moment for them. It was disco rejecting its own roots -- the gays. Kind of like telling the Colonel he couldn't eat at a fried chicken restaurant or street musicians they couldn't play jazz on Bourbon Street.

The injured parties can take solace that they are not the first to be thrust into such a ridiculous position. Take the Sunset Strip hippies, for example. Before the '60s, Sunset Boulevard in Hollywood was just another rundown neighborhood lost in the suburban sprawl of Los Angeles. But for some reason bands of untidy young people, later to become known as hippies, began congregating on the sidewalks and in the bars along Sunset Boulevard, and the area gradually became known as the Strip.

The shopowners quickly realized that hippy coin was better than no coin and began to cater to the psychedelic flower children by converting their businesses into boutiques, head shops and Go-Go dance bars. Then the masses became infatuated with the hippy mystique, and the Strip became congested with all kinds of hippies. Many of them rich hippies.

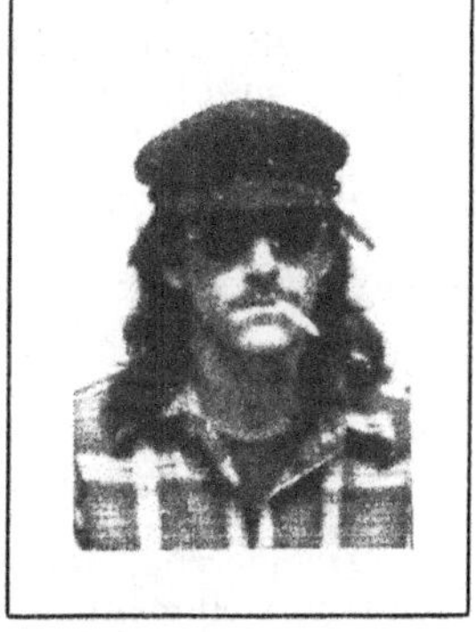

Rich hippies who came with dates and bought mixed drinks and paid cover charges to mingle with the "real" hippies, who were mostly outside hawking the *Free Press.*

The derelicts on the Strip were pleased with the notoriety, at first. But they soon came to resent the thousands of phonies who had invaded their turf. Like park pigeons, they began to feed off the intruders, by pushing dope, begging for spare change and hustling ass.

The new clientele -- the weekend hippy and the full-time plastic -- found it easier to mingle with each other than with the hard-core, who had turned them on to the scene in the first place. The drug addicts, frustrated artists and lost souls -- the original hang-outers whose nickels and dimes and whose culture had created the economic base for the neighborhood -- became a nuisance after they had served their purpose. The storeowners realized the derelicts might in time scare the new patrons away, and the merchants decided to act. They convinced the city council to pass loitering and curfew ordinances. The police began enforcing the ordinances. A series of riots followed. When the smoke cleared, the hippies were gone.

The irony of the Sunset Strip story is that after the hippies left, the phonies began to feel that only phonies go to the Strip, and they stayed away, and the turf was overtaken by, you guessed it, the gay community.

Just a couple of years ago, before the New York City gays and blacks turned the disco scene into the latest rage, discotheques were nothing but crummy nightclubs too cheap to hire a band. Nobody would ever have dreamed of paying a cover charge to listen to records or of dressing up in outrageous glitter and platform shoes if it were not for those two oppressed cultures which paved the way.

The New York disco scene from 1971 to 1974 was underground because blacks and gays felt the only way for them to get loose was behind closed doors and in private clubs, away from the straights. Inside those abandoned factory lofts and private clubs, the disco scene took shape -- the omnipotent deejay, the mind-blowing sound systems, non-stop music, and the emphasis on dancing dancing dancing.

It was inevitable that big-time promoters would step in when they saw the discos were beginning to affect the record industry; when they saw how many people were getting into the bizarre world of unisex fashion and glitter whether they were gay or not. That's when the disco scene went above-ground and began its present economic boom.

I'm not suggesting that the gay community has provided the economic base for Merlin's. Hardly. But Merlin's has spent tens of thousands of dollars to refurbish the club to look like a disco. And just who the hell does the management of Merlin's think created the disco scene? Prohibiting people of the same sex to dance to disco music is like telling a hippy he can't play with his strobe light. Not only should Merlin's let the unisexers do their thing, but it ought to be paying half the fairies in Greenwich Village a share of the profits.

The New Victorians

The language is being censored. Not by the government, but by well-meaning reformers who are on a tangent from their struggle to improve social conditions and have begun hacking away at the English language.

There have always been those who strived to purify the lexicon. But most have been harmless Edwin Newman types -- cloistered academics, religious fanatics or old fuddy-duddies. The New Victorians, however, are liberal and even radical activists who are using semantics to fight discrimination. But in the process they are taking the vitality out of the language, and perhaps society.

At the vanguard of this New Victorianism is the feminist movement, which alleges someone was stacking the deck

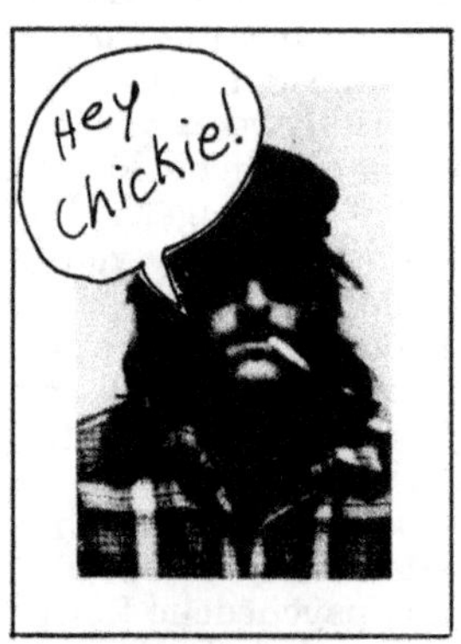

when it was decided to use "man" instead of "woman" or "homo sapiens" in sentences like "God created man in his own image," "all men were created equal" and "man the lifeboats."

The relevance to these quirks of English, say the New Victorians, is that the words we use help shape our ideas and attitudes. So, like the Newspeak of "1984," feminists have attempted to manipulate our thoughts by banning such subliminally sexist terms as "mankind," "history" and "repairman." Then they get to a word like "chick." The New Victorians already have succeeded in banishing "chick" from chic conversation. The argument is that anyone who says "chick" is a sexist because the word relegates a total human being to a sex object.

I don't know about "history" and "mankind," but I think I can say from personal experience that thinking about women as sex objects did not start with the word "chick." It started in a gland that doesn't need words to express itself.

Some people may not like what "chick" connotes, but, like Archie Bunker's humor, the word allows us to express emotions rather than talk around or repress them. Besides, you don't have to be a sexist to use the word "chick" anymore than Charles Dickens had to be a bigot to have created Fagin, or Mark Twain a racist to have invented nigger Jim.

Isn't it ironic that blacks can call each other "nigger," homosexuals can call each other "queer," and women can call each other "bitch," but the people who, after all, probably invented many of these pejoratives are castigated for using them?

The reason profanity and slang have stayed with us is not merely because the uneducated peasants persisted in using them, but also because words like "fruit," "spade" and "lady" sometimes express more than their legitimate grammatical counterparts. Many slang words are more colorful and have a better sense of rhythm than the prissiness of formal English or the sterile rhetoric of the New Victorians.

The results of the New Victorians' efforts have not been to eradicate racism and sexism but rather to make us suppress certain emotions, attitudes and prejudices. It has turned us into a nation of closet cussers.

It wasn't so long ago that the free speech movement in Berkeley sparked the youth revolution. Liberation has taken a 180 degree turn when the vogue is now to repress all the profanity that just a few short years ago was known as exercising freedom of speech.

The Doctor and Eye

Last Saturday night I had the occasion to go to the emergency room at Memorial Hospital of Carbondale. I had chipped my spectacles and feared I had a glass splinter in my eye.

Every time I blinked I imagined a tiny glass speck making little scratches on my cornea. I felt no pain, only a disconcerting itching in my eye. But I could not decide whether it was my imagination or not, and I knew I would not be able to relax until a qualified professional checked it out.

I burst into the emergency room with an urgency obviously not shared by the receptionist. "Havaseat," she said distractedly, a telephone propped next to her ear.

"Welcome to the bureaucracy," I thought. After about 60 more anxious blinks, she asked me what my problem

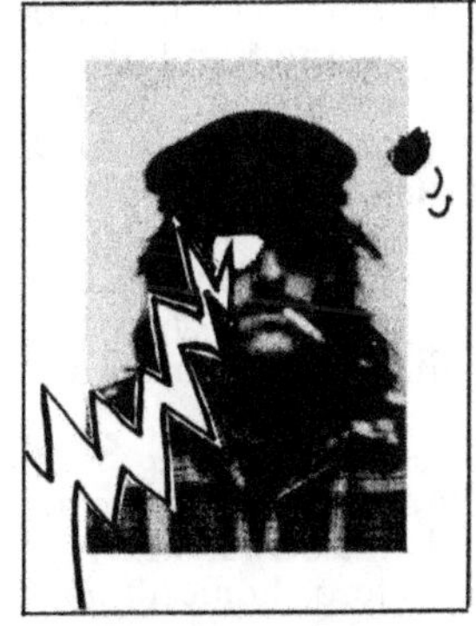

was. I told her about my chipped glasses and the itch and how I probably shouldn't even be there, but it was my eye, for chrissakes, and I wanted somebody to look at it.

So she went and got Dr. Roseman. "Whatzamatter?" asked Dr. Roseman, and I went through my story again.

After telling me to lie down on the table, he stuck a piece of litmus paper in my already irritated eye, dying it orange. One of several attending medical students flicked off the lights, and Dr. Roseman peered into my peeper.

"See that?" Dr. Roseman asked the med students. "Now you know what a corneal scratch looks like."

"Swell," methinks. "That sliver of glass is probably lodged in my eyelid and they think they're studying a cadaver.

I voiced my concern to Dr. Roseman, and the next thing I knew he had turned my eyelid inside out. He held it captive for awhile -- showing off to the med students, I suppose -- while I laid there feeling like a rodeo calf that had just been roped.

"Nothing there," he said at last, and relinquished his hold on my eyelid.

I gulped, blinked, and my eyelid snapped back into place. I could stand the suspense no longer. "What have I got, doc?" I asked.

Dr. Roseman turned to the med students again. "Remember when we were talking about good patients and bad patients?" he began. "Just a few years ago, this," he said, squeezing my shoulder, "was a bad patient. Always bothering the physician with questions the med student was instructed to lie about or ignore. And the good patient was the passive one who said, 'yes Doctor, anything you say, Doctor.' The medical profession has got to change, and I like to think that in the last few years it has begun to change its ideas about good patients and bad patients. And to see that good patients are those who take responsibility over their own bodies and question the doctor's prognosis. Question the treatment and what kinds of drugs are being used."

I sat there and beamed at the med students, feeling like a prize lab specimen. Until I realized that Dr. Roseman had just done what he said doctors shouldn't do -- avoided my question. "So what have I got already," I asked again.

"You've got a corneal abrasion at 6 o'clock," Dr. Roseman responded.

"And what does that mean?" I pressed, taking more responsibility for my own body.

"It means you may have had a piece of glass in your eye, but I doubt it because the most obvious symptom of something in the eye is excruciating pain."

"Well, what if there is still something in my eye?" I asked. "What do we do then?"

Roseman turned to the medical students again. "And never answer 'what if' questions," he lectured. "Because 'what if' has nothing to do with anything."

But I wanted to know what would happen if worse came to worst. Would they strap my arms and legs to the table, as I was writhing in "excruciating pain," prop open my eye with a prong and gingerly pluck glass crystals off my eyeball with a tweezers?

Dr. Roseman thought that was pretty funny. "It's because of your neurotic heritage that you want to know," he kidded. "In all probability you never had anything in your eye to begin with."

Just about the time he had calmed me down, he pulled out some gauze and tape. "I'm ninety-nine percent sure you've got nothing in your eye," he said. "But just to make sure we're going to patch it and send you to an opthalmologist."

"If you are so sure I have nothing in my eye, why are you doing all that?" I asked, alarmed again.

"Just to be on the safe side," answered Dr. Roseman, which was rational enough, but left me thinking I'd been hoodwinked into wearing a sadistic placebo for asking too many questions.

I wore the patch until it drove me crackers, then ripped it off and spent the rest of the weekend feeling paranoid and guilty. I went to the opthalmologist Monday, he found no evidence of anything, and I never did find out whether that piece of glass ever existed. Dr. Roseman is probably right that it never did.

But I still got this nagging theory about a tiny sliver of glass, tucked away somewhere in my eye. Each time I blink, it jars it just a little. And sooner or later one of those blinks will jar it loose, sending it raggedly skidding across my eyeball like a mini piece of shrapnel.

I'm still waiting for that blink and that "excruciating pain" to hit me. So I can tell Dr. Roseman "I told you so."

On Meditation

The ancient art of meditation is making quite a comeback on college campuses these days. Under new names like Transcendental Meditation, Divine Light and Scientology, meditation is rapidly becoming a fixture in the usually fickle world of pop culture, alongside such mainstays as pot, frisbees and jogging.

Unlike most youth culture fads, which are either illegal, obscene, or both, meditation is legal, free (sometimes) and doesn't entail injecting toxic substances into the body. And it has the unqualified endorsement of just about every poet, philosopher and sage who ever lived.

Some view the current popularity of meditation as the eve of a spiritual awakening. Others, however, suspect it is just one more escape devised by the "leaders of tomorrow" to help them avoid the harsh realities of the modern world. If the '60s were a rejection of the banal apathy of the '50s, so the '70s may someday be interpreted as being a negation of the permissiveness and activism of the '60s. Viewed in such a light, meditation neatly fills in the need of those who desire to retreat from the arena of social change and experimental lifestyles: What could be more safe and wholesome than sitting alone and thinking about belly buttons, nonsense syllables, or just plain nothing?

Because meditation is so wholesome, it's hard to see how it can become a bad

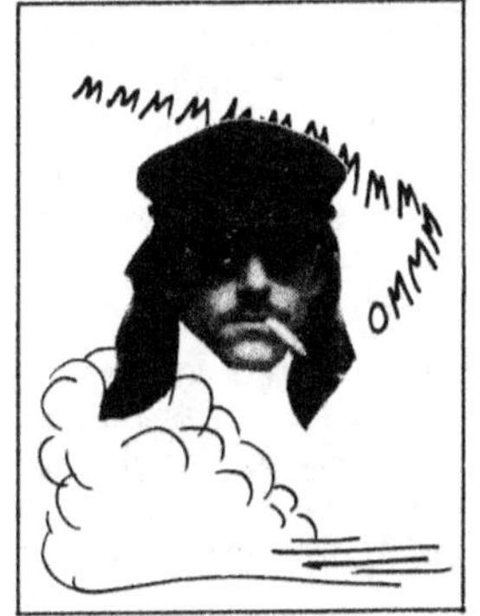

habit. But if the search for the inner light causes someone to withdraw from the material world -- and such "profane" manifestations of it as the competition for jobs or grades, the challenge of trying to improve the human condition, or the emotional knots of an intense relationship -- then that person may be using meditation as a crutch.

This is not to say meditation is inherently evil. There is mounting scientific evidence that it is healthy and reduces stress. It might even produce "altered states" and put you in touch with God.

But if you find yourself taking refuge in non-thought and using meditation as an end in itself, well, maybe you're just playing with yourself.

Here Comes the President

"Mommy, I can't see," cried the little girl.

"Don't worry Sissie, the President hasn't landed yet."

The scene was last Saturday afternoon at the Williamson County Airport where some 8,000 Southern Illinoisans were doing their version of waiting for Godot. In a scenario to be re-created throughout the week, thousands of curiosity seekers streamed across the field hours before the candidate was to arrive, abandoning their cars along the highway like so many

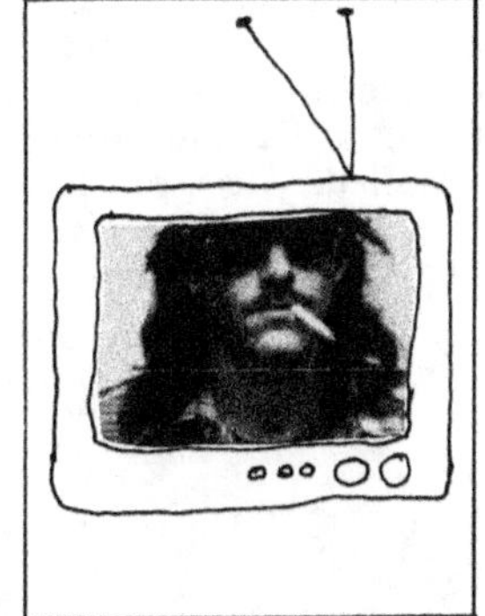

empty beer cans.

The Gerald Ford Show was less substance than surreal, but what it lacked in circumstance was more than made up for in pomp. High school marching bands with goose-pimply baton twirlers kept arriving and playing "Banana Man" while the public address system periodically informed spectators of the location of the outdoor porto-toilets.

An anti-abortion group stood against a wall and mutely waved pictures of bloody fetuses, while an elderly collection of VFW types with medals, ribbons and war wounds were ushered across a restraining rope to front-row seats.

Even Mike Freedom Man Belchak showed up in full regalia -- cardboard box suit, dunce cap and a dollar bill hanging like a carrot in front of his nose. After the Secret Service previewed his act, Belchak wandered harmlessly through the crowd while a thousand camera shutters clicked like castanets around him.

"Here comes the President!" someone cried, and 16,000 eyes grew round, straining to see the silver bird flying low over the runway. Only it wasn't the President; it was the national press corps. Three Greyhound buses lumbered out to pick up the reporters and drive them all of 300 yards to a press stand, which in less exciting times served as a flat-bed truck.

While the press was primping for the President, another silver bird appeared on the horizon. Smoothly it sailed onto the runway and taxied up to the crowd. The front door opened, Secret Service agents popped out, then Sen. Chuck Percy, and then the surprise guest politician, Secretary of Agriculture Earl Butz. Finally the President emerged, walked down the steps without incident, addressed the high school marching bands and VFW types, smiled and waved and waved and smiled. He and his entourage walked parallel to the crowd, and, separated by a mere rope, he pressed flesh with his beloved grassroots and they with their beloved leader.

It was almost anti-climactic when Ford got around to delivering his speech, and, knowing this, Ford kept it low key. Boy was it low key. Even as Ford was speaking of "the great people of Southern Illinois," some of them were beginning to move toward the exits. Along the fringes of the crowd, people were walking around with puzzled looks on their faces. Perplexed, not about the man Gerald Ford, but about the whole phenomenon of electing a president.

"**I** don't know why I came here," remarked one man as he loosened up joints stiff from the cold and from trying to stretch a five-and-a-half-foot frame over a six-foot shoulder. "To get a look at him, shake his hand; maybe get a picture."

There are a lot of reasons to go to a political rally, but one of them isn't to become informed on the issues. For the most part -- and especially for the incumbent, who is insulated by security measures -- the political rally has become a meaningless ritual, a facade.

Many have suggested that America should face up to the impracticality, the exorbitant expense and downright foolishness of these political mass communions and abolish them altogether. The only problem with that is the alternative -- to completely lose touch with our rulers and allow our images of national leaders to be entirely shaped by the media.

Maybe it's just a few skin cells or a glimpse of a forehead from beneath someone's armpit, yet it's still reassuring to know the President of the United States isn't really made out of a bunch of little dots on a TV screen.

Afrophobia

Let's not beat around the bush. We are talking about white people who have an irrational fear of black people.

The afrophobic finds the everyday chance encounter with a black person an unsettling experience: Just passing a black person on the street or standing next to one in a bar can bring on vertigo, sweaty palms, shortness of breath, even paralysis. But the anxiety of passive proximity is miniscule compared to the afrophobic's terror of an actual collision where, say, a tall, well-groomed, black, proud and beautiful person asks him for a match.

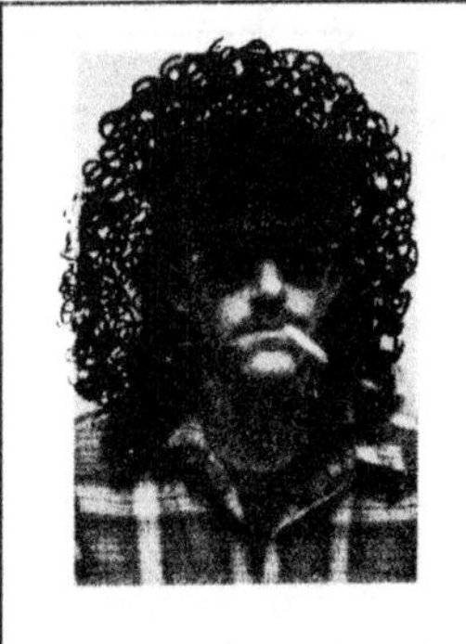

Afrophobia is really a sub-category of a set of phobias, call them social phobias, where someone is unjustifiably afraid of members of a particular social or ethnic group. There is upper-class phobia, lower-class phobia, sexy-girl phobia, handi-capped-phobia, and, of course, homo-phobia.

The afrophobic isn't racist in the conventional sense. He or she may hold no grudge, carry no bias, display no malice. Just a blind, irrational and uncontrollable terror when in the vicinity of black people.

To deal with his fright, an afrophobic will use a variety of defense mechanisms. Avoidance is one of the most common. So is transference, whereby the fear is transferred to an emotion easier to cope with -- namely hatred.

There are other reactions that are less obvious. What one is most afraid of can also become an object of awe and fascination. And some afrophobics will seek out the company of blacks as friends or lovers out of masochism or guilt rather than compatibility or genuine desire.

Most blacks will cut the afrophobic some slack. But some will seize upon his weakness and use it to their own malevolent ends, which only reinforces the phobia.

Whether an afrophobic hates blacks or not, however, he is a racist in the fundamental sense that his personality disorder disrupts communications and upsets relations between members of different races: An afrophobic just can't help viewing a black person as some sort of "fright object" rather than as a human being. Therefore, each afrophobic should attempt to find a solution that works for him or her. The technique suggested below may not be for everyone and it doesn't come with a guarantee. But it is relatively simple and shouldn't get you in trouble.

Neither avoid blacks nor take one to lunch. Don't make a cause out of it. Just go about your normal life, and when you encounter a black person, become aware of your body -- the pitter-patter of your heart, the unevenness of your breathing, the shaking in your hands. Try to control that nervous laugh, and meet the other person's eyes as long as you can. Don't project bravado you don't feel. Be cool, be bland, try to relax.

It may take one encounter or a thousand, but somewhere along the way you should develop better control over those nervous gestures. And looking calm is halfway to actually being calm. The appearance of calm usually makes social interaction less intense, which should add to your confidence. And who knows, maybe one day you'll arrive at that magic moment when you step back from a conversation and realize that you are actually relating and have forgotten about the color barrier.

Until that day arrives, however, just do the best you can. Don't feel guilty, don't decide it's easier to hate than fear. Don't force it.

And if you happen to be on the other side of the fence, just try not to laugh. Give the goof a break.

1975-1977

The nonSequitur Story

The next three selections are from nonSequitur *magazine. As good a place as any to start the* nonSequitur *story is with Earl Vinecour. During the mid 1970s, "Earl the Pearl" was the loose-living rabbi who officiated services at Beth Jacob, the local synagogue, and headed Hillel, the SIU Jewish student organization. Vinecour was a young and liberal rabbi, though a passionate Zionist, and he was also something of a finagler.*

In 1975, unbeknownst to me, Vinecour and my parents conspired to get me involved in something constructive and to meet nice Jewish girls by making me the editor of Kol Shalom, *a Jewish newsletter mostly ghost-written by Vinecour. In 1974, SIU's student government had appropriated $1,500 to the* Kol Shalom *Journalism Club, another Vinecour front. Student government was downright stingy about using any of its*

ample student activity fees for student publications, but Vinecour had weaseled the money by aligning Kol Shalom *with* Uhuru Sasa, *the Black Student Organization newsletter. BSO sent a contingent of ominous-looking lobbyists to a student government meeting and harassed the senators into appropriating money to both groups. The university later froze* Kol Shalom's *funds, saying university money could only be used for "non-ethnic" activities. And in its infinite wisdom, student government made a policy that it would fund only one "non-ethnic" publication, i.e.,* Uhuru Sasa, *thus putting any other group wishing to start a publication in the uncomfortable position of having to compete with the Black Student Organization for money. (BSO would usually defend its funding by charging that potential encroachers were racists, a position* nonSequitur *found*

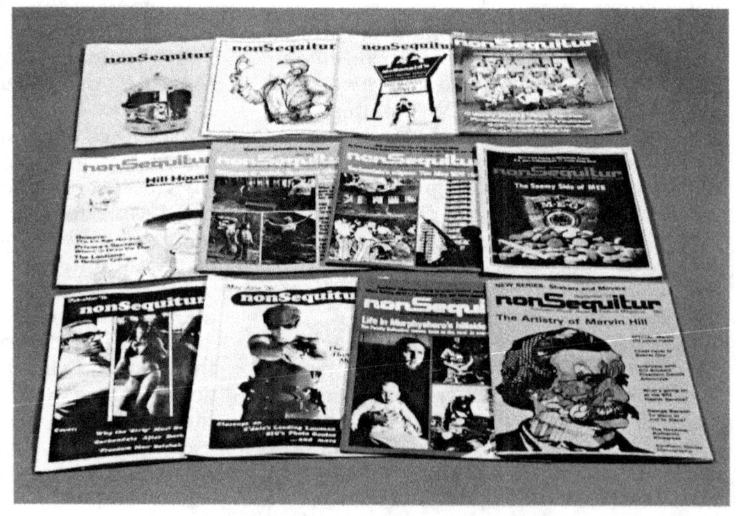

itself in a year later.)

Nevertheless, Vinecour hoped to get his hands on the $1,500 already appropriated by making Kol Shalom *a non-ethnic publication. I was only too willing to assist. My first editorial decision was to gain credibility in the non-Jewish community by interviewing a Palestinian student. Even though, to placate the Jewish community, I also interviewed Hy Ruffman, the head of the regional Jewish Federation, Vinecour decided stories about Palestinians weren't the kind of material he wanted for* Kol Shalom. *He handled the problem in a characteristically sneaky way. He urged me to continue with my project using university money while he would publish* Kol Shalom *as a separate newsletter with money from the Jewish Federation.*

So there I was, an editor without the slightest idea of how to put out a newspaper. Luckily Charles Casey, a journalism graduate student with whom I had gone to high school, happened along, and he co-edited the first issue. I also owe a debt of thanks to Daily Egyptian *business manager Adrian Combs who played a pivotal role in getting the funds released.*

From the beginning, Casey and I agreed on little, an editorial schism that was to continue as others replaced him. I wanted to name our fledgling publication something like "Lame Duck," an oblique reference to our precarious funding. At the other end of the spectrum, Casey preferred a name more easy going and general, like "Sunset." One night we were throwing names around at our typesetter's, the Author's Office, when print shop co-owner Jim Cook came up with "Non Sequitur." The name had the right mix of sophistication and off-beatness, and "nonSequitur" was born.

In some ways the first issue, laid out on Casey's kitchen table, is my favorite, although it was mighty raw from a technical standpoint. Casey knew another grad student, Jim Santori, who knew people like Jack Helms, Bill Federman and Ron Bath, who knew John Barry, who knew Andy Piper, who knew Ed Dunin-Wasowicz and as they came on board, the magazine rapidly improved in quality.

Debra Storhaug was also an immense help in keeping things organized and dealing with my ego during and after the stormy editorial meetings.

In 1976 Mssrs. Santori, Bath, Helms, Barry, Federman and I took the big step when we entered into a partnership with WTAO-FM owner Bill Varecha and took the magazine off campus. For the next Year WTAO salesman Jim duBois played a vital role by selling just enough advertising to keep us afloat. No one was ever paid a salary.

In nonSequitur *we combined hard news reporting with features and new journalism and presented them with stylish graphics. The articles ranged from a three-part series of in-person impressions of Northern Ireland by journalism graduate Tim Powers to a satire of a local wet T-shirt contest, "Chest Fever in Beaver City." The best of* nonSequitur *deserves an anthology of its own, but as I'm paying for this book, I just included my own stories in this one:*

In 1976 Debra Storhaug, John Barry and I flitted around the edges of the Republican National Convention in Kansas City. Presidential nominating conventions are perhaps the most over-reported news events in the country, and "The Rubbish and the Rubies" was my attempt to inject some fresh analyses into a stale story.

"The Great Washington D.C. Fiasco" was written after an ill-fated "junket" to the nation's capital, in which a contingent of Illinois journalism students including myself had mistakenly thought we were going to meet with President Jimmy Carter. We didn't, but as "Fiasco" shows, you needn't let the facts get in the way of a good story.

"Who let Frank Hall Down" is about a friend of mine who has had to deal with mental illness. I am happy to say Frank (not his real name) has come back from his setbacks and is coping today.

Most likely it was a lack of interest in the business side of publishing by most of the people involved that brought nonSequitur *down. But I am proud to say that most of the* nonSequitur *alumni have gone on to distinguished careers. Barry and Bath are newspaper photographers in Iowa, Federman works for the* Wall Street Journal, *and Santori is one of my editors at the* Southern Illinoisan.

1976

The Rubbish
and the Rubies

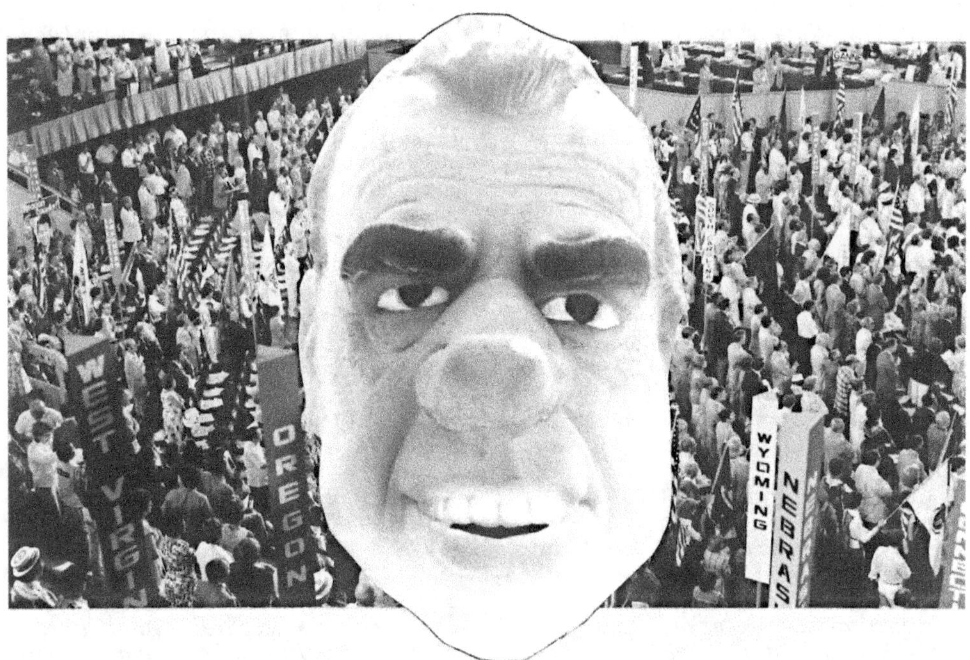

Typically ass backwards we split for the 1976 Republican National Convention in Kansas City, not knowing what we would find there nor what we were looking for.

There were three of us; a photographer, an observer and a scribe. John Barry was the photographer, out to capture on film the phenomenon of a presidential nominating convention, shoot as many public faces as possible and hopefully get down to the convention floor to snap the perfect image.

Debra Storhaug, a political agnostic, just wanted to be near the hoopla and the excitement. It was left to me to transcribe and try to distill a meaning from the gush of events that was to engulf us over the next five days.

We were armed with two flimsy angles by which to get from the outside of spectators and hangers-on to the inner circles of high political intrigue. One was a recently expired *Daily Egyptian* press card, and the other was the name of an up-and-coming politician from Lincoln, Ill., who we hoped would escort us behind the scenes. I had belatedly written off for press credentials and been refused. We had been unable to reach our contact. We were going in blind.

Sunday

The *Kansas City Star* shed some light

on the matter. President Gerald Ford was due to arrive at his temporary residence, the Crown Center Hotel, at 5 p.m. Our contact was also staying at the Crown, so we decided to break the ice in K.C. with a presidential reception.

When we arrived, the Hallmark greeting cards-owned Crown Center was crawling with every sort of cop from Secret Service to Pinkertons. The lobby was full of delegates, spectators, TV cameras, campaign workers and several hundred "Presidentials," teenagers bused in to cheer on cue.

There was a bar in the lobby, and not to our surprise we finally located our contact at the watering hole. His name was Scott Warner, and at 23 years old he said he was the youngest Republican officeholder in the nation. Warner is a city alderman in Lincoln and hopes to be its next mayor.

Scott worked in the law firm of John Gehlbach, an attorney in his 50s who walked around with a silver pin in his lapel signifying that he had made a $1,000 donation to the Ford campaign. Scott knew Clark Horvath, a mystery man who worked for President Ford's campaign organization in Washington, D.C. Horvath also wore a silver pin, along with a red glass dot on the identification card hung around his neck. That dot gave him access to the two top floors of the hotel -- the headquarters of the White House staff.

More and more people were crowding into the Crown lobby, and Warner was buying us drinks on what he claimed was the president's expense account. We were joined by some of Scott's and Clark's young Republican friends who all seemed to be officers in an organization called "Youth of Illinois for Ford." A band had been set up in the lobby, and warmed up the audience with a rendition of "Jumping Jack Flash." A stir went through the crowd as the Secret Service ushered Nelson Rockefeller through the lobby. The crowd went wild with chants of "We want Rocky." The booze continued to be deposited in bladders, and tongues began to loosen.

One of Warner's friends took me earnestly aside and tried to convince me that Jimmy Carter was a hawk. "I just have this real strong feeling that he will get us into another war . . " He looked into my Semitic eyes and added, "in the Middle East."

Horvath rolled his eyes. "Let's not forget why we're all here," he chided. "We're all professional hand-clappers."

Finally the president and his family arrived to a flood of hot TV lights and a thundering ovation. Gerry Ford introduced the family, gave a mini-speech, and within 10 minutes it was over. Time to head upstairs to Horvath's room and do some more drinking. On the table in the room was a porta-bar that folded into a briefcase. "Don't drink my Early Times," the owner of the briefcase shouted from the bathroom. I jiggled my ice cubes and attempted to continue interviewing.

"How come you became a Republican?" I asked Warner.

"Because 80 percent of my county is Republican," he answered, paused, and as an afterthought added, "and I agree with the philosophy of the Republican party."

Scott's sugar daddy, Gehlback, made some cheap ethnic jokes, and Scott negotiated a dinner date with Debra. I started to question another Young Republican who belched in my face. It was becoming obvious that if there was a "head honcho" within our grasp it was Horvath. Warner was trying to latch onto Horvath's karma, the Young Republicans were hanging on to the hanger-on, and there I was, getting burped at by a hanger-on of a hanger-on.

Monday

Sometime during Sunday's inebriation, Horvath told us where to go to get limited-access press credentials, which came in the form of 3-by-5-inch cards that we were to hang around our necks. In a Republican dress code, where suits, ties and dresses were *status quo*, it was those precious cardboard identification tags that separated the annointed delegates, press and security personnel from the tourists.

We went to the Municipal Auditorium, which housed the Republican National Convention Headquarters, as well as the media headquarters. The assistant college press supervisor told us that without prior reservations there was little he could do. Bravely I showed him my recently expired *Daily Egyptian* press card and hoped for the best. Not exactly the *Washington Post*, but what the hell.

Fate was on our side. The assistant happened to be Arabic, and when he saw the word "Egyptian" he was instantly sympathetic. In a thick accent he said he was slightly familiar with SIU through a friend who once was in the Arabic studies program, and that was enough to get us our passes.

Credentials in hand, we sped over to the Hilton Plaza, where most of the Illinois delegation was staying, and where Ronald Reagan was to put in an appearance around 4 p.m. The room where Reagan was to appear was filling up with people. It wasn't a particularly big room, and it was made smaller by a roped-off area in front of the podium and stage in the rear where the behemoths of the media, the television cameras, were poised. Much of the rest of the space was taken up by lesser representatives of the media and some teen-aged hand-clappers known as the Youth For Reagan (YFR). There were fewer of them, they were younger, but they made up for their smaller numbers with greater decibels of enthusiasm.

The room quickly became hot, crammed and stuffy. There was a lot of jostling going on, and tempers were short. Some guy in a baby blue cowboy leisure suit with white rhinestones was warming up the crowd with boasts that as head of the Screen Guild Reagan had acquired first-hand knowledge of foreign affairs by "fighting the Communists in Holly-wood."

The Young Americans for Freedom ecstatically waved their signs and syncopated "R-R-R-E-A, R-E-A-G-A-N, Ron-old Ray-gun!" But that singularly vulgar remark, dredging up and even bragging about the McCarthy era, the Red Scare and the blackballing of intellectuals, liberals, socialists and radicals in the arts, revealed a lot more about the Reagan philosophy than his decision to pick liberal Richard Schweiker as a running mate or his Pepsodent smile and Knute Rockne hair. His popularity also told a lot about the character of the American electorate. Americans, indeed all people, prefer their leaders to be strong macho warriors as opposed to effeminate, intellectual sensitive leaders.

Some Hollywood lightweights like Efrem Zimbalist Jr. said some words, then Schweiker and Reagan made their appearance to shouts of "We need Reagan" and "We like Schweik." Their speeches were of the "go team go" variety, no substance, no revelations. The entire production was meant for the TV cameras, and if a glimpse of Reagan and Schweiker wasn't enough to get your rocks off, it left a foul taste in the mouth.

Tuesday
To save time, I was dropped off at the Plaza to see if the Illinois delegation would come through with guest tickets while Deb and John went back to the media headquarters to get a daily schedule. The funniest thing happened on the way to the Illinois delegation. I ran into Ronald Reagan again. And just about the time Reagan came out, Gerald Ford went into the Illinois caucus.

At the end of the caucus, like a small-town revival, several officially uncommitted (unofficially committed) delegates testified they had seen the light and came out for Ford or Reagan. Finally I got in to check on our tickets, and the Illinois delegation had indeed come through. We were going to get inside the convention hall!

The next stop was Yippie Park, at the War Memorial. There was a tiny contingent of Yippies, while the majority of dissidents were gay, with a few Jesus People and passersby thrown in, along with several surly individuals who might be classified as truly dangerous. All told there were fewer than 50 hardcore, including the band. Things were so docile the police weren't even around.

It was getting late in the afternoon. The Yippies were finishing their signs and last-minute preparations. They climbed into their beat-up vans and jalopies and headed off to Kemper Arena where they would stand behind a double-high chain-link fence and keep up a steady stream of anti-establishment racket. We changed out of our T-shirts and back into our suits, climbed into my Dad's borrowed Buick and clutched our convention tickets, which would put us in touch with a different kind of racket.

The atmoshere inside the convention hall was like a big sporting event. We felt awe looking at the convention floor, just like first seeing the field when you enter a baseball stadium.

Almost as exciting as seeing the politicians was picking out the hotshot TV reporters through our binoculars. The anchor booths for the three networks were glass-enclosed areas on the mezzanine level. It was gratifying to watch Brinkley blow his nose or Cronkite wipe sweat off his brow after the TV cameras had been catching the delegates in inelegant poses the night before. Like at some sporting events, the best seats were across from the TV and not in the gallery. Through our binoculars we could see everything, but we couldn't tell what was going on. When they began the roll call vote on whether Ford would have to name his running mate, there wasn't even a scoreboard with a running tally.

From our vantage point the delegates on the floor looked like a bunch of ants swarming around. Over at the New York delegation, we could see a tipsy Nelson Rockefeller holding up a broken telephone, and we could see another clump of ants forming around the Mississippi delegation, but we had no way of knowing what was happening.

Mike Wallace was standing with the Mississippi delegation getting the scoop. Suddenly Debbie spotted Scott Warner standing next to Wallace, eavesdropping on news in the making. Somehow Warner had gotten down on the floor. When he returned upstairs, John took off after him, hoping for a chance to get that perfect image. I stayed put, collecting random impressions and getting more melancholy by the moment.

For about the 50th time I asked myself what I was doing in Kansas City. After all, half of the greatest politicians in America were gathered here, as were representatives of a thousand news-gathering organizations. An event protected by thousands of cops and focused upon by the eyes of the entire world. I had come so far, to K.C. and inside the arena. I should not stop here. I should chase after John, descend to the summit, practice my craft, buttonhole somebody down there, ask them some inane question.

Suddenly Debbie spotted John through the binoculars. There he was, buzzing around on the floor, like a honeybee, collecting pollen with his camera as fast as he could focus his trembling eyes. The honeybee had communed with the ants. I, too, should join them in the holy act of newsmaking. But my mind was not in a honeybee mood. To extend the swollen metaphor, I was a praying mantis, preying on the events and lives of others; a cannibalistic journalist.

Who the hell was anyone trying to kid anyway? Who could believe the president was being chosen before my very eyes? How could a decision like the fate of a nation be made at a circus like this? No! It had to be hype. The hugest pseudo-event of them all. And everyone, all the politicians, police, reporters, hippies and hand-clappers merely reinforced the facade.

And to hell if I would lend one iota of credence to this sham by participating in it. Courageously I clung to my pillar of sarcasm and my bleacher seat. The hell if I would lower myself to become a media groupie.

Wednesday
By Wednesday morning things had changed; I was hooked on the convention, and getting tickets became our primary concern. Unfortunately, everyone else felt the same way because it was the night of the big showdown between Reagan and Ford. At the Illinois delegation the list was discarded and instead a raffle was held to determine who got the 25 tickets 300 people wanted. After we lost the raffle, we went to the California courtesy room, located next to the Illinois room, to eat the free fruit and buy a drink.

The network news had just come on, and several sullen Reagan supporters had gathered around. Uncle Walter intoned that in the wake of the defeat of Reagan's effort to force Ford to name his running mate, Schweiker had volunteered to withdraw from the ticket, but Reagan reaffirmed his support.

One of the Reagan supporters watching television asked why Reagan didn't accept his resignation, looked around and apologetically added, "I guess I'm not supposed to say that." No one said anything, but it was clear they agreed.

The bold Schweiker move by Reagan campaign manager John Sears was, in the final analysis, a brilliant gamble but a fatal political blunder. The liberal Pennsylvania senator was not popular with hardcore Reagan conservatives, and he failed to impress northern liberals a whit. The move may have been detrimental to Reagan, but it was probably for the good of the party and the nation. Reagan's appeal was his uncompromising, saber rattling xenophobic image. Those who responded to his cause were the "anti-people" -- anti-E.R.A., anti-amnesty, anti-abortion, anti-busing, anti-detente and anti-gun control. But the anti-people tended to be over-zealous in a generic sense. The fanaticism of their support was reflected in the passion of the Reagan demonstrations. Sure, the Reaganites yelled louder because they were behind, but there was also a disconcerting messianicism to the Reagan supporters.

Certainly there were many Reagan supporters attracted to the man for legitimate philosophical or political reasons, but the fanatical Reagan supporters, especially the Young Americans for Freedom, gave the Reagan movement a slightly fascist under-current. It would be sympathetic, and probably inaccurate, to suggest that Sears saw the fanatical drift of the Reagan contingency, and for ethical reasons sought to divert it. More likely, Sears realized that a minority of zealous support was inferior to a majority of lukewarm support, and he attempted a last ditch effort to align the right with the left to head off the middle. But his strategy was doomed for the same reason the leftist radicals have been unsuccessful -- a non-polarized society. The result has been the selection of moderates in both parties. Neither Carter nor Ford can be seen as "cause" candidates.

Thursday
Over the course of the week, we had been immersed in the Republican universe, and had even started to think a little like Republicans. Evil old Reagan had become a sentimental friend, if not favorite, and Ford a moderate, level-headed conservative who had managed to delay the inevitable shift of the GOP to the far right. It was therefore a somewhat shattering experience when we turned on the tube Thursday morning to learn that Ford had decided to play politics as usual with the selection of Kansas Sen. Robert Dole as his vice-presidential running mate. About the only good thing about Dole, as a youthful President Ford Committee staffer told me, was that nobody knew who he was. "That will make it easier to market an image of him."

What vacillations Ford must have gone through as he agonized over the John Connallies, Howard Bakers, Anne Armstrongs and Elliot Richardsons. Each of them had his strong and weak points, each represented a definite campaign strategy. What Ford finally opted for was the most cautious of political decisions; an attempted synthesis of all the possibilities, which ended up looking like a disjointed Dadaistic painting.

Robert Dole. The hard campaigner of a Connally, the flippant conservatism of a Reagan or Agnew, and the entertainment capacities of Milton Berle. Possibly the most imponderable of all the perplexing elements that went into the Dole decision is the part his war wound may have played. Dole's right arm is partially paralyzed. Thus, he will conduct the entire campaign as a left-wing hand-shaker.

The soapers jammed the airwaves, so we headed back to the city. John's search for the perfect image had come down to the last day, and it was imperative we find a way back into the convention hall. John and Deb theorized the dejected Reaganites might not use all of their passes. We headed to Alameda Plaza, Reaganland, where hopefully there would be some sore losers and spare tickets.

Our only hope seemed to be to throw in with the Youths For Reagan who had evolved a technique known as "scrounging." About 50 of us climbed on a bus and headed to the arena with 15 tickets. According to the organizers, the ones who got the tickets would head into the arena and scrounge tickets from people already inside who had extras.

One of the leaders of the Youths For Reagan strolled down the bus. "California residents get first dibs," he said. After he had dispensed about a dozen tickets, Debbie got his attention by asking if all the Californians had gotten their tickets, honeysuckle hanging from every syllable.

"I'm trying," he answered, as he delivered a precious ticket into her tender grasp.

"Feminine charm scores again," I thought sarcastically.

When we got to the arena, John used the ticket. He approached alternate delegates, and inside a half hour he had secured two more tickets. Meanwhile Deb had scored two tickets from the YFRs. Since we had beat the system, we generously gave them to fellow scroungers. We'd made it to the finale!

The crowd stirred, the aisles jammed with Ford supporters. Cary Grant was at the podium, rambling about how wonderful women were and how much he loved them. He introduced a weaving Betty Ford who came out to wave and exited stage left without saying a word. The lights dimmed, the crowd hushed, and what followed was a slick home movie of the first family. Then the president appeared and laid a stirring speech on the good folks of Peoria and answered Carter's call for a debate. Ford then trotted out Betty again, and the rest of the family, Dole, Rocky, the cabinet, and even Ronald Reagan, hoping to cash in on his charisma.

The joint was a madhouse, a last orgasmic demonstration of shouts and signs, party hats, emotional outbursts of conditioned response. "What malarky," I again thought from my perch in the peanut gallery. "What pomp. What a mockery of democracy."

But as the meaningless noise continued I thought about how so many other nations choose their leaders. Instead of battling with horns, signs and buttons, they use guns and grenades to solve their political differences. If America can sublimate its political energy through such harmless activities as pep rallies instead of riots, balloons instead of mortars and party hats instead of military uniforms, then more power to the absurd American way.

Epilog

The convention was over, the politicians and delegates had left the arena. From behind his glass booth, Cronkite sipped beer from a plastic cup while a few lingerers poked through the garbage, looking for souvenirs. The network floor reporters huddled for their convention recaps, and we wandered among the rubbish and the rubies, looking for one last crystal in the debris.

The Roger Mudds and Sam Donaldsons looked mellowed out. "Cassie's (Macken) down for the eight count," laughed Tom Brockaw. Morton Dean thought it was "a hell of a convention," and even seasoned John Chancellor wandered onto the floor looking dazed.

Some cops were off on the side using their riot clubs to play catch with a balloon. The cheering became an echo, and ghosts from the '60s took up their own chants -- power to the people, Ho Ho Ho Chi Minh, and the whole world is watching . . . Was there ever really a difference between the stoned freaks of a decade ago and the Republicans of today? At the Democratic National Convention in Chicago in 1968 many of the young people had been used by the Yippies the same as the teen-age Ford supporters were used by Ford campaign workers today. Only instead of balloons, it was baggies full of shit they were instructed to hurl.

Still, it was for a cause, like peace, equality, and liberation, rather than a candidate like Gerald Ford. But drop the romanticism, Mac. The good guys seldom win, and the world is not always a choice between good and evil. Sometimes it's a choice of lesser evils.

Maybe we can live in a polarized world with choices like Nixon or McGovern, or a stagnant world with choices like Ford and Carter. The former is more exciting, the latter safer. There is more to gain in a polarized society, but a lot more to lose.

And considering the batting average of the good guys, maybe this is one season we can take solace in the fact that there ain't a dime's worth of difference between the candidates.

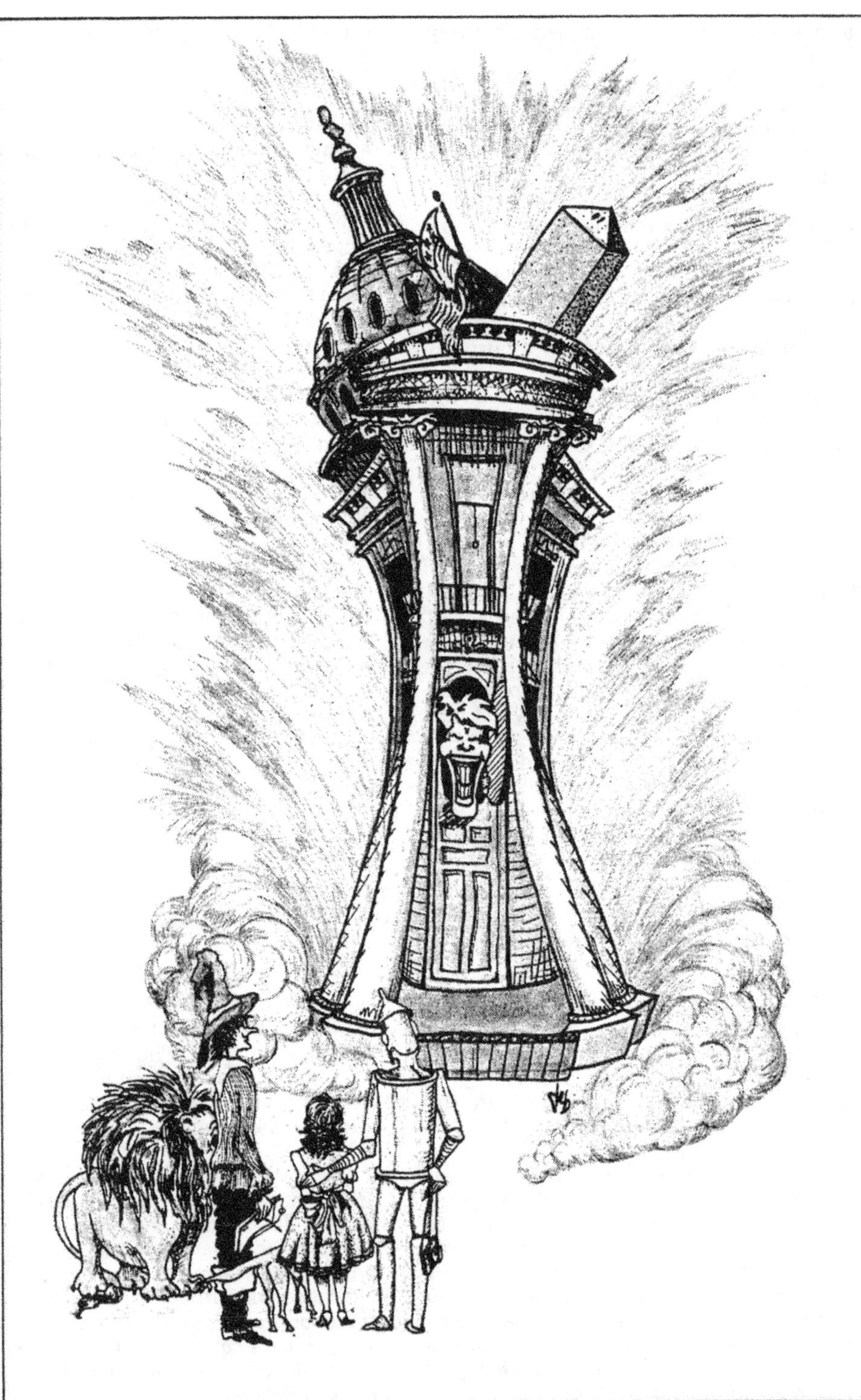

The Great Washington D.C. Fiasco

Imagine you had a chance to ask one question, face to face, with the president of the United States. That's just the opportunity a group of Illinois journalism students, including yours truly, recently thought they had as a result of a chain of circumstances that ultimately resulted in The Great Washington D.C. Fiasco.

It all started innocently enough when a youthful journalism student from Peoria, George Sloan, attempted a noble enough endeavor -- to get an interview with Jimmy Carter. Shortly after Carter's inauguration, Sloan wrote the White House requesting an interview with the new Chief Executive. Sloan, like hundreds of other unaffiliated small-time reporters who had similar notions, received a congenial reply signed by Press Secretary Jody Powell saying he was sorry but the president did not grant one-on-one interviews.

Unlike the hundreds of other people who ask for an audience with the president, Sloan persisted. He wrote Powell back and suggested that because Carter did not grant one-on-one interviews, perhaps he would consider meeting with a group of Illinois journalism students representing college newspapers from throughout the state.

Several weeks later an ecstatic Sloan got a reply from Powell saying that, yes, the president would consider meeting with such a group. Sloan claimed he was certain the letter came from Powell's office because the word "for" was spelled "fro." So Sloan, taking the communique at face value, set about contacting the various journalism schools in Illinois. It was late March, and I was dreaming about the folds of an over-stuffed brown leather chair when *nonSequitur* news

editor Jim Santori awakened me with the news that if I wanted to see the president I had to fill out a form for the Secret Service. Jim was calling from the *Daily Egyptian* newsroom, which was abuzz with speculation about the trip.

My first reaction was complete disbelief that I or anyone else from SIU would attend a press conference in Washington with the president. After a respectable amount of time so as not to appear curious, I strolled into the newsroom and attempted to get to the bottom of things. If it were any other president, the idea would have been unthinkable. But Carter's "open administration" made it seem remotely possible. And as former *Daily Egyptian* reporter Scott Singleton put it, "Hell, if he'd talk to a town meeting in Clinton and a kidnapper in Cleveland, why not us?" Thus the seeds of The Great Washington D.C. Fiasco were sown.

As arrangements for the press conference continued, more letters were exchanged between Sloan and the president's press secretary, and about 50 journalism students from about 10 Illinois colleges and universities signed up for the trip, which, by the way, was find your own transportation and pay your own expenses. Looking back, it's hard to accept how we seduced ourselves into believing we would actually get to see Carter, how we were willing to settle for halfway promises and verbal assurances that everything was proceeding smoothly. Indeed, there were many (especially the parents of the would-be White House correspondents who were asked to finance the venture) who cautioned us that something seemed fishy. But what the heck, it was time for a vacation anyway, and even if the odds were a thousand to one, how could any self-respecting go-for-broke journalist pass up an outside chance to get a fluke interview with The Most Powerful Man On Earth? As the day of the press conference, May 19, 1977, approached, the group of 50 had dwindled down to about 20 diehards, half of whom came from SIU.

The cracks began appearing in the dike after we arrived in Washington. The day before the press conference, Sloan announced that instead of going to the White House we would be incarcerated next door in the Executive Office Building and subjected to a procession of cabinet deputy undersecretaries and political party underlings. Sloan said Carter was "iffy" but Press Secretary Jody Powell was still "probably." It became official when on the day of the big fiasco we were ushered into the room of the Executive Office Building that epitomizes broken promises -- the Indian Treaty Room. With a secret smile indicating some sort of Washington in-joke, our tour guide, Deputy Presidential Press Secretary Jim Perks, told us we were sitting in a historic room, but no Indian treaties had ever been signed there.

He also made it plain that we would not be seeing peanut face. But he said you never could tell when Jody might suddenly pop through the door, speed-rapping and chain smoking, as if Powell really was the little elf the media portrayed him to be.

So the ground rules had changed from what do you ask the president to what do you ask, for instance, Bob Howell of the Justice Department or Robert Barry from the Office of Soviet Affairs at State. It's not that we were unappreciative or that the speakers weren't interesting, but without some recognized name to quote there was no way any of us was going to end up with a very sexy story.

By mid-afternoon we were getting pretty fed up. We had sat through five lengthy but unproductive interviews already, and in what seemed like a fit of arrogance, the Republican National Committee had dispatched what looked to be a 16-year-old Young Republican to practice his rap on us. I was blowing lazy smoke rings at the ceiling and wondering whether anyone would mind if I put my feet on the historic Indian Treaty Room table when I decided it was time to take matters into my own hands. I'd call Jody Powell's office and tell somebody off.

The press secretary's secretary told me Powell was not available and was about to hang up when I went into my sob story. "Look," I began, "you people may not be aware, but there's a contingent of journalism students next door who have come all the way from Illinois at their own expense because your office told them they would be having a visit with the president. Now I realize we're not from CBS or *The Washington Post*, and I realize the president, after all, is a very busy man. But between the 20 of us we have invested several thousand dollars and traveled thousands of miles, and it seems to me that the administration could pop for just one political superstar, just to make our trip seem worth it, you know."

The secretary assured me she would see what she could do and put me on hold. Several minutes later she told me there just wasn't anyone in the office.

"Look," I pleaded, getting desperate. "I like Jimmy Carter and I certainly wouldn't vote against him because of a silly incident like this. But this is just the kind of thing that might make our families and all the people we've told about the trip hold a grudge.

"Besides," I added, playing my trump card, "what if the White House press corps got ahold of this? They'd eat you for breakfast in Peoria."

Instead of putting me on hold, this time the secretary put her palm over the phone. I could hear her talking to someone and then what sounded like a muffled, baritone, "aargh."

"You're in luck," the secretary told me. "Jody unexpectedly came into the office, and he says he'd be happy to drop by for about 15 minutes."

We were prepared to be hostile, but when a deadpan Jody Powell said, "Hi, I'm Jody Powell and you're not," we were like mush in his hands.

"The White House Press Corps is a bunch of buffoons," lectured Powell, "though it's not entirely their fault. The several hundred accredited reporters who dog the president like a pack of hyenas are under incredible pressure to beat each other out. They usually get the same thing at the same time, which is merely the official version or what I choose to tell them. So even though the White House beat is at the top of the news profession, it's really a crummy job."

Powell looked contemplative for a moment and shrugged his light brown hair off his forehead. "God, I wish there was something I wanted out of those guys," he mused. "I mean, every one of those bozos would give his left nut to get on my good side, not to mention the lady reporters," he chortled. "Just to get that leak a few minutes sooner. For a little extra background or an extra juicy quote.

"Are they objective?" Powell repeated the question. "Let me put it this way: every one of the reporters who covered the candidates during last year's primaries thought that if the candidate they covered got elected, they would become the next White House correspondent for their network or newspaper. And people wonder why Frank Reynolds cried when Reagan lost the nomination in Kansas City."

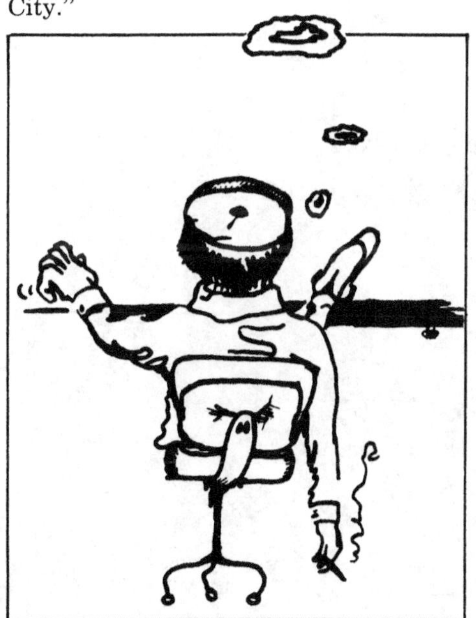

When someone asked about ABC White House correspondent Sam Donaldson, Powell's eyes flashed. "Hoo-ee," drawled Jody. "He's the most meshuggeneh of the bunch." Powell went on to say that in his opinion Donaldson has a terminal case of "Plains Fever," which he said was caused from eating too many free peanuts and having too many beers with brother Billy.

"Sam has a great sense for the absurd, and Plains was perfect for him. ABC should assign him there forever. But I don't think Sam will ever forgive Jimmy for being from Plains when the other reporters got to cover their candidates in Los Angeles, Washington and New York. But that's just one of those things I gotta put up with."

When asked about Carter pollster Pat Caddell and his report that suggested Carter continue to promote style over substance, Powell didn't back down. "That's just hardcore political reality," stated Powell. "Hell, when Eric Severeid does it they call it 'political analysis.' But when we do the same thing they call it 'manipulative' and 'cynical.' Crap. Most of those White House reporters wouldn't know substance if they stepped in a pile of it anyway."

I watched my smoke ring disintegrate as it lazily floated toward the ceiling. The 16-year-old Young Republican was still droning on about how the GOP was going to appeal to blacks and young people.

Alas, there was never a telephone call, no such conversation, no such meeting with Jody Powell. Only the figments of my bored imagination. But let that be a lesson to all you Jody Powells. In this enlightened age of gonzo and new journalism, if you guys aren't going to give us the news so that we can inform people, then by golly we'll make it up so at least to entertain them.

And for everyone who is not Jody Powell, if anyone ever tells you you've got a chance to talk to the president, get it in writing.

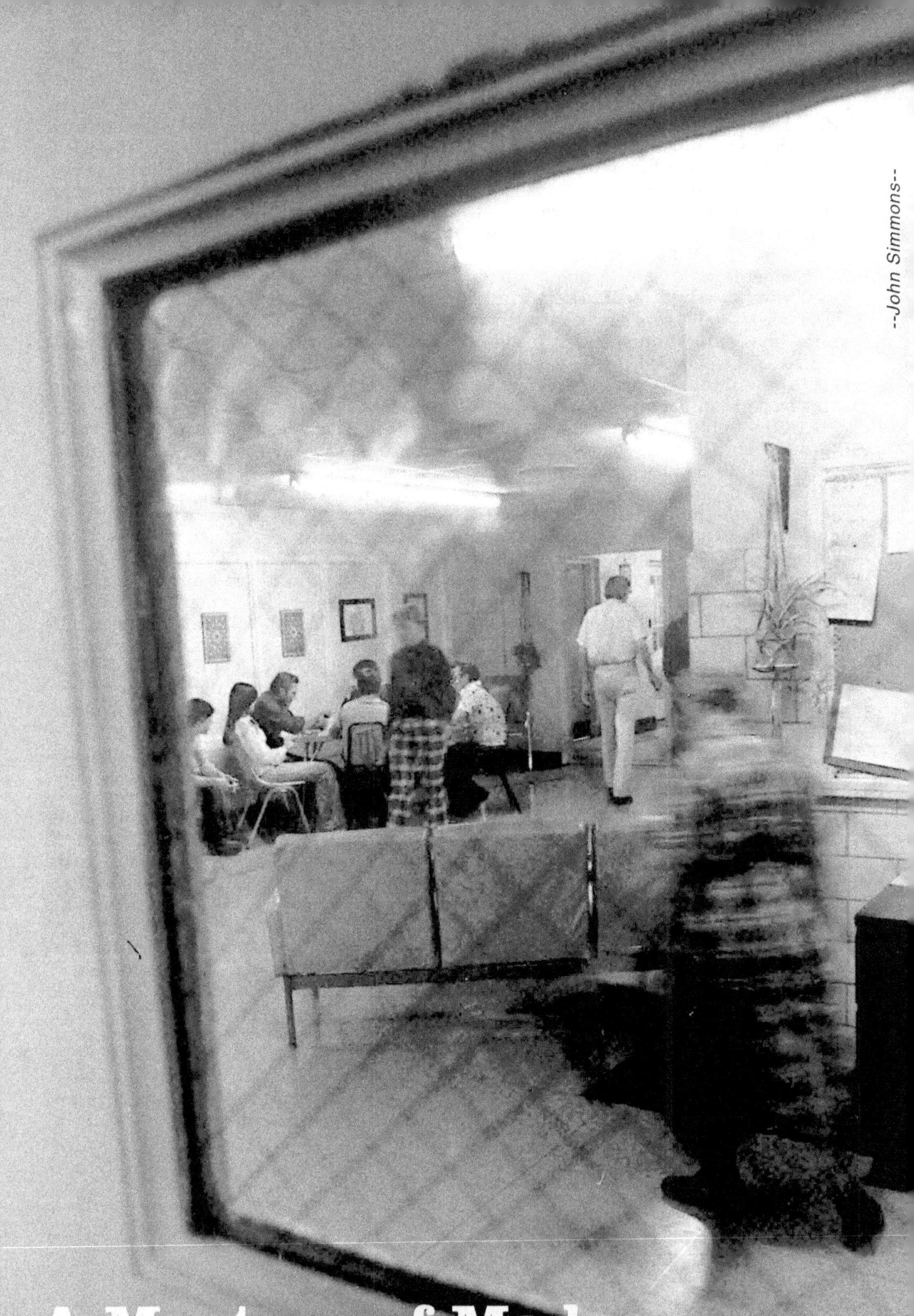

A Mystery of Madness:
Who Let Frank Hall Down?

A close friend of mine presently resides in the state mental hospital in Anna. What drove Frank Hall mad is a question that haunts me deeply. I've known Frank on and off since 1964 when we were on the same little league team. We were on the high school student council together, chased the same girls, flipped out on the same drugs. I had many chances to reach out to Frank as he transgressed from somber introverted student to acidhead, Jesus freak, capitalist and finally paranoid schizophrenic. So I wonder often what I or anyone else could have done to save him from his fate.

Frank grew up in Carbondale with his sister, mother and stepfather. Both of his parents were teachers of moderate income, and Frank's upbringing was . . . well, it was normal. In high school he was an honor student, president of the student body, quiet but popular with a seemingly bright future.

It was also normal, upon graduation from high school, at least in 1969, that Frank experiment with the hippy lifestyle -- marijuana, LSD, and whatever else was going around. Frank got stoned a lot, and he could get pretty far out on LSD, but so was everyone else at the time. He joined a rock-and-roll band, slept around and found a girlfriend while his parents, like most parents, put pressure on their son to straighten out his act.

Frank and his girlfriend decided to take the obligatory trip to the West Coast. They left in search of the end of the rainbow. Several months later, out of money, out of luck and out of options, they returned as born-again Christians.

They separated and Frank rapidly became a dyed-in-the-wool Jesus freak -- hanging out with other Jesus people, constantly studying and preaching the Bible, and abstaining from drugs, alcohol and sex.

Frank's parents found Frank the Jesus freak no less repugnant than Frank the acidhead and began to press him to accept psychiatric help. And most of his friends, who had drifted back to more middle class values, also found his Jesus rap a drag and began to shut him out.

Frank clung to his religious fervor for several years, but eventually it became obvious a new pressure was weighing him down. Frank's parents had consulted psychiatrists who told them to cut Frank off financially unless he accepted psychiatric help. Their reasoning was that to continue to support him would only prolong the inevitable.

Suddenly Frank's thoughts of miracles and divine plans were replaced by other grandiose ideas -- mostly schemes to make lots of money. He wanted to escape his poverty, increase his self-esteem and become more respectable to others, but he was frustrated in his efforts. Always interested in design and architecture, Frank applied for jobs with city planning and private construction, to no avail. And he had no more luck than anyone else in the Carbondale job market.

One night Frank pleaded with me to give him $25 so he could leave town because his parents wanted to put him in an asylum. I told him he was paranoid, and when he said that if I was really his friend I would do this one big favor for him, I consented half out of guilt and half to get him off my back.

Two weeks later I was only mildly surprised when I learned he had been taken to Wohl Hospital in St. Louis for tests, and then transferred to Anna.

I visited Frank last summer while he was there. Amongst the aged and obscene alcoholics, chronic manic-depressives and catatonics endlessly repeating their incomprehensible motions, Frank attempted to keep busy reading, writing and planning how he would make it once he was released.

Although the drugs the doctors had prescribed calmed him down and made him more rational, they also made him sluggish and listless and blurred his vision. And although his therapy seemed to be working, he began to think of himself, and others began to think of him, as a mental patient.

After several months, Frank got out of Anna and he seemed to be better. He was laughing for the first time in years and put on some weight. He stayed with me for a week then moved into a halfway house. Next he got a job with an insurance company, which sent him to a school to learn the trade. When the insurance job didn't work out, he got another job with a solar energy company. But the company went out of business, and Frank was out of money, and going hungry, again. It was obvious he had suffered a relapse the day he walked into the *Daily Egyptian* office and announced that he had been appointed president of Southern Illinois University.

When I ran into Frank again, he was running for political office, attempting to sell a design idea to Bucky Fuller for a million dollars, hassling females, bumming meals, incessantly talking and becoming an unbearable pest.

When his friends could stand it no longer they threw him out, as did various area social welfare agencies. He was ineligible for food stamps and most of the crisis centers offered only overnight lodging. It was then that Frank began exhibiting new and, for the first time, aggressive behavior patterns; yelling and threatening to sue all those who disagreed with him.

One night he went to his parents' house to beg for money. Still following the advice of physicians, they refused and attempted to get him to leave. Blows were struck, and Frank was soon arrested and charged with assaulting his parents. He spent the next week in the Jackson County jail because no one would post his bail.

Perhaps his last remaining friend, I was Frank's final refuge from the police, the doctors and "normal" people who wanted him taken out of society and put away. But I, too, was fed up. I felt guilty that I couldn't help him, that I couldn't stand even to be around him, and that I, like everyone else, had come to the conclusion that incarceration in a mental institution was the only solution.

Finally, one morning when he came to my house and demanded to enter, I chased him off with a baseball bat. With nowhere left to go, Frank stole a bicycle and pedalled from Carbondale to Anna, where he signed himself into the mental health center for the second time.

Occasionally Frank calls me collect, and I always accept the call. He tells me they are treating him well, that they feed and shelter him, that they even have

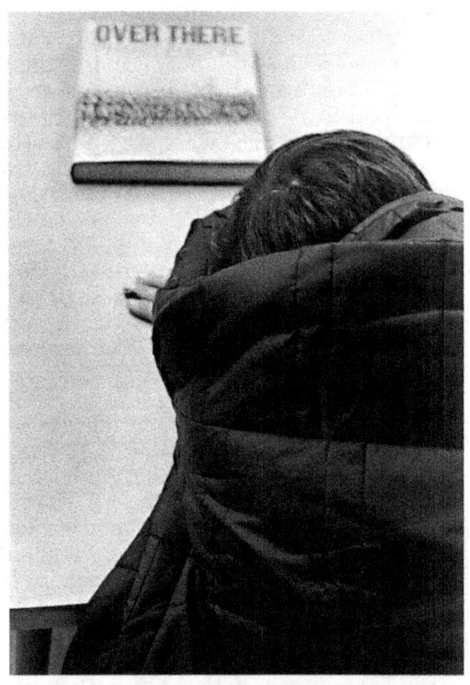

crafts and bowling. He says that in some ways it's better for him in there than out here. "Because at least there are some real people in here," he tells me. But they still think he might run away and keep him in a controlled area.

I tell him I'm glad he's happy, at the same time I'm aware that the more he gets used to being institutionalized, the less likely he is going to want to come out.

And often I wonder why he is where he is. Is Frank Hall genetically insane? Is it something in his upbringing, sex life, psychedelic drugs or born-again religion that sent Frank over the edge? Maybe it is the condition of poverty itself -- exposure, malnutrition and alienation -- that brought Frank down. Maybe a combination of them all.

But mostly I wonder about the future. I have faith that Frank will come back out a second time. And when he does, will his family and friends, strangers and employers be a help or a hindrance, and will Frank's own soul be strong enough, patient enough, and resilient enough to make it in this jungle we call "society?"

The Hite Report Report

This article was written shortly after Shere Hite packed a ballroom at SIU. It was stolen from the desk drawer by friend Deb Browne, who had co-founded the Southern Observer *newspaper here and needed some last-minute copy. It was printed in the November edition of the monthly paper under the title "The Grump Report," by Ralph Grump. The rest is self explanatory . . . or shall we say exploratory . . . or explicatory . . .*

Shere Hite says 70 percent of American males cheat on their wives, cohabitators and girlfriends. Ms. Hite, the author of "The Hite Report on Female (and Male) Sexuality," made this startling pronouncement at a recent lecture at SIU.

She bases her assertion on the same material she used for her books -- the results of several thousand questionnaires sent to a rough cross section of Americans. Some may question the validity of her research. But even if you make allowances for the roughness of the sample and macho exaggerations, even if you assign an ample margin of error of, say, 25 percent, it still appears that a heck of a lot of guys are fooling around on their mates.

Much of Ms. Hite's SIU lecture was a pseudological -- and, for me, unconvincing -- explanation of that fact. She used the familiar feminist catchwords like "macho" and "sexist" and even resorted to some Freudian mumbo jumbo about parental role models.

According to Ms. Hite, the typical American family consists of a "weak" and "repressed" wife who is mistreated by her "controlled" and "uncommunicative" husband who "on a regular basis" has sex with other women, doesn't tell his wife

about it and doesn't feel guilty about it. The son in this family -- I hope I get this right -- hates his father for the way he treats his mother, feels the urge to protect his defenseless mom, and then, when he grows up, goes out on his wife because he resents her for being like his mother. Or something like that.

Only briefly did Ms. Hite mention the "resurgence of primordial theories" that provide an alternative explanation for

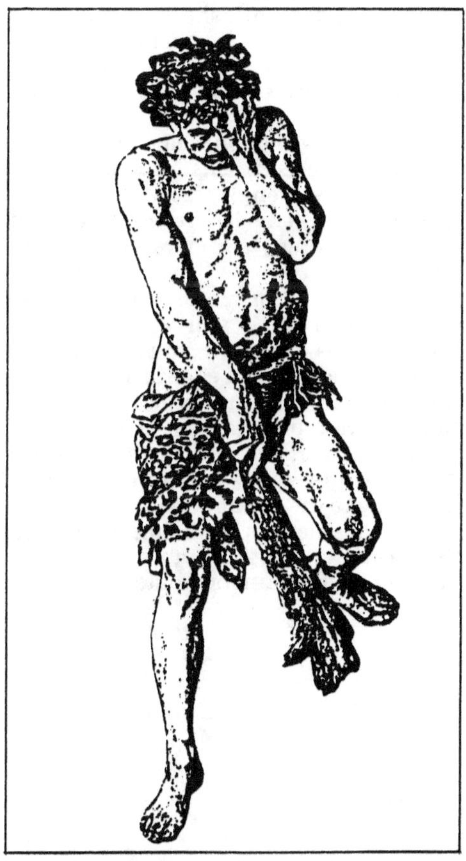

contemporary sexual behavior. The primordial theories are no less pseudo-logical than Ms. Hite's, but from the maleist perspective they are a lot less degrading.

Back in the cave-dweller days, or perhaps even the tree-dweller days, when homo sapiens or some Neanderthal ancestor did a lot of premature dying, there evolved separate instinctual "sex strategies" for male and female cave-persons to propagate the species. Because life was so short and threatening, the best chance a caveguy had of doing that was to knock up as many young caveladies as he could and hope some of them lived long enough to bear a cavebaby.

A cavewoman, on the other hand, saddled with the evolutionary boobie prize of gestation, had to develop a different modus operandi. She would seduce the hunkiest caveguy she could find and hope he liked her enough to protect her from the elements and other horny caveguys while she was vulnerably pregnant. To seal the deal, men and women developed the emotions of love and possessiveness to go with their ravenous libidos.

Voila. Men go out on women more than vice versa because this primordial sex strategy was engineered into their chromosomes long before the advent of society, marriage, pornography, the pill and sexism.

Granted, the primordial theory has some logical gaps you could drive a brontosaurus through, and it does not justify infidelity in an egalitarian society. But theories of natural selection assume that we were not made in God's perfect image. Rather, we are mere imperfect adaptations, slowly evolving and adjusting to the dynamic equilibrium of a mostly hostile world. Being imperfect, there is no reason that our sex instincts and our love instincts would always be compatible, however convenient that might be.

Many of us hot-blooded males truly love our mates. We don't hate them in any sense. We don't think of them as property. We don't think it is macho to cheat on them. We'd rather throw ourselves in front of a bus than hurt them or allow them to be hurt, physically or emotionally.

And yet, we still feel this incongruous urge to have sex with other women. This urge is a source of frustration, grief, guilt, shame and humiliation. It tempts us to compromise, deceive, and sin against our own moral codes. When we don't hate ourselves for our fantasies, we resent our mates for standing in the way of us acting them out. And it robs us of fulfillment from either our mates or our illicit lovers.

Whereas Ms. Hite and many of her sisters might say this propensity for males to cheat is a "freedom" bestowed on them by a sexist society, I envy those all-too-few persons who are emotionally free from this desire and dichotomy in their lives.

The solution to the male promiscuity problem, says Ms. Hite, is equality between the sexes. If men would drop their sexist mindsets and if women would become more assertive, it would just disappear.

I doubt it. As more women become "liberated" from the home, take on careers, outside interests and become more like men in those kinds of ways, I suspect they will fool around more, too. And it would take a more totalitarian form of repression than women's lib to stop males from doing the same.

Besides, if 70 percent of American males are cheating on their mates, just whom does Ms. Hite think they're cheating with?

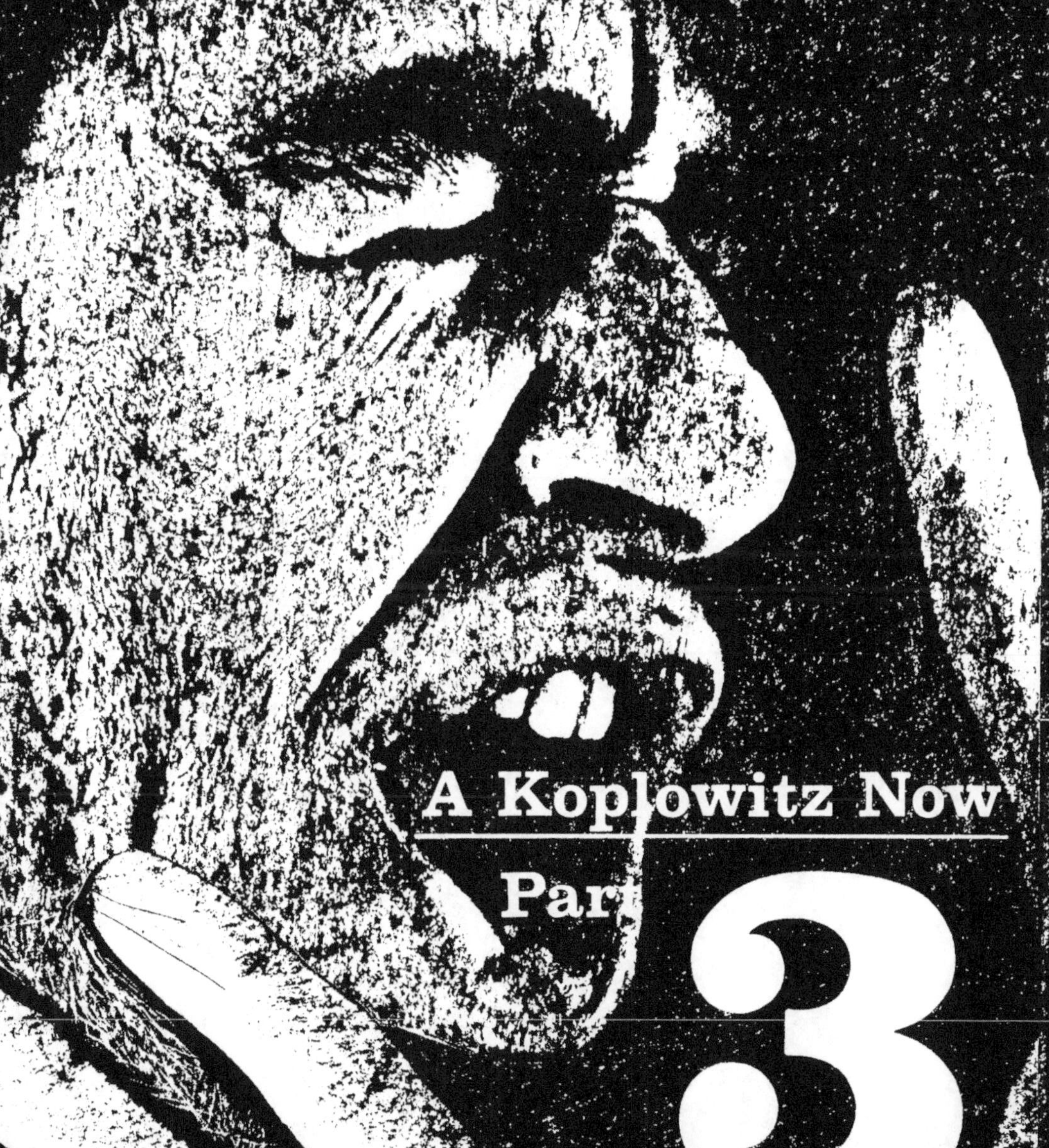

A Koplowitz Now
Part 3

The Blue Period
1969-1974

Have you ever wondered whether the product of felicity was less poignant than that of madness? I did. So between about 1969 and 1974 I attempted to drive myself insane by depriving myself of all the things that had made me comfortable -- my parents, my girlfriend, school, money and friends. It was a desolate, sordid period. And as the layers of my middle class identity were stripped away, the "real me" that began to emerge was more of a Frankenstein than a Zarathustra. I stuck it out for about five years, long enough to decide that if the function of government is to protect us from each other, then the function of society -- families, friends and lovers -- is to protect us from our selves.

Not surprisingly, my "product" during this period reflected my loneliness and alienation. "The Horny Blues" is a poem I penned at sunrise in 1971 while sitting in the nude on my bedroom floor. I was on a William F. Burroughs stream-of-consciousness kick at the time, and the result is not what you would call pretty. But neither is sexual frustration, and that is what I was attempting to describe.

"Kidnapped by Jesus Freaks" is taken from a letter written to a friend in 1972. It is a true account of a night spent at a religious commune in Corvallis, Oregon, which was the first but not the only time I have been the unwitting object of a cult seduction. I also spent two days and a night with a tribe of fundamentalist Christians in New Burnside, Illinois, who had me helping them tear down condemned houses for building materials for their little colony in the wilderness; and several days with some eclectics in Richmond, Virginia, who called their religion the Unity Grace Movement and used intensive group therapy sessions to cultivate adherents.

"An Occurrence in August Heat" is a short story written in 1973. Based on a not-so-true encounter with a couple of door-to-door Morman missionaries, it's an exercise in wish fulfillment, aimed at every bright-eyed zealot who ever tried to "save" me.

"The Kid" and "The Fly" are the opening chapters of "Kid Clyde: An Existentialist's Horror Story," an unfinished novel. Both stories are loosely based on my experiences in Portland, Oregon, where I had gone to live in 1972 because I didn't know anyone there.

The last story, "Of Mice and Moonlandings," is from a diary entry in 1969. There was a "teen town" dance in Carbondale the night before man first landed on the moon, and for some reason I found that terribly significant. The resulting essay is as close to an ending as I could find for this anthology. Enjoy.

The Horny Blues

Ah. At last. A virgin notebook. Five in the morning, tripped out, stopped by the man, shut down by chicks, home at last and there she sits: The Last Virgin Notebook in Carbondale. Well, maybe tonight will be the big fuck huh, the good fuck this time? Look. I'm no hotsnot. All's I am is a Sam with a load. All's you is is a Sue. Sue Notebook. You been sitting around uninked, Sue. What for? To get uninked somemore? Hell no, says Sue, but not just any Sam will do: Turn me on with a little Shelley or Blake, she spake. Ink is just ink, but whatever you want it to be honey, anything anything at all you want that's what it is it is just for God's sake get it out of my sight. You say you don't need no tips from Sammy's meat, no gentle prod or electric rod you say you got something better say silence and death that welcome abyss sure honey, whose chariot? Father Time is just another line to avoid the blister and scratch me mister stab me spear me skewer me eat me what'd ya use for a fork pork you still around Sam don't you realize a climax is s'posed to end you but the pen's still got ink stink what for what more who needs it?

Watchin my ball point twitch with my nerves and my eyes and the heat and the time a well oiled keen o machine what's it good for but comin to tell you to unnerstand it's standard comes with every model we make yes yes guaranteed against wear and tear for the life of the occupant so use it damnit, crush it with those meat choppy legs smother it in dose thighs cram it down those tits till it don't salivate no more please, take a piece, a little teensie weensie piece, c'mon honey a peak, just a peek between the lines it's easier isn't it to wait for life than wait for death? Who's waitin train's leavin right off into thin air so what's this platform doin here in fuckass plastic wood veneer and what the HELL am I doin standin on it Christ it's down to piteous who's ta do the pitying but the pitiful where's the rest where'd they all go Sue? Home. Ta bed. It's late. They is catchin them Zs. God bless them Zs. And damnit, fatigue wins in the end don't SHE in the buttfucking end just another meddlesome middle class cuss on a February morning toast at sunrise to an early death and Mae West gack bleck gawd the pen still runs on and on and it doesn't even have the dignity to do it without effort. Sam you oughta just write it off Dear Valentine be my Kleenex tonight turn out the light ganight.

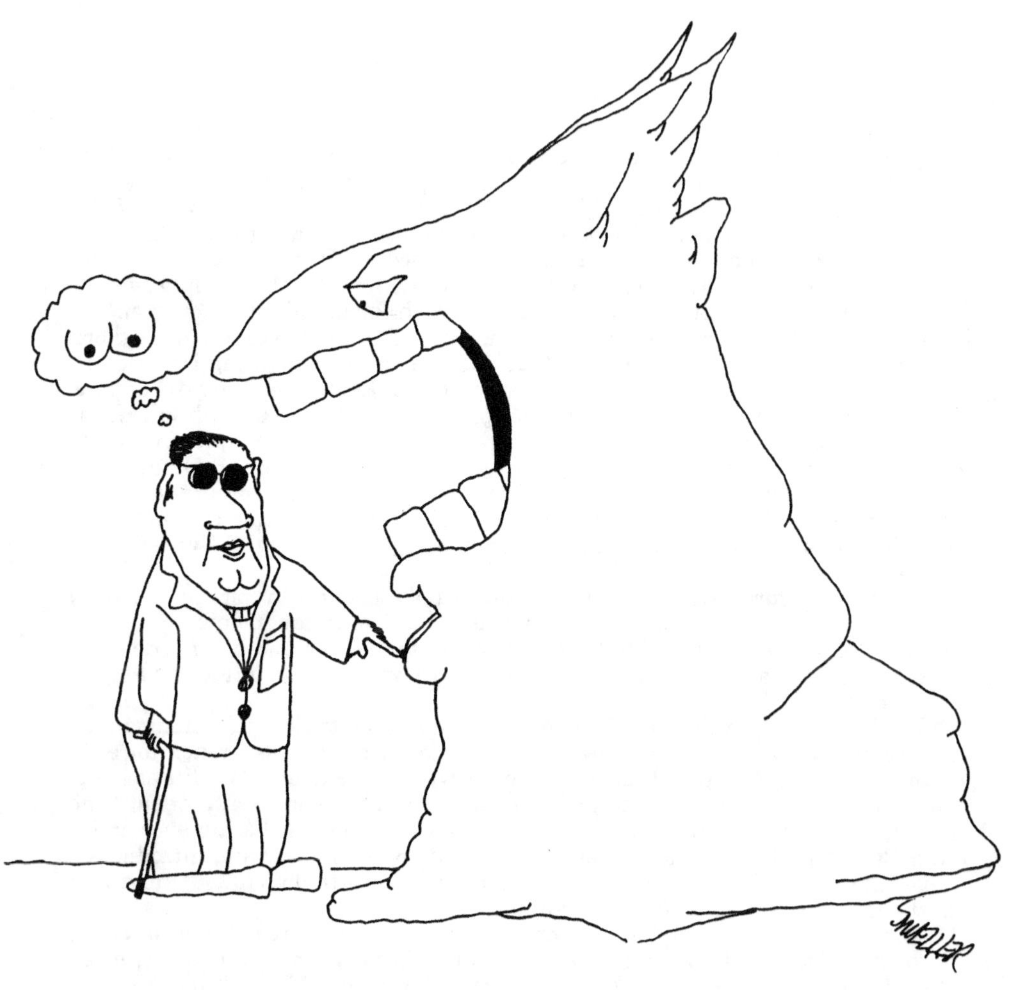

Kidnapped by Jesus Freaks

Dear Lewi,

Oregon is beautiful, though not quite as awesome as I had anticipated. It reminds me of West Virginia or Pennsylvania -- mountains, pine trees, overcast weather and logging trucks. Last week I hitchhiked from Portland to Corvallis to look for John, a lost friend from college. The trip went well until I reached the outskirts of Corvallis where carloads of collegiate hippies passed me by flashing peace signs.

Finally I'm picked up by these two real sociable dudes who start telling me about their commune and offering me a place to crash for the night. They even take me all the way to where I'm going and wait while I run in to see if John is there. He isn't, so I decide to take them up on their offer. I can tell something isn't quite right, but I can't put my finger on it. Once we reach the commune, I get the picture.

There's a sign painted over the front porch proclaiming the place is "Shiloh House." On the mailbox are the words "Jesus lives here." Inside are all these pictures of you-know-who in various well-known poses, and quotes out of the you-know-what burned onto stained wood plaques. There's also a bunch of screaming brats, indicative of a lack of birth control, and one labrador retriever who just couldn't get enough of smelling my balls or licking his own. Egads, I thought, I've been kidnapped by a band of Jesus freaks.

Sure enough, before long the two guys who picked me up begin coming on lightly with the testimonial overture waltz. But they still don't seem too insane. I mean, they're not being pushy and they are going to feed me and bed me down, and I still contend that people have a right to believe whatever, so biting my tongue, I try to be civil.

Shiloh House starts filling up. In twos and threes they trickle in, introducing themselves and being very loving toward me. To steady my nerves I reach for a cigarette, but I'm out. A jeep pulls up and out pop seven more at once. They file past and greet me. Then out of the group emerges this one dude with a short scruffy beard and Charlie Manson eyes -- really spooky eyes, man -- who comes lumbering over and real humble-intense like sits down next to me on the porch railing and introduces himself as Steven. Steven sits down closer than I like, so close that if I hadn't moved my feet at the last moment he would have sat on them.

Unlike the others, he immediately launches into some hardcore religious lines like "have you tried Jesus, pal?" For some reason, my first impression is that he is a faggot. I try to get a grip on myself. Faggot vibes from a Christfreak? It can't be. After a short interchange, he's gone, but I'm still acutely aware that I'm out of cigarettes.

Someone yells "soup's on," which means it's prayer time, and then the dinner procession begins. I am hustled to the front of the line so I am out of the kitchen first and find myself with a choice of 32 vacant seats at these two long rows of picnic tables. I choose a seat in a corner of the room and pray Charlie Manson doesn't sit next to me. He doesn't. He sits across from me and continues his diatribe.

The food is fantastic, and I want to compliment the chef. But I am so afraid that she'll correct me and say "don't thank me, thank God," that I never get

around to it. After dinner I take off my shoes, sit on the porch and conspire to
procure a smoke. I'm sitting out there, minding my own business, when all of a sudden
the night comes alive with Jesus freaks. From every conceivable direction -- down the
sidewalk, through back yards, out of cars -- all these people converge to where I'm
sitting, introduce themselves, lay a Jesus rap on me and enter the house.

After about 50 people are inside, I decide upon a course of action. Boldly I enter
the house. Standing in the middle of the front room, with 50 glassy-eyed Christians
looking on, I bravely ask if anyone has a cigarette. Those who don't pretend they didn't
hear me grimace as if I had told an off-color joke. Finally, someone says piously,
"we don't smoke."

"No problem," I say and retire to the couch. But damn if the Jesus flytrap sitting
next to me doesn't start up with the rap, and finally I bluntly tell him to can it.
I retreat to a desk in the back of the room to write. Ha.

From my new vantage point I observe the following conversation:
"Your name is . . . Michelle?"
"Huh uh, nope."
"Cheryl?"
"Tee hee, no."
"Shirley?"
"Nope."
"Oh pshaw. What's your name?"
"Christine."
"Praise God."
"And your name is . . . Steven?" (For yes, indeed, it was none other
than goony Steven.)
"Praise God," says Steven. "Praise God for people who remember names."
"I never remember names," says Christine. "It was a miracle."
"Well praise God for that."
"Amen."
Yuk.
Next come some two-chord Jesus songs, some more prayers, and then it is Bible
study time. Somebody says let's talk about Jonah and the whale, and one and all whip
out their Bibles and peer at the prescribed page. Except yours truly, of course,
who is peering intently at an organic substance he'd just dug out of his nose.

At this poignant moment subtle Steven strolls across the room. Heads look up and
the speaker stops talking as Steven selects a Bible from a nearby bookcase.
The room falls completely silent as he makes a beeline for me and opens the Bible
on my desk. He takes 23 seconds to find the page (I counted), gives me a patronizing
look and returns to his seat. The Bible class continues, as does my claustrophobia.

I'm cut off from my shoes, not to mention the door, by 50 nodding Jesus junkies.
Realizing it is either my shoes or my sanity, I sacrifice the former and slither out
the back door, over a fence, and off to buy a pack of smokes. I return several blistered
toes later to find blissed out Christians sprawled on the front lawn languidly listening
to a guitarist playing more Jesus music.

Inside, people are milling around a core of eight or so who are sitting at a table
trading personal Jesus experiences. Then goony Steven latches on to me again and
offers me a piece of strawberry pie. I sit to eat and another disciple, Rod, comes over
and joins me. Steven also sits beside me. Like, on the arm of my chair. As I'm eating,
Rod and Steven bombard me with Jesus riffs, then Rod backs off and remarks that it
must be hard for me to stay in a house full of Christians when I'm not one. I tell him
I think Jesus people are cool, but I don't like it when they get pushy. He says he
understands and wanders off.

But not Steven, who remains parked on the arm of my chair, intently watching me
eat. "So you didn't find your friends?" he asks rhetorically. "You know, I kind of
had a feeling you wouldn't. That instead you would receive a sign that you should be

searching for a more dependable type friend."

Before I know it, he's peppering me with some really hard-sell Jesus jive. He starts rappin' about how sinful he was before he was saved. And how he still has horrible temptations and the capacity to sin, to be perverse, even to murder, he says.

When I can get a word in edgewise I ask him what he thinks of Tarot cards. He testifies that he has tried cards, stars, I-Ching, yoga, etc. etc. but they are all idols. I mention something about Hinduism and he starts telling me about his trip to India. Suddenly it dawns on me that Steven must be making up some of his rap. Nobody has been through all that. In his fervor he must be "lying for the Lord" or something. Very strange.

After a while I realize I'm having no effect whatsoever on the course of the conversation so I quit even nodding my head and sink into a sullen reverie. The lines start to run together into one long nauseating monologue. "Have-you-ever-tried-Jesus-is-the-light-and-the-way-have-you-ever-confessed-to-Jesus on and on . . . "

I am shaken out of my delirium by his request that we "get down on our knees and pray to Jesus."

There was something queer about the way he asked me to get down on my knees . . . I remain seated, and he rambles on some more, getting more frustrated. Finally he says, "I can't save you, I can only tell you the word."

Real softly I say, "yeah, well, so now you've told me," and he finally walks away.

But almost before I can sigh he's back. "Say, uh, do you know where you're going to sleep?" he asks.

"Well, uh, I guess right over there on the couch," I say.

"Say, naw, pal, we got an extra bunk downstairs. Why don't you use that?"

"Okay."

So Steven picks up my pack, carries it downstairs for me, and deposits it in one of the tiny plywood-walled rooms with a bunk bed within. I say "thanks," he says, "sure," leaves and shuts the door behind him. I sit on the top bunk for a moment, and then he returns. It is at this point that I realize that hospitable Steven has taken me into his own room. Groovy.

"Us fellows gotta get up at the crack of dawn to go to work," he says. "So do you mind if we go right to bed?"

We both strip together. We're down to our underwear now. He's sitting on the lower bunk and looking expectant. I jump directly over his head and land deftly on the top bunk. Somewhat deflatedly he lies down and douses the light. There is a long moment of silence, and then I feel a sharp kick to my mattress in the area of my buttocks.

Rather than cry rape I keep silent. He might have called it turning the other cheek. I finally had an edge on him. I had shamed him. I drifted off to sleep.

The next morning, after he left for work, I poked around his room. Among other items I noticed an AM radio. When I turned it on it was on the local hack Jesus station. But what was really impressive was that he had torn off the tuning knob.

H.B.

An Occurrence In August Heat

The two Mormon missionaries were a long way from Salt Lake City. They weren't even sure where. Not that they cared. Just another doorbell attached to an innocuous-looking frame house somewhere in the middle of August in Southern Illinois.

A haggard woman in hair curlers answered the door. "What's your pitch?" she asked.

"Good day. I'm Tim, he's Chris, and we'd like to share with you the good news of the Church of Latter-Day. . ."

"Well look fellahs, I'm in the middle of cleaning the house, but my son is home and he might be interested in talking with you. He ain't got many friends and all he does is lie around the house all day an. . ."

Presently a tall skinny boy about the same age as Tim and Chris came to the door. He was shirtless and the elastic of his underwear peeked out from above a pair of faded corduroy pants. He had an abundance of pimples and a goiter that bobbed up and down when he spoke. "Howdy," he said, thrusting four bony fingers and a thumb in their direction. "Name's Harold. What's yours?"

They rejoined. "Look, why don't we go sit out on the patio for a spell; rest the soles of your shoes and all that. Jeez. It sure is a hot one today ain't it? Could I offer you something to drink, a soda or something?"

"Don't drink soda," they answered in unison.

Harold snapped his fingers. "Of course. Of course of course of course. Say Mom," he hollered back into the house, "we got any of that lemonade left? Could you bring us out a couple of glasses of lemonade? Bring me out a beer," he added. "You don't mind if I have a beer d'ya?" They nodded.

"Well, I guess you guys have had lots of experiences since you began your missionary service," Harold said as they found seats on the patio. "Memorable moments to recount to your grandchildren and all that."

"Well, yes, we've met a lot of people during our travels," said Chris. "Some of them have been very kind to us."

"Do you think your Mormon rap got to very many? I mean, do you think you've been successful in converting anyone to the faith?"

"It's hard to say," answered Chris. "Sometimes you get the feeling that the person you're talking to is really starting to become interested in what you're saying. But the second you leave them you never know if they just forget about you or what. So it's hard to say."

"Yeah, that's real true I guess. I hope you don't mind all this shop talk boys, but aren't there some times when you just *know* you've scored?"

Tim took a scholarly sip of lemonade and answered slowly. "For the most part, everyone that receives us into their home is receptive to us. But once in awhile, once in a great while we will be with one or a family, and they are especially warm and cordial, and I can just feel that they have been moved."

Harold smacked his lips together and ran his tongue over them. "Ya 'moved em' huh? Moved em! Heh heh heh. Say, listen, you ever been propositioned by any of them?"

Tim looked perplexed by the tone of his voice. Chris said, "Beg your pardon?"

Harold took a swig of his beer. "Aw, c'mon, you know, you must know. What I mean is, have you ever knocked on a door and some young housewife or teenage daughter answers. She's home alone and she invites you in to talk. She starts running her hands through her hair and leaning forward or crossing and uncrossing her legs or something and before you know it you start feeling all funny inside. Then she asks you to take off your jacket and helps you loosen your tie and maybe she puts her hand on your leg, you know."

Tim's eyes were fixed on a TV antenna off in the distance, but his face was red. Chris couldn't conceal a smile from spreading across his face.

Harold chortled. "Chris, you know what I'm talking about, I can tell."

"Well, I must say there sure are some strange people in this world," he said and began to blush.

"Yeah?" Harold asked expectantly.

"Well, there was this one lady just yesterday. You could smell the alcohol on her breath, and she kept laughing all the time and just kept looking at me, you remember her Tim?"

"How about the one that every couple of minutes would undo another button on her blouse and make some comment about the heat?" answered Tim. He wasn't looking at the TV antenna anymore.

"Wow," remarked Harold between sips of beer.

"Say," giggled Chris, "You remember the girl that had on that short red skirt and those stockings that look like chicken wire? She'd uncross her legs, lean back for a second and stretch, and then wink at me."

Tim had a faraway look in his eyes. "There was this one lady in Ohio who said her husband is in Korea. She had on this sweater that whenever she'd lean forward you could see a whole lot of her. Well, as I was talking about the second coming, she leaned really far forward so that I could see just about everything. Then, after I got a whole eyeful she slowly shook her head and said, 'really.' She must have done that at least three times to me."

"She did it a couple of times to me, too," chimed Chris.

Tim took another gulp of lemonade. His jaw was working up and down.

"Say," said Harold as he leaned forward. "Did you ever make out? I mean, didja ever go all the way with any of them?"

Tim looked like he had just discovered his trousers were unzipped and there wasn't a table in front of him. Chris, also, was visibly shaken, but with a self-righteous voice managed to say, "Of course not!" He crinkled his eyes and proceeded to look insulted.

"Oh, c'mon now, really? You're putting me on. I mean, you guys must have fallen at least just once, just to find out what it's like, didn't you?"

"No, never, not at all," shouted Chris. Tim seemed on the verge of tears.

There was an uneasy pause during which a cigarette mysteriously materialized in Harold's hand. The sun continued to beat down like The Rolling Stones on a librarian. "Look," Harold persisted, "you can tell me. I won't tell a soul. I promise."

It was Tim's turn to react. Chris could only stare, open mouthed, his arms dangling at his sides; he thought he saw Harold light his cigarette without the aid of a match. "I guess we have given you the wrong impression," said Tim, "by the way we must have sounded and all. I am sincerely sorry for the manner in which we have been talking. I mean, we're really not like *that* at all."

Harold leaned back and took a deep drag on his cigarette. "Why not?"

Tim's face assumed that from his mouth would come words expressing the obvious antithesis of 'why not,' but no words came. His features slowly relaxed into a facial glob expressing little more than that there seemed to be a strange odor in the air.

Chris looked Harold in the eye and brought out his trump card. "You have a foul soul," he stated.

"That's not nice," Harold said evenly.

Chris deflated and discovered he was beginning to feel extremely uneasy. This wasn't going at all how it's supposed to, he reflected.

Tim studied a pattern of sickening dots and dashes that the sun shining through his glass of lemonade made on the concrete. The heat and brightness and the buzzing of

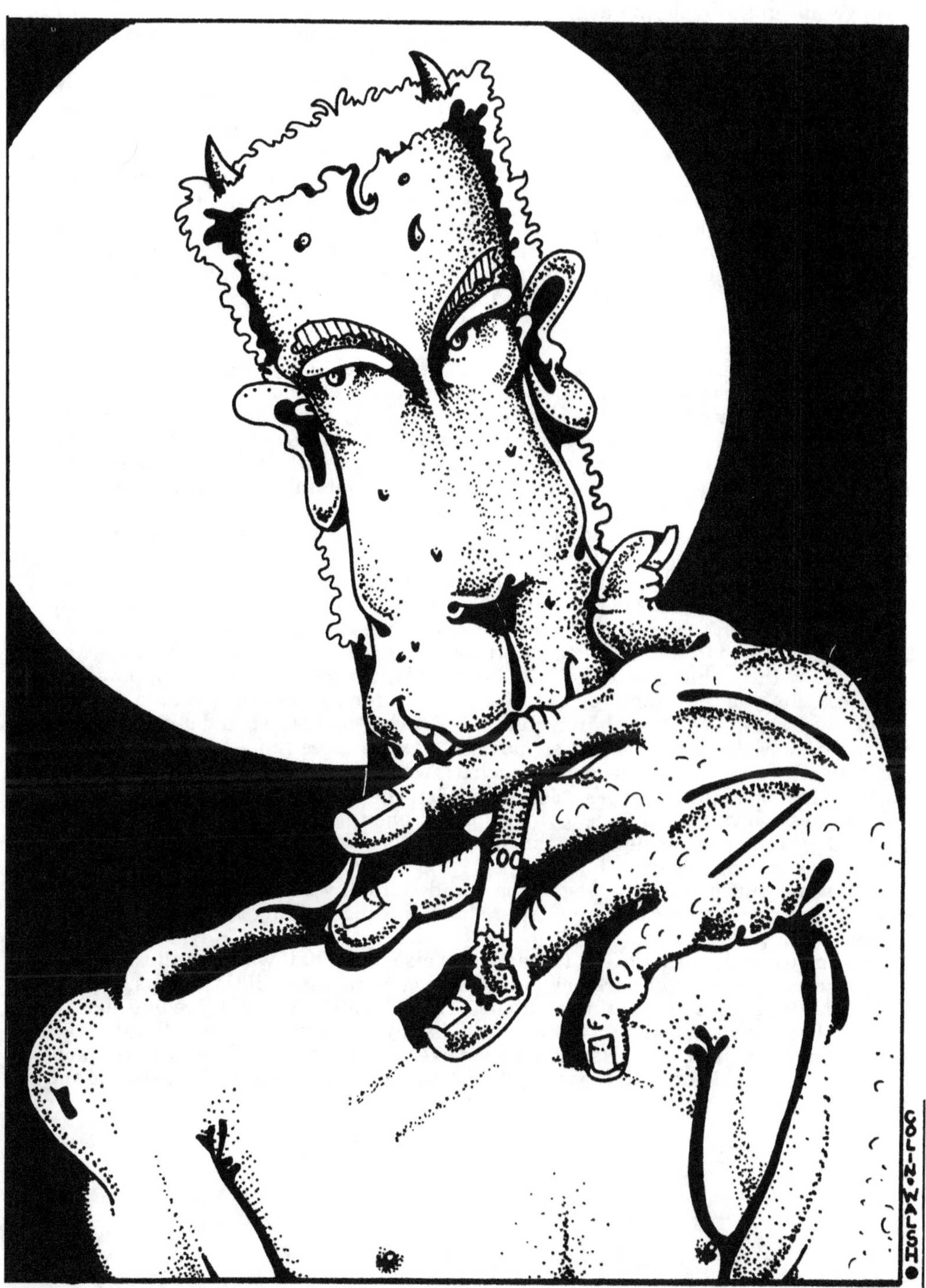

invisible insects seemed to weigh him down like a massive, soggy, wet paper bag. He felt himself sinking into a swoon. He watched through glazed eyes as Harold blew a strange-smelling smoke ring at him

"Say," said Harold, as if to change the subject, as if to get on to lighter conversation. "You ever smoked dope?"

Tim felt his body become clammy, chilled, wet and feverish at the same time. He couldn't tell whether he was gripping the arms of the lawnchair or if in fact his body had gone completely limp and numb. "Heh, hey, wha ish dis, what ya tryin' ta do here?" he stammered.

Chris, lost in the heat and his thoughts, hadn't caught the last exchange. But he was suddenly aware of a silence and the prickly feeling of his companion. He somberly peered at Tim and slowly switched his gaze to Harold. He blinked several times and had to wipe away a blurred vision of first, a convict in chains, and second, a scaly grey humanoid with pointed scarlet ears and red forked tongue, abruptly crushing out a cigarette and then staring back at him appraisingly.

Chris had had enough. "Uh, Harold, I can see that at the present time you aren't interested in discussing the Lord Jesus Christ and His everlasting grace."

"Damn right I ain't," retorted Harold with suddenly steely eyes. "Listen, chump, what makes you think you know the score so well? I mean, this Jesus Christ cat, what makes you so sure He ain't just a pawn in someone else's game? And what makes you so sure He ain't programmed you with a lot of false information? What I'm asking you is what if Jesus Christ is actually the Antichrist? Where does that put you?"

It all became clear to Tim, and he vocalized the resolution to his swirling emotions. "You are the Antichrist," he blurted.

Harold let the accusation hang for the most tantalizing of moments. He leaned forward confidentially, his voice lowered to a hissful whisper. "How do you know for sure that Satan isn't the real Christ and Jesus isn't really the devil? And how do you know that in the battle for the souls of the mortals, all your Sunday School teachers aren't really the archangels of the Antichrist, and that they haven't been hypnotizing you, seducing you into wasting your lives at the throne of the Antichrist?"

His voice sank even lower, barely audible. "Maybe you boys should slip over to the other side. Besides," he laughed soundlessly, "we're more fun." His hand dropped lightly upon Tim's knee as one would touch a fawn, and gently stroked it several times. He looked frankly into Tim's eyes. "Just surrender," he purred, "like you did to Jesus..."

Tim's heart, beating wildly, leapt to his throat, making him breathless. Chris' heart dropped to his bowels and he had to flinch to keep from pissing it out. "Good day sir," he cried hoarsely, and leaped to his feet.

Tim, somewhat unsteadily, also rose, as did Harold, who extended his hand and started making mundane closing chatter, "sure was nice talking to you boys, thanks, see you later, good luck . . ."

Tim and Chris, ignoring Harold's hand, and his mouth, half-walked half-ran off the backyard patio out into a large expanse of other backyards, thorn bushes, cyclone fences, barking dogs and drainage ditches. Harold watched as the receding figures' images became distorted in the waves of balmy August heat, and finally were swallowed up by the foliage. He put his hand over his eyes to shield them from the sun. "Now, what should I do with the rest of this day," he mused. "Maybe I'll go inside and masturbate."

Kid Clyde: An Existentialist's Horror Story

Chapter 1: The Kid

The money had been depleted over a short and worthless span of thwarted self-indulgence. And with the money seemed to go the last vestiges of self-esteem. Clyde began thinking of himself as "the kid," his life as "drifting," and what might be called schizophrenia began to pick over the carcass of his psyche.

Clyde called them "voices." God damn voices. Contradictory and caustic voices, shouting abuse at one another, forming allies, holding conventions, trials, seances, depressive warfare and an occasional beer-bellied belch, snort or guffaw.

Whatever happened to the Captain? Was there ever a Captain? Who was the Captain? Was he King Kong, was he Father, or was he the head shrink, residing over an endless and inconclusive group therapy session?

And what about those voices? Were they like the tones of a chord, pieces of stained glass? Or mud on the pane, pimples on the face? Maybe hidden among them was the proverbial "still small voice," or, in optimistically Darwinian terms, a fantastic battle of the bullshitters would erupt at the cosmic poignant moment and a victor would emerge, ole King Kong himself. Or maybe it was to find the correct mixture, the harmony, flow . . .

Clyde didn't know, and he knew he didn't know, but he wasn't sure. All he knew for sure was that one night he languidly reached down to scratch his balls, and lo and behold, his probing fingers came upon a bulbous globule. Was it an insect bite (and thus would go away); a wart (and thus would remain); or a tumor, resulting in a major aberration in his mode of living, back to St. Louis for the operation and a nervous breakdown on his mother's couch, to a future tainted with forever pissing through a straw (is life without it worth it, he asked himself), to the terminal question.

Things were certainly becoming sticky. So he'd hang out at the ice skating rink at the mall -- at first he was able to pretend he was Santa Claus on the park bench, smiling benignly at good-mannered pigeons with a palmful of tasty morsels. But spores of capri pants and death-masked faces somnolently parade past the expanse of his eyeballs; now it is a high schoolish embrace at the edge of the ice, the asshole redshirted "rink patroller," high and aloof, coming out of his Athenian skating pose to look down upon the fallen skater, a spongy breasted sophomore in clingy knit sweater and stretch pants. With obvious leering eyes combined with a patronizing and policemanlike attitude, he stands over her as she struggles to regain face on the ice; waiting for a wrong move, there, she falters, he grabs her arm, she cries out, "Hey, leggo, I can do it myself," and sags against him in sensual abandon.

The kid had to turn away.

For some reason, possibly the vicarious jubilation, he couldn't part with a fascinating speculation as to the end of the matter, the resolution, the final form. Would it be played out in dramatic existential squeeze, a violent outburst, baptism by fire or a ritual metamorphosis? Would it come by dramatic recovery, as in debilitating illness; by manhood, as in middle of a knife fight; or by surrender, as in sweet Jesus? What about suicide? The thought of seeking a solution in any of those places made him physically ill. Though the kid had flirted with them all.

But what the hell, right, ya know, just what the hell. So he continues to gaze unsuccessfully at the ectoplasm of his fantasies, and spill his unwanted seed upon deaf toilet paper, continues to eat, to breathe, to laugh between the queesies in the presence of transient company, continues to run.

He was up before the alarm. "Jesus. Eight o'clock in the morning. When was the last time the kid was up by 8 a.m.?"

Courageously staring down his haunted eyes behind shaving-creamed reflection, deft hands over barren terrain, and inside the neurotic pep talk; "Ho hum de dum, oh, shavin' in the mornin' to look mah best, aren't ya glad ya took a shower last night? So's you can get right back out on that pavement, just like yesterday, and the day before, except today's the day the kid scores that job ya been so worryin' about. Just gonna get those cosmic forces together and go out and do that thing. No moanin', no complonin', all optimistic and slick and clean and charming and positive . . . Hm, now where to furst? Oh yeah, the service station on Broadway. Don't forget the want ads . . . damn hair, oughta get it cut so's it don't look so scraggly . . . and those shirt wrinkles . . . just gonna hafta do with what ya got. Go get em kid!"

He walked over to the pancake house, then realized he was too knotted up to eat. He suffered through a cup of coffee and a greazy doughnut and hit the street. It was still early in the day, but the summer sun already seemed to be high in the sky, burning holes in the mucousy mist that hovered over the city. The kid tried gas stations, department stores, laundries, bakeries, dairies, factories, restaurants, car washes, construction companies, cigar wholesalers, grocery stores, and some businesses that manufactured god-knows-whats. He met a succession of personnel directors and secretaries with interchangeable faces, and he filled out endless applications with the same questions on them, plus an occasional zinger: "Why do you want to work for Forkfoster Rug Cleaning Co.?" all without incident.

He found himself in the local bowery district, before a day labor place. Inside, a man behind a counter offered him a job punching a button in a factory for two bills an hour. "The easiest job we got, really easy, all you do is stand there and push a button for seven hours. Starts at three o'clock. Shall I sign you up?"

The kid had the man sign him up, then continued on his search, encountering representatives from the printing and stationery industry, maintenance engineers and assorted other pointy-nosed people whose shallow and arbitrary minds stood between him and his survival. Finally he could go no further. He spotted a cafe, dragged himself up the two ornate steps and through the unoiled swinging door, blessed the gush of vibrant air conditioning that turned his sweat cold and then looked around uncertainly. He trudged over to a table next to a pretty young woman who was delicately consuming a cottage cheese and fruit salad. She mildly grimaced at the intrusion and turned back to her pear slices.

"When was the last time the kid had a woman?" he tried to remember as he surveyed the menu and out of the corner of his eye noted a run in the girl's stocking. He muttered some mild, somewhat humorous complaints about the existential absurdities of job hunting in the hopes that maybe he could "get something going."

Surprisingly, she responded.

"Looking for a job are you? There's really very little more depressing than looking for work."

He was startled by her voice. It had sounded so soft and silky he wanted to stroke it. "Yeah, I guess so. I just can't believe how long I've been at it with just no luck at all."

She seemed truly moved by his predicament. "Have you tried an agency?" she asked. "Agencies are usually pretty reliable, and they do the looking for you . . . "

He almost didn't notice that she had stopped talking. In the short time her lines had taken, he had become entranced by her thin bones, snowy white skin, fair brown hair, shimmering nylons and short dress. Muscles contracting, throat constricting, wanting to simply and brutally lunge at her. He had to swallow twice before he could speak. "Um, yeah, but they cost money . . . "

"Not always. Sometimes the employer will pay the fee for you. That's how I got my job."

"Where do you work?" he asked, not really caring, but anxious to keep her attention.

She rambled on about her secretarial gig, and he strained to come up with a way to transfer the conversation from the cafe to a more intimate locale; maybe a movie theater, a park, or her apartment. Did she have a boyfriend? Who was she living with? What kinds of movies get to her, who are her favorite authors, what are her fetishes, was she attracted to him yet? How to keep the ball rolling? How? Ask for her address? Try to make a date?

" . . . take your shirt," she was saying.

"Huh," he said and started to laugh.

"It's wrinkled."

"Yeah. Wal I realize I don't look my best right now, I've been out in that sun for five hours, you know . . . "

"It wouldn't take long to find an iron and go over that shirt," she responded, somewhat crisply. "I mean, if I were interviewing you for a job, that's the first thing I'd notice. Just trying to be helpful." She polished off her salad, paid the tip and headed for the counter.

The kid stared at her vacant seat until the inevitable asthmatic old man took her place, and then he stared at nothing at all.

On the street again, and the sun has fried the city. People rushing through intersections, heads down, cars using horns instead of brakes, no one giving an inch, no slack, and a thin layer of sweat and grime lubricating all surfaces. Music blaring out from store fronts, delivery trucks vying with the private sector for the occasional open space, and the meter maid indiscriminately reaping the rewards. Ebony pimps with purple cowboy hats, bell-bottom slacks and dayglow vests; antiseptically cleaned and powdered career girls; and crotch-tugging businessmen craning their necks to catch a flash of beaver as the middle-aged-but-well-preserved housewife bends over to reach into her trunk for a package.

The kid arrives at the day labor place 45 minutes early and checks in. "Everything is cool," says the man behind the desk in an inscrutable AM radio voice. The kid sits down on a stoic wooden bench and chooses a smoke out of his dwindling pack. As his sweaty fingers touch the cigarette, the moisture turns the paper transparent. Outside, a pickup truck rolls up to the curb. Through the smudgy plate glass window the kid sees two fat redneck Indians, one in his 50s, the other in his prime, hop out, leaving a rugged but voluptuous Indian woman alone in the front seat. Shortly they return with a can of soda and a pack of cigarettes, which they give to the woman, and then they depart again to a nearby bar. The woman notices the kid on the wooden bench, lazily stretches, adjusts a bra strap and opens her can of soda. He spends 10 minutes studiously ignoring her.

But the Indians don't return, and it's very hot inside the day labor place, so he goes outside and props himself against the building, staring more openly at her. She notices him, stretches again, lights a cigarette, and ceases to notice him at all.

Some tramps show up at the day labor place, some proud, some groveling, some down and out hippies, a couple of alcoholics, and some cruel looking teen-agers boasting about imaginary women and brawls. The two Indians return to the pickup truck and the one in his prime drapes his arm around the woman and smears a wet sloppy kiss over her lips, cheek and half of her nose. She presses her breasts against his chest while the other Indian gazes out of the car window with a silly grin on his face, and they drive away.

Three o'clock comes and goes. Once again the kid inquires about the job. The man tells him so and so is supposed to call at any time. He goes back outside to sit on the sidewalk. Three grubby hippies approach, carrying backpacks. "Spare change?" one of them asks.

Clyde asks them if they think he's sitting outside a dumpy day labor place because he has spare change.

The second hippy draws himself up to his maximum height, although he is still slouching under the weight of his pack, and asks how he would like to "get rolled."

Too fatigued to be afraid, too irritated to be tactful, Clyde looks up and says "yeah man, I'd like that just fine. It's the best offer anybody's made me all day."

After a pause the third hippy asks him for a cigarette. He gives him his last cigarette. They depart without as much as a have-a-nice-day.

An hour passes and the kid returns inside. About 20 sullen, heat-exhausted men are trying to out-wait each other in the wan hope that something will turn up. But as the hours melt into the heat, magnifying the futility of their positions, they begin to mutter to themselves, swat at flies and send somewhat humanistic glares at each other.

A hulking wheezing Indian has sat down next to the kid and has been trying to think of something to say for 15 minutes. The Indian takes off his beat-up shoe, and then his sweaty filthy stinking gym sock. He picks at a series of blisters on his toe, and suddenly several droplets of white pus that look like tiny pebbles spurt from his foot.

"Somethin' won wif mah foot," he says to the kid, who out of the corner of his eye has watched the entire display with disgust, and then nausea. "Here, looka mah foot," he says, and shoves it within five inches of the kid's face.

Clyde forces the kid to gaze upon the Indian's foot. "Yeah, there sure is," he answers with less pathos than he feels.

"I guess I've taken my share of abuse for this day," he mutters to himself. "I mean, I mean, just what's going on here? That's enough for today."

He left.

Chapter 2: The Fly

Eventually the kid secured a job at the Forkfoster Rug Cleaning Co., of which little need be said beyond the fact that it was minimum wage, but steady money, and the first tentative step toward a stability from which, Clyde hoped, the lucid and contemplative mind might be cultivated.

For a somber month he diligently served his function without complaint or distinction, putting in his hours during the day and coming home to his silent basement apartment in the evening; to a six-pack in the refrigerator or a subjection to the neighborhood bars and the crass assortment of hard-faced creatures who haunted them. The occasional movie, inconsequential walk in the park, Emily Dickinson gazes at shouting children on bicycles, one flower in a row with a bent stem, the sound of motorcar tires swishing on wet pavement, cringing at the intrusion of a diesel switching gears, tentative greetings or furtive sideglances at passersby; as often as not a nightcap replaying worn out memories of long defunct affairs.

One day a co-worker suggested he come over and "groove on my new quadrophonic stereo system. Maybe we'll get high and boogie."

The kid arrived promptly at 7 p.m. Co-worker lived in one of those apartment buildings where you had to ring the bell, wait for the buzz and lunge for the door and wrench it open, or else do it again. He had to do it again. The second time the door was opened by a gaunt blind man who introduced himself as Co-worker's father. He led the kid back to a small apartment and a mangy smoky-eyed collie who began to bark. The kid tried to tame the dog, tried to pet it, to establish eye contact, to show that he was an OK guy, but the dog would have none of it. It was more content to bark.

Over the racket of the dog, Co-worker's father, staring at a point on the wall beyond the kid's left shoulder, said his son would be home shortly. He then launched into his life story, which consisted of an upbringing in Liverpool, puberty in the navy, a whirlwind courtship with an Irish lass, a blinding explosion in the North Atlantic, the birth of a son and the death of his wife from cancer 15 years later.

The kid lit a cigarette, the dog continued to bark, and the man continued to talk at the wall. In time the old man jerked up his head, laughed about something and withdrew to his bedroom. The dog decreased its bark to a threatening growl and the kid's cigarette ashes were deposited at regular intervals in a chipped ash tray.

Suddenly the door buzzer sounded again. The man stumbled out of the back room and lurched toward the intercom, almost falling over a chair while the collie yelped and weaved between his legs. The kid calmly held on to his cigarette with two hands. Co-worker entered, and the telephone rang, which set the dog off to new heights of barking. Co-worker nodded at the kid, petted the dog, answered the phone and greeted his dad, who began telling him various people had called and the things that had happened to him that day. Co-worker grunted into the phone, remarked that he would be right back and beat a hasty exit from the apartment.

The man yelled at the dog for snarling at Clyde, who was just reaching for his cap when Co-worker returned. The family unit then went through its greeting ritual again as the kid slumped back into his chair. Finally the dog found a place on the floor to scratch and the man retreated to the back room. Clyde and Co-worker nodded at each other again, and then looked away. Neither of them had prepared anything to say.

So Co-worker turned on his amp, fiddled with the dials and moved some wires around, and a baritone voice filled the room, espousing the virtues of Coca-Cola from four resonating speakers. The kid remarked what a fine sound system it was.

Co-worker got out the tea. "Domestic, grew it myself, from Cambodian seeds," he said, and they proceeded to get wrecked.

As the marijuana seeped through Clyde's brain, the blaring noises, jagged motions and fragmented dialogue receded. He felt as if he was in a Ford LTD commercial and had just rolled up the window as a freight train rushed by. A tremor of paranoia passed through him as he wondered whether, out there, he was going to have to cope with something. He looked at Co-worker and sighed with satisfaction that he appeared on the nod, his head cocked back on the couch, a contented smile on his face, seemingly not the least bit concerned about who the kid was, where he came from, or was he happy.

Clyde drifted off into thoughtlessness. His heartbeat became waves lapping against the shore, the limbo of his existence a lazy hammock on a summer day, and the God damn voices but a muted buzzing of distant bees. He sailed into the void until several nerve endings on his knee got his attention. He lazily looked down and observed a large housefly. Approximately three times the size of an average housefly. Reflexively he shrugged his knee. But the fly just flew up in the air, made a loop the loop and resettled on his knee. A pang of irritation shook the kid's composure, but he decided to ignore the insect. Somewhere along the line he had heard that houseflies don't bite, so theoretically if he allowed it squatter's rights no harm would come to him. After a while the fly would have to get bored with his knee and fly off to rejoin his buddies roosting around the garbage cans. He closed his eyes and slowly counted to 10. He pretended the room, lights, heat, body, mind and fly were all nothing more than run-away hallucinations, and that if he thought about it right, the fly would cease to exist.

Steeling up his cosmic mind he opened his eyes. To his dismay, the fly had crept halfway up his pants and was headed towards his crotch.

"Jee-zus," Clyde groaned to himself. "There's nuthin that fly can do to the kid. Just forget about the damn fly."

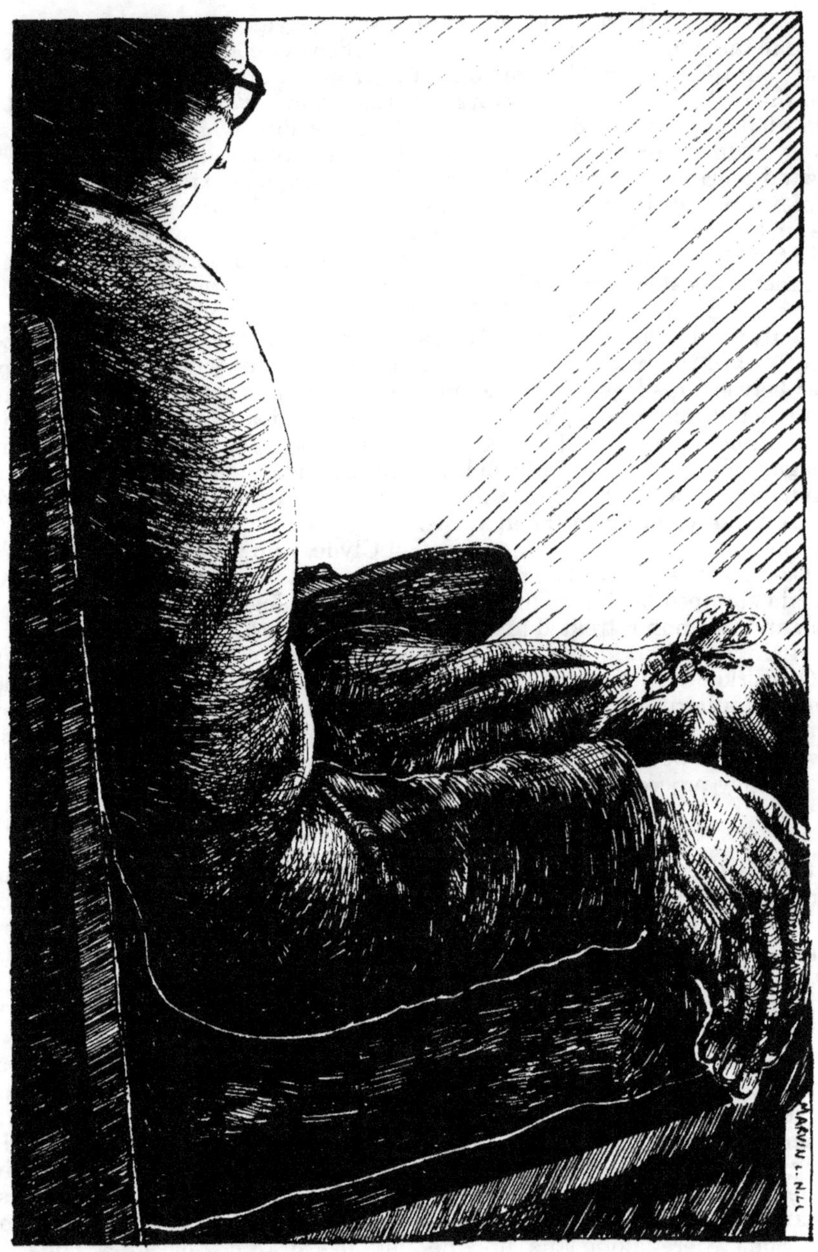

But he couldn't. He flicked at it several times, but it only returned. Then a weird thought struck him. He heard Co-worker's father moan from the bedroom, and Clyde imagined that when the blind man was staring at the wall with the simple but radiant smile on his face that he was actually looking at his deceased wife, Co-worker's mother. Her ghost still lived in the apartment, still rattled the teacups and came to her husband in the night, still had a hold on her family. Clyde could almost sense her presence in the lace curtains, the carpet, the stale air, and, with a bolt, in the fly.

After a moment he laughed at the absurdity of his imaginings, but his uneasiness remained, as did a feeling that this particular housefly was possessed of an essence more personal, more ominous, than your everyday housefly. To get some sort of reassurance that the fly was just a housefly, he turned to Co-worker and said "Weird flies you got here."

Co-worker looked over at him with lazy eyes. "Yeah. They like to get stoned."

Which was no help.

Bam! And then it hit him. All this paranoid and neurotic thought had been induced by an entity the mass of a fly. A fly! If an insect could scatter the kid's forces, what possible chance did he have against Vietnam, gnawing social obligations, bulbous globules or his own inner voices? His mind rebounded to thoughts of ghosts in his own life -- inherited and incurred guilts, unfinished situations, incomplete endings, impulsive desertions, wrong decisions, defeats, debts, rapes and the unknown circumstances of his own end. That old high school girlfriend and a woman in Omaha; a frail schoolmate whose nose he once bloodied and whose fiance he later screwed; the pissing away of a college education and an apprenticeship in the family business; the younger brother he had attempted to castrate for 18 years; a fist fight he had lost in front of a crowd over nothing; a sexy older woman in a sports car who had picked him up hitchhiking and who had wanted it but he didn't have the nerve to ask; a particular full house that didn't beat a straight flush; a blood-curdling scream and then an escaping assailant rushing past him, and the kid not lifting a finger; an agonizing series of artistic frustrations, sexual fiascos, aborted enterprises and worthless and guilty victories.

The fragmented events, people, pieces of color and emotion had all merged into a single poltergeist, whom he had created or offended at some point, and who now stalked him like a shadow, taking different forms at different times, and tainting his future with the certainty that the monster would always show up, always be there to expose shortcomings and weaknesses, cracks in the armor, and knock down all the walls he might try to erect in between.

He felt a trembly numbness and an icy steadiness at the same moment. He turned his gaze once more on the fly. He studied it intently, the veins in its wings and the strangely human way it rubbed its front feelers together. Were those antenna motions for feeding, for spreading disease, or for sending messages? The possibility that the fly was conscious and trying to communicate with Clyde sent fresh shivers up his spine. Did the fly carry a message, a meaning? Did it hide the resolution to its own enigma? Was it a mournful ghost haunted by the same restlessness as the kid? Or was the fly an evolutionary anachronism, an appendix, a wisdom tooth, alchemy, and innocence . . .

Of its own volition, the kid's left hand suddenly smashed the insect into a crunchy mush on his leg. He heard a corresponding thud in the back room as if the old man had rolled over in bed and fallen on the floor.

Co-worker was startled by the sudden commotion. "Hey man, what're ya doin? You OK?"

The kid rubbed his clammy palm on his leg and flicked the fly onto the carpet. "He made me do it," he murmured, "he made me do it."

Co-worker frowned briefly at the fact that Clyde had messed up the floor. The kid tersely lit a cigarette and tried to look nonchalant. Co-worker sank back into his stupor, and the quadrophonic FM station droned Moody Blues. But inside the kid's mind he was screaming. He was dying to know if the man in the other room was all right, but too embarrassed to ask. Gingerly he retrieved the fly and transferred it into an ash tray. Its legs were still twitching. He repressed a desire to cremate it with his cigarette.

Clyde shrugged and attempted to regain his pre-fly tranquility. He was diligently tapping along to the music when out of nowhere a fly divebombed into his face, bounced off the lens of his glasses, and z-z-z-ed off.

The kid grabbed his cap and made for the door. Co-worker took it for granted he had said good-bye and muttered "dig ya later." A piece of dust or something blew out the door just before the kid closed it behind him. He didn't stop looking back until he had made it to his apartment, climbed into bed, and pulled the covers over his head.

Of Mice and Moonlandings

July 19, 1969. Carbondale.

Sometime tomorrow the first *homo sapiens* are going to land on the moon. I don't understand the significance of that, but it must be important. Tonight I went to McDonald's, the usual launching pad for my group. That may seem insignificant. But at least I can relate to it. My group: The local cluster I orbit with because I can't stand to hang out with anyone else. Sometimes I can stand my group. Sometimes. Saw Dillow, Potts and Lewi. Somebody paid somebody for a nickel of pot. They blasted off to "look for chicks and get drunk." VanMeter, Dickerson and LeMedico showed up. They got ahold of some beer and some chicks and took off, too. So, the air traffic controller went to U.D.'s and bought a 49-cent notebook and a 19-cent Bic pen. He's sitting in Spudnut's now. The place has changed. Nobody comes here anymore. I'm alone. And bored. Now that high school has become a past-tense experience, maybe the juvenile cliques we all belong to will just fade away. My group calls itself "The Action Faction." We wear these silly tweed caps and adhere to a nonsense set of bylaws called the Soft Bread Axioms. Oh well. I think I'll take in another vestige of high school adolescence -- a teeniebopper dance. All the snotty bitchy boppers with their over-developed bodies and under-developed minds will probably drive me crazy. See you later.

LATER:

Well, the boppers drove me crazy. The dance was at the Carbondale Teen Town, a reconverted warehouse across the street from its adult counterpart, the Elk's Club. The band tonight, Odds and Ends, was like every other band that plays here. They think loud equals good. The drummer even had the skin off the front of his bass drum. Back to the boppers: The girls who go to Teen Town dances are between 13 and 16 years old. They wear these short skirts and T-shirts that stop about an inch below their breasts. I love, desire, crave, am obsessed with their bodies. The thing is, they aren't overjoyed with mine -- 105 pounds, 5-foot-6, squinty eyes and no "cool." I'd sure like to get down with one of them, but all they seem to be interested in is horses, dancing, tanning, Clearasil and who's going with whom. Sex, pure animal sex, doesn't enter into their heads. This narrative is getting to be a drag. I'll quit for now.

July 20, 1969, 3:17.40 p.m. Central Daylight Saving Time.
The moment man landed on the moon.

People keep blubbering about how proud they are to be an American, and Walter Cronkite just came out and said it. "God was riding with the astronauts." But it was man, not God, who put an earthling on the moon. And if it weren't for the "godless" Russians and Sputnik, America never would have spent all that money on a space race. If there is a God, I'm not so sure he, she or it really wants us

messing around up there. Though it may have been a paranoid desire for strategic
superiority that motivated this country to go to the moon, it was the exact opposite
of human nature that actually got us there. It was science, technology and
mathematics, fantastic machines and emotionless computers that allowed Neal
Armstrong to step on the moon. Men are vulnerable. They make errors, act on
impulse and are tempted by earthly desires. It was man without imperfection who
landed on the moon, and I'm not sure something wasn't lost in the process.

Well, man is on the moon now. They unveiled a plaque, planted a flag and got a
phone call from President Nixon. According to Uncle Walter, they are collecting
rocks and stuff now. The moon, a new frontier, the limits of man's ultimate efforts
to date. It makes the events of a summer's evening in Carbondale seem trivial and
unimportant. Why doesn't everyone just forget about their selfish desires and work
for the common good of mankind? Unfortunately, lust, violence and goofing off are
a basic, intimate part of the human condition. They are what life is all about. Out
of humanity can come superhuman achievements like the moon landing but only if
the defects of humans are removed. And let's face it, without the petty human
dilemmas such as sex, love and the big date on Saturday night, who really cares?

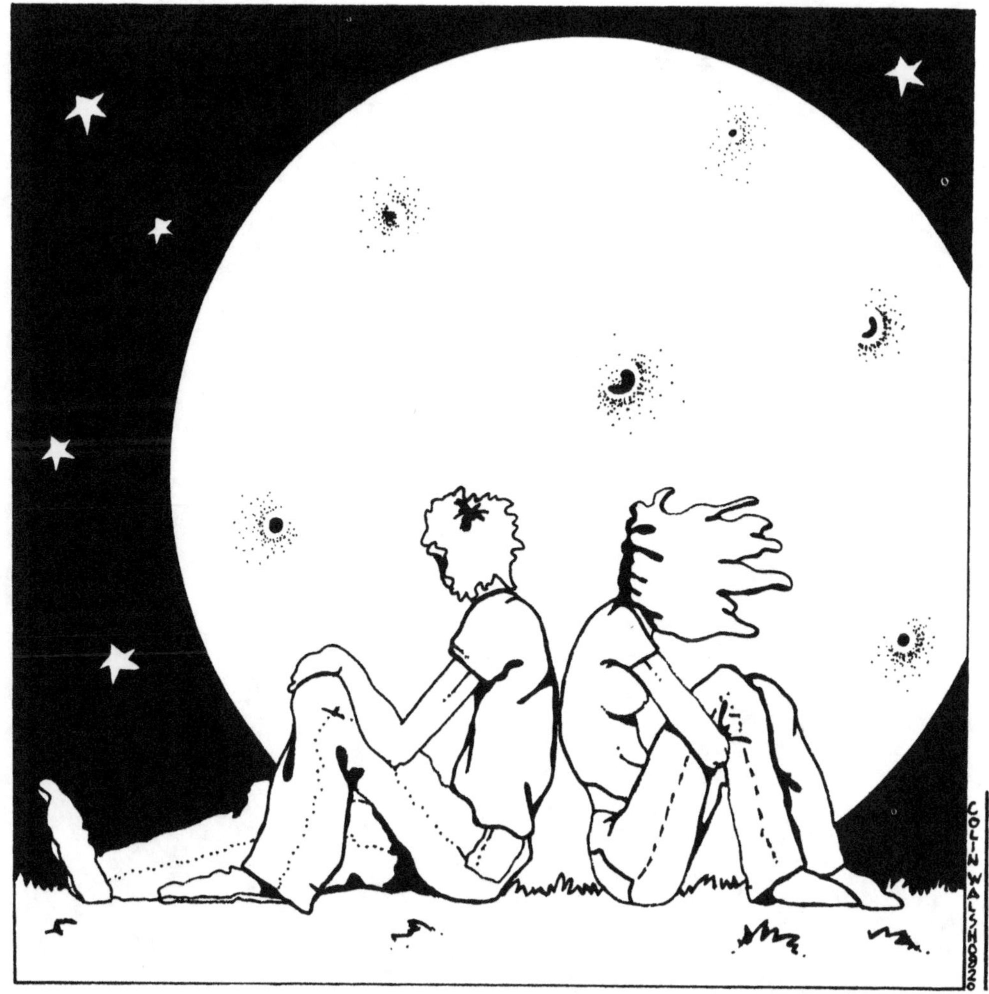

Addendum

Part

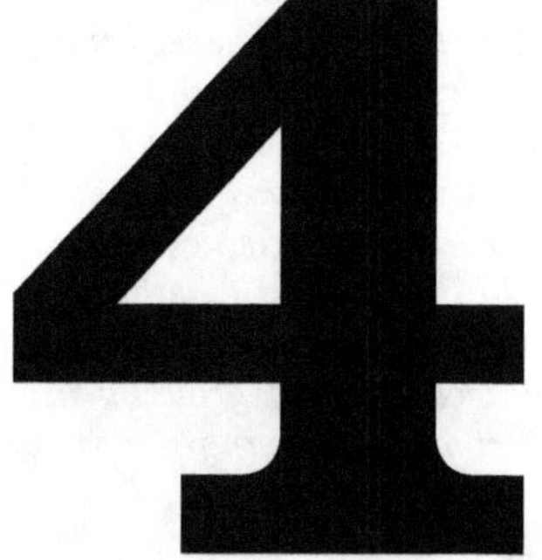

1959

Carbondale Before Dark

A tree stump clinging to a tiny grassy island, marooned in a parking lot a quarter-mile southwest of where I once went to school -- University School, aka Pulliam Hall, the building with the iconic clock tower on the campus of Southern Illinois University-Carbondale -- is the last vestige of where I grew up from 1952, when I was in diapers, to 1964, when I was in puberty. Like other homes in the neighborhood, during the 1960s, ours was eminent domained by the university for the higher public purpose of providing academicians with a place to park their cars. SIU eventually demolished the house, yard and street, leaving behind a solitary oak tree that had been in our front yard. It survived on the island until May 2009, when it was felled by a derecho storm.

In February 2008, when the university began tearing down the last 13 houses on my old stomping ground, an SIU Daily Egyptian *reporter interviewed me about what the area had been like in the 1950s and '60s, when I was living there and attending U-School, a nursery-12th grade training school for teachers that began closing in 1968. I'm afraid I wasn't much help to the reporter, and after getting off the phone I felt like I'd let down the 'hood, which had been unexceptional to grownups, but a virtual never-never land for kids.*

As the author of Carbondale After Dark, *I'd told the story of the town's notorious strip. Now that the last of my childhood strip was disappearing, it seemed the least I could do was put together a few sentences to mark its passing. I also found myself reminiscing about growing up in the rest of Carbondale during the 1950s and '60s,*

when the town was undergoing a seismic shift in race relations.

I won't pretend to know what it was like to be black in Carbondale. For that, I suggest Traces in the Dust *by Melvin LeRoy Green Macklin. His copious history of the town's black community has a prelude called "The Wonder Years," in which he describes his 1950s upbringing in the "Hoodlums" neighborhood on the far northeast side. For more stories on Carbondale in the 1950s and '60s, check out* Short Stories from the Neighborhood, *edited by Bob Pankey and authored by members of the CCHS class of 1969 on the occasion of our 50th high school reunion.*

In 1959, Carbondale had 15,000 residents and 12,000 SIU students. I was 8 years old and living in a bucolic neighborhood west of U-School so full of kids it might have been called a baby boomer incubator. Besides the Koplowitzes, other families in the area west of SIU, east of Oakland Avenue, north of Chautauqua Street, and south of Mill Street, included the Bedwells, Borkens, Byers, Camps, Cherrys, Connors, Crandles, Crenshaws, Ethertons, Flys, Galleglys, Heislers, Jordisons, Lavenders, Limpuses, Logans, Malpasses, Olsens, Pages, Pattersons, Prossers, Randolphs, Robbins, Sheltons, Smalls, Steinbergs, Swansons, Tobermans, Troutts, Vanmetres, Wellers, Whams, Whitmans and Wrights, and those are just the ones I remember.

Our address was 906 W. Grand Ave., the middle house of three on the north side of Grand, between Elizabeth and Forest

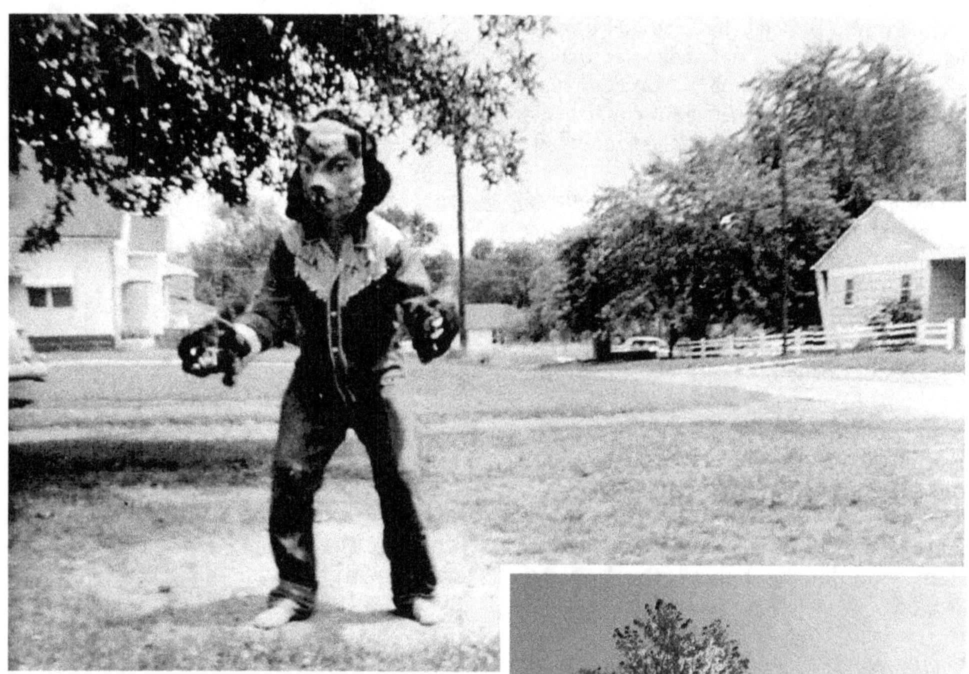

ABOVE: My neighborhood circa 1959, looking east toward SIU from the front yard of 906 W. Grand. My friend, Dave Small, 8 (Tom's younger brother), is wearing a werewolf mask and claws. Branches from the oak tree at top left. Photo taken by me with a Kodak Brownie camera. RIGHT: The neighborhood-cum-parking lot photographed by me in 2008, looking south toward the Communications Building, with oak tree at center left.

streets. Our square, white, frame house was modest, with a leaky basement and an unfinished attic. My younger brother Sandy and I shared one bedroom, our parents, Audrey and Julius, the other. We all shared the bathroom. We also shared a single black-and-white console TV connected to an antenna on the roof. Periodically, a repairman would drop by with a suitcase full of vacuum tubes to fix it. And we shared a single, black, rented telephone, wired to the wall, that had no buttons or even a dial. To make a call, we'd pick up the handset and a human operator would say, "number please." Unless a neighbor was on the party line, and then we'd eavesdrop.

The furnace in the basement had been converted from coal to fuel oil, and during the winter a man in a tank truck would drive down a cinder alley alongside our house and stick a hose through the coal chute to fill our tanks. New Era Dairy milk trucks also used the alley, to deliver and pick up bottles, as did peddlers and trash collectors, sometimes in a wooden wagon pulled by a couple of mules.

Carbondale was covered with foliage that attracted birds, especially robins, cardinals and blue jays, while milkweed vines drew monarch butterflies. The town was also edible. Kids would pilfer from apple trees and chew on mint leaves a neighbor grew. We dangled the stems of wild wheat grasses from our mouths like they were cigarettes, and in the fall, maple seeds fell to the ground in pods that whirled like helicopters. We'd pinch the pods to squirt the seeds at each other, then suck on the leafy part until it was just the right consistency to make a perfect kid's noise -- somewhere between an air horn and a fart.

The neighborhood store was Kelley's, a mom and pop grocery in a wooden pole building around the corner on Forest Street. Owned by the family that later managed the Giant City State Park Lodge, Kelley's was my first hangout, where my recreational drug of choice was glucose in the form of Popsicles, candy bars, soda pop and bubble-gum. After school, the concrete porch in front of Kelley's would be full of kids getting their sugar fixes.

Spring and summer afternoons we'd chase after the ice cream truck, and at night we'd bicycle behind the "mosquito truck," a jeep with a loud contraption on the back that spewed a dense, white, smelly, plume of smoke that was probably toxic DDT. In the fall, families would drive past dorms and frat/sorority houses to view yard decorations that combined Halloween and Homecoming themes to depict the dastardly things the football team was going to do to the opposition. The best part of winter was Christmastime, with more festive yard and store decorations, and a live manger scene on the lawn of Holden Hospital, next to the Dairy Queen, which had been turned into a Christmas tree lot.

The hub of downtown was actually called The Hub, a cafe owned by Nick Masters on the southwest corner of Illinois Avenue and Main Street. It's the same building one of the town's founding fathers, Daniel Brush, once had a general store. Beneath The Hub was a lounge called the Rathskeller, aka Rathole, one of the few downtown taverns in the 1950s besides the Levee, a black strip across the train tracks on North Washington Street.

Before South Illinois Avenue became known as the strip, it was dotted with eateries including the Alibi, Varsity Grill, Lavender's and UD's, where in my adolescence I played a lot of pinball. We went to the movies at the Varsity Theater, where blacks were supposedly segregated in the balcony, although white kids would sneak up there to make out. We also made out at the drive-in, which in those days meant drive-in movie theaters, like the Waring (later Campus) on old Route 13 halfway to Murphysboro, and the Egyptian, south of Herrin, which claimed to have the biggest outdoor screen in the country.

The first fast food drive-in I remember in Carbondale was the A&W root beer stand on East Main Street, where instead of a drive-thru, carhops would deliver the frothy brew in frosty glass mugs on metal trays that attached to the car window. Next came a Frostop on the north side, a Dog n Suds on the west side, and a McDonald's where Lenus Turley Park is now, across Glenview Drive from the town's first strip mall, the Murdale Shopping Center, which opened in 1958.

U.S. 51 used to be a two-lane highway that traversed Normal (University) Avenue. At the main gate to SIU it would jog west on Grand for a block, then turn south on Thompson Street, where the Faner Building is now, and head out of town west of the old campus and what would become the SIU Arena. Shortly before I was born in 1951, the highway was rerouted east to Illinois Avenue, clearing the way for the college to expand west. U-School became the first major addition to the campus in 1950, followed by Woody Hall, which was a women's dorm and cafeteria.

If the definition of a private school is having to pay tuition to get in, then U-School was a private school. However, being attached to the university, it was anything but parochial, with student teachers and experimental teaching methods. Many of the students were the children of SIU faculty, so the student body was more transient and cosmopolitan, yet more insulated, than the townie schools.

In addition to small and big gyms and small and big auditoriums, U-School had small and big swimming pools. The brick entryways to the grade school classrooms were adorned with six small corner castings or renderings of classic fairy tales, including "Hansel and Gretel" and "Three Billy Goats Gruff." The nursery school and kindergarten were in the same classroom, which had a one-way mirror so adults could spy on us from an observation room. There was a shallow, indoor fountain stocked with turtles and tadpoles, and a hive encased in window panes, where we could watch bees make honey. The highlight of those years were the field trips -- in nursery school we

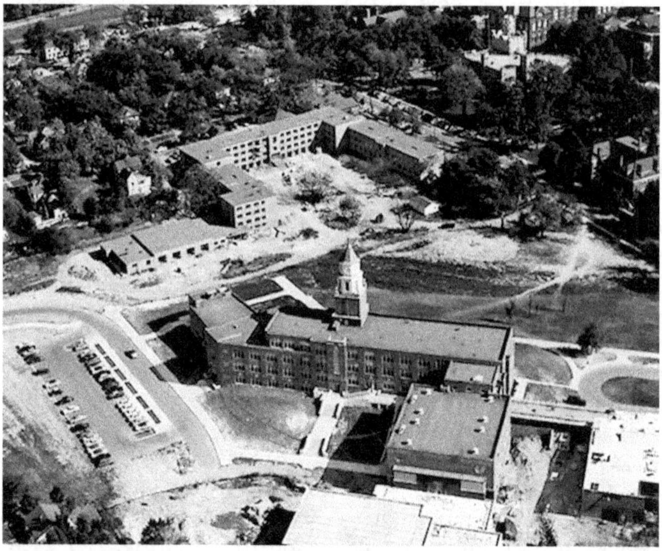

Taken in 1952, this aerial photo shows the newly opened U-School with Woody Hall under construction. Altgeld Hall and part of Old Main can be seen at upper right. A section of Grand Avenue runs on a diagonal from center top to middle right, which is east to west. Following the diagonal, my home was three blocks west, past houses, a marsh and some woods.
--Photo by SIU Photographic Services. Courtesy of SCRC, Morris Library, SIU-C--

took a train to Anna and back, and as kindergärtners we rode a bus to the St. Louis Zoo. Dr. Mott taught nursery and kindergarten, Mrs. Goodwin first grade, Mrs. Bricker second, Mrs. Treece third, and Mrs. Meehan fourth grade.

In high school I spent a lot of time at a place called the typing room, where students learned to use more than their thumbs to tap letters on something called a typewriter. The typing room doubled as the newsroom for the *Tower Times* mimeographed student newspaper, which is why I hung out there with fellow nerds, although at the time we considered ourselves pseudo-hippies.

Since U-School was on the grounds of SIU, the entire campus was our playground, including Old Main. Built in 1887, it was the oldest building on campus until June 8, 1969, when it was apparently torched by an arsonist, motive unknown. Altgeld Hall, built in 1896 to resemble a medieval castle, had a natural history museum with dioramas and a gift shop that sold packets of Confederate money. We also explored the nooks and crannies of Shryock Auditorium, got lost in a grid of World War II barracks that had been turned into married student housing, and infiltrated the labyrinthine steam tunnels beneath the campus.

West of the Quad, past the Baptist Foundation and SIU President Delyte Morris' home, was the new Morris Library, which had three floors of open stacks and a basement with microfilms of old newspapers. The Life Science Building, with its odoriferous labs, was the westernmost building on the campus. Beyond that, Lawson Hall was houses, the Wham Building a dry marsh, and the Northwest Annex was woods.

Itchy Jones and the rest of the Saluki baseball team played at Chautauqua Field, where the Communications Building is now. Between the baseball diamond and a state public health lab was a crawdad-laden ditch fed by a bug-infested drainage pipe large enough for an 8-year-old and his pals to crawl into. Beyond right field,

Greek Row and Thompson Point dorms were construction sites where we had epic dirt clod fights.

Between U-School and my house was a densely wooded area with winding footpaths worn through the ivy. Where the Wham Building is now, the woods gave way to a muddy field filled with cattails and reeds taller than an 8-year-old. Between the field and the woods was a rutty, barricaded dirt road called Lake Street, which is what it turned into when it rained. Parents warned their children not to go into the woods, so despite the poison ivy, ticks, pollen and chiggers, it was a forbidden pleasure. On the southeast edge of the woods, atop a steep hill fortified by thorn bushes, Virginia creepers and climbing ivy, was a burned-out house. With a basement, two floors, an attic, and rooftops to explore, there was plenty of room to play hide and seek, light fire crackers, and indulge in other risky behavior. We called it the haunted house, although it was mostly haunted by us kids. The authorities eventually got wind of the goings-on at the haunted house and tore it down.

On a more wholesome note, Sandy and I became Cub Scouts. For the regional Cub Scout Jamboree talent show competition at the Carbondale Armory, the town's all-white troop covered our faces with shoe polish and put on a minstrel show. Sandy got a solo, pantomiming Al Jolson singing "My Mammy." Even back then, the show was panned for being racially insensitive.

Most of the kids in my neighborhood attended grade school at Winkler Elementary, west of Oakland on Freeman Street. They went to middle school at Lincoln Junior High on South Washington Street, between Freeman and College streets, where the police department is now, and then to Carbondale Community High School, which was on North Springer Street. The black kids went to Attucks on the northeast side, across East Main Street from Woodlawn Cemetery. Like U-School, Attucks was both an elementary and high school, plus a community center.

The schools, my neighborhood and the west side in general were mostly white, except for Martha Johnson, our maid, who lived on the northeast side, but spent five days a week at our place, cleaning and corralling me and my brother. Back then, blacks were called colored people. We were one of the few families in the neighborhood to have a colored maid because our mom worked with our dad at Kay's, the dress shop they owned across from the (old) train station. (They later opened Kay's Campus Shop at Illinois and Freeman, above what was then Crazy Horse Billiards and Gatsby's bar.)

As a child, I can't say that I distinctly liked or disliked Martha, which is what we called her. She was the boss when my parents weren't around, and I respected her the same way I did my parents -- grudgingly. Martha was poor but she wasn't bitter. She was basically a decent person, and I love her now like a third parent.

When Martha was in her 50s and I was still in my single digits, she seemed ancient and intimidating. Her face was dark and wrinkly, and her body was short and wiry. She had rock-hard biceps from scrubbing our floors on her knees and wringing out our clothes by hand before pinning them to the clotheslines in our backyard. As well as cooking and cleaning, she bathed Sandy and me when we were little. She taught us Negro spirituals, like "Mary Had a Baby," and read us our Jack & Jill and Humpty Dumpty magazines. She'd smell up the house with collard "greens," watch her "stories" on our TV, and as she ironed she'd talk to herself about things that had happened at church, repeating conversations and cackling at the funny parts.

Martha lived in a nondescript home with asbestos siding on Wall Street, at the northeast edge of town, next to relatives who had a small farm with mules and chickens. There was a barber chair on her front porch where her former husband had cut hair. Most days Martha took a Yellow Cab to our house, but some evenings my parents would drive her home. Sitting in the backseat with Martha and my brother,

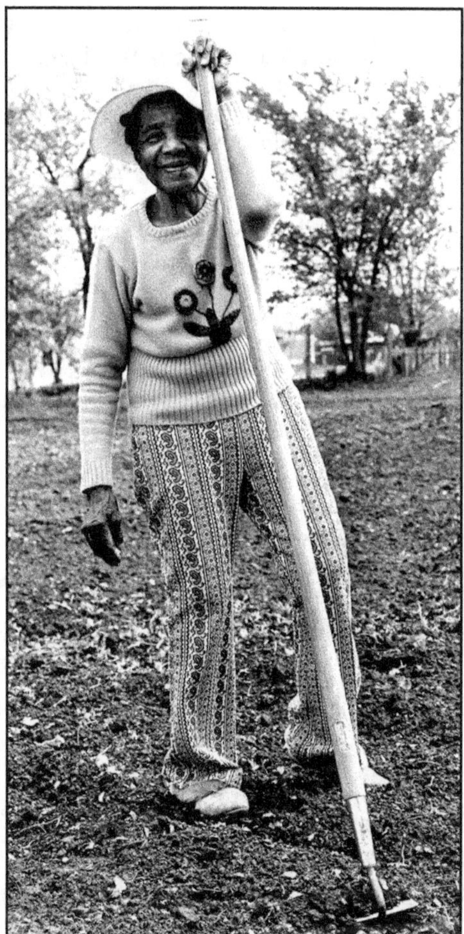

Martha Johnson outside her home on North Wall Street. Photo, taken by me In 1976, also appeared in the *Daily Egyptian*.

I'd peer wide-eyed out the window as we crossed the railroad tracks and came upon sheds and clapboard houses with sagging porches. I remember the embarrassment all around the car when I stuck out my finger one evening and asked "what's that?" and my dad awkwardly tried to explain what an outhouse was for and that yes, Martha had one. At first I thought he was joking.

One summer, when I was about 10 years old and school was out, I fell in with some slightly older boys, some of whom were black, and we were sitting on the rocks at U-School's playground when I first reflected on the word "nigger." I'd heard the term before, but it wasn't part of my vocabulary. (When John F. Kennedy was elected president in 1960, a politically incorrect limerick made the rounds that poked fun at the new president's diction and idealism, but today would simply be considered racist: "Do your work with great vigor, or you will be replaced by a nigger.")

I don't recall how we got around to the subject, but one of the black kids said a nigger was a very bad person. I said something like, "well, isn't it a very bad colored person?" and he disagreed, saying anyone, black, white, blue or green, could be a nigger if they were evil.

Unfortunately, I didn't get the message. A day or two later, I was outside and Martha told me it was time to go inside, but I didn't want to go inside. Instead, I walked into our garage and hissed under my breath, "nigger."

"What did you say?" Martha asked as she came in the garage after me, more sad than angry. I don't recall what happened next, whether she bawled me out or if I apologized. I do recall feeling very ashamed, and I've never again used the word in anger.

Sports were a big part of our lives. We played baseball and football on the lawn in front of the state public health lab at Oakland and Chautauqua. We also played in front of the University Baptist Church at Oakland and Freeman, and in a neighbor's yard on Elizabeth Street. A precocious older childhood friend, Tom Small -- a bad influence who turned me on to pinball and girlie mags -- dubbed it Sad Sack Field.

My next exposure to black people occurred when I joined Little League. My friend Tom was a gifted athlete, and my dad made sure I got on his team -- the Cubs. There were eight teams in the Atom League, which was the youngest division of Little League at the time. Seven of the teams were all white and one was all black -- the Sox. At the end of the season there was a tournament, and Tom pitched the Cubs to the championship game, where we met the Sox, who had just as talented a pitcher, Lester Taylor.

It was a tight game throughout, with Tom and Les matching each other strikeout for strikeout. For most of that season I had been frozen at the plate, never swinging, hoping for a walk, and I did the same thing in the championship game. But during my last at bat, I unaccountably took a swack at the ball and sent a squibber toward the mound. I saw Lester reach down for the ball, saw it dribble out of his glove, and realized I should be running to first base. I took off, but he recovered the ball and threw me out by a half-step.

In the seventh and final inning, Tom's arm gave out. He walked a batter, which in the Atom League was as good as a triple, because the batter soon stole second and third. Tom got a strikeout, but the next batter hit a grounder up the middle. From shortstop, I watched as the ball skipped over second base into center field. Game over. Tom stood on the pitcher's mound, crying. The rest of us threw our gloves in the air. Time for ice cream. I don't remember feeling upset that we'd been beaten by some colored kids, but it did occur to me that they sure were good at sports.

A couple years later, when I was in the Bantam League and Tom had moved away, my new team played another black team -- well, pretty much the same team, except older -- and they were still good at sports. By this time I had come to seriously dislike playing the colored team, not because they were black, but because they all seemed to hit the ball to the shortstop, and I was the shortstop. One night we played the colored team on their home field on the northeast side, off Wall Street near the all-black Thomas Elementary, now Attucks Park. The diamond hadn't been graded, so before the game, we all went onto the infield to toss dirt clods into the outfield. But we couldn't get them all, and sure enough, midway through the game, a batter hit a grounder to short that ricocheted off a clump of clay and smacked me right on the schnoz.

I stood there for a second, stunned, as blood began to gush down my face, and then I just started bawling. My dad ran onto the field and carried me off. My only solace was that it had happened on the east side, where nobody I knew except my teammates had seen me crying in baseball. Until the next morning, when Martha arrived at our house and saw my shiner.

"I heard some white boy got hit in the face by a baseball last night and cried all the way home," she said. "That was you?"

What could I say?

In the early 1960s, the civil rights movement came to Carbondale in the form of SNCC, the Student Nonviolent Coordinating Committee, a chapter of which formed on the campus. One of SNCC's first actions, in 1965, was to picket the Family Fun restaurant on the east side, which had blacks working in the kitchen but none in the dining area. The faculty father of one of the three other Jewish kids in my class was in SNCC, as was his son, who was my friend. But I also had friends who were against integration, and my parents, although sympathetic to civil rights, didn't want anyone telling them who they had to hire. Many of the local Jewish families were of the merchant class, and after services at Beth Jacob Synagogue on a Sunday when SNCC was picketing, the congregation drove en masse to Family Fun, where we crossed the picket line to have lunch, except for my friend and his dad, who joined the protesters.

Soon SNCC was sending "salt and pepper teams" to apply for jobs at other businesses. If the owner didn't hire the black, SNCC would threaten to picket. My parents found a way around the problem -- they hired a colored woman. And they soon found that integration wasn't so bad, as other colored women began streaming into the store to buy clothes from the new colored saleslady.

There were just a few colored kids at U-School, and I didn't have much contact with them. That changed in 1968, when U-High was phased out and most of its students transferred to CCHS. Attucks had closed in 1964, so now everyone went to the same high school. (U-School's grade school closed in 1971, marking the end of neighborhood schools in Carbondale, as students were bused to achieve racial balance.)

However, except for some of the sports teams and P.E. classes, high school remained largely segregated. I still didn't have many blacks in my classes, and the races mostly socialized separately. My favorite teacher, English instructor Mary Sasse, started a human relations club to try to bring everyone together. I joined the club, as did my girlfriend, Kathy "Weegee" McNeill, but then I got jealous and made us quit. I was all for social equality, just not with my girlfriend.

In *Traces in the Dust*, Macklin observes that integration was a mixed blessing for Carbondale's black community. He says the closing of Attucks "spells an abrupt end to the close-knit, community structure Blacks had known for generations." He adds that desegregation, "for which Blacks had fought, ultimately proved to be a two edged sword. While it ushered in a supposedly 'new age of progress and opportunity for African Americans,' it also launched the Black community in Carbondale on a journey never witnessed before -- one which was to forever detract from the Black way of life."

During my last years at U-School, I entered the sphere of another precocious older boy, Jerry Magnus, who experimented with pot, went to protest rallies and put out underground newspapers. I transferred to CCHS in 1968 as a junior, but kept in contact with Jerry, who stayed at U-School and decided to do an underground newspaper on race, with an opinion survey, articles on local race relations, and other provocative stuff. He also wanted to write about the East Side Rangers, a group of young, black males who said they weren't a gang but a militant civil rights organization. Jerry invited me along to observe the group at their weekly meeting at City Hall, then located on East Main at Marion Street. I was apprehensive, and so were my parents, but I was as curious as I was scared, and my parents let me go on one condition -- that I park the family Buick on the west side of the tracks.

During study hall a few days later, I spotted someone I thought I'd seen at the Ranger meeting, sitting at a table in the high school library. It was none other than my Little League nemesis Lester, who had become the star center on the Terriers basketball team. I gingerly sat down across from him and asked if he would participate in a survey about race relations. Les glared at me but didn't say no, so I read the first question: "Do you think Teen Town should be integrated?" Without saying a word, he reached across the table, took my pencil from me, snapped it in half with the fingers of one hand, then stared at me as if I were the pencil.

We never finished the newspaper.

*Dedicated to Mary Sasse
(1932-2019)*

1983

Bucky's Dome

Much of Carbondale After Dark *was written by me and laid out by Deb Browne in futurist Buckminster Fuller's geodesic dome home while we lived there in the early 1980s. After moving out, I wrote a story about the dome and sold it to a magazine called* Technology Illustrated, *which unfortunately folded before the article could be published and I could get paid. My review was mixed, but to be fair, the dome was in pretty bad shape before we moved in, and by the time we left it was in worse shape.*

Fuller built his dome home in 1960, on the northeast corner of Forest Avenue and Cherry Street, just a few blocks from where I was growing up. After SIU President Delyte Morris resigned under fire in 1970, during a backlash to the student power movement, SIU became a less hospitable place for unconventional and often liberal thinkers like Fuller, and he left Carbondale forever in 1972. (He died at age 87 on July 1, 1983; his wife Anne died two days later.)

The dome became a rental property, and like Fuller's legacy, his home suffered from neglect. Few city or university officials were interested in preserving the structure, and some derisively called him Fucky Buller.

In 2001, Fuller protege Bill Perk purchased the property and donated it to a nonprofit, RBF Dome NFP, with the goal of restoring it. Since then, the group has repaired the exterior, rebuilt the interior, and put on a new roof. In 2015, the city finally designated the site as a historic landmark.

Some say geodesic dome inventor R. Buckminster Fuller was a genius. Others say he was a fool. After having lived in his house for four years, I feel qualified to say he must have been a bit of both.

From September 1979 until November 1983, I rented the same dome home that Bucky and his wife Anne Hewlett-Fuller inhabited from 1960 to 1972, while he was a professor at Southern Illinois University in Carbondale. The 39-foot diameter dome is one of the first ever made into a home, and the only house the Fullers ever owned. (Before building their home, they erected a prototype at the south end of the strip that later became Synergy, a drug treatment center.)

Living in Bucky's dome was fun, often exhilarating, even transcendental, which is no surprise. Though many of his ideas seem complex or far out, Fuller was at heart a pragmatist who believed in the essential goodness of nature.

Alas, as a place to live, the dome had its limitations, like few vertical walls upon which to hang pictures. The 1,400-square-foot dwelling was modest, with just two closets, one bedroom (but two bathrooms), no basement and no garage. Drafty in the winter, muggy in the summer, it had a tendency to leak. With all its odd angles it was hard to keep clean, and arranging furniture was a challenge. It had also been through a lot of weather and a certain amount of neglect.

My first encounter with Bucky's dome was on a field trip in the third grade. It was still being built, and my most vivid memory of the day is of the teacher warning us not to touch a mysterious pink substance on the walls that looked like cotton candy and seemed to be called viper glass. (Years later I realized she'd been talking about fiberglass.)

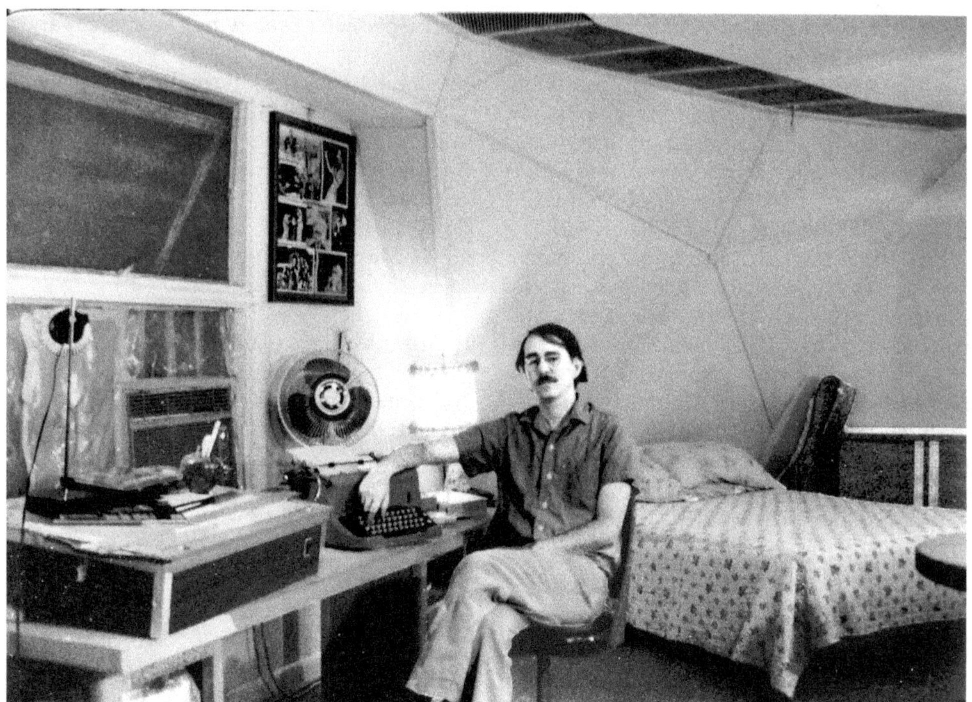

The author at his typewriter in the dome, circa 1982. Deb's light table is at the left. *--Deb Browne--*

The construction of the dome certainly illustrated Fuller's principle of "more with less." According to news accounts, the shell was assembled in less than eight hours on April 19, 1960. Hundreds of spectators were on hand, as was Fuller, who proselytized to the crowd as workers bolted the triangular components together.

Though the 10-sided structure looked strange, it was made out of conventional building materials and cost only $8,000 installed. The parts were made by the Pease Woodworking Co. of Hamilton, Ohio -- later Cathedralite Domes -- one of about a hundred companies then leasing Fuller's dome patent. In addition to fiberglass, the prefabricated kit included 60 triangular plywood panels on two-by-four frames, standard windows and doors, interior finish and kitchen and bathroom fixtures. When neighbors complained the spherical home broke up the boxy symmetry of the neighborhood, Fuller added a tall redwood fence to block the view.

The Fullers painted the outside of their new home turquoise and white, and the inside all white, accentuating its airiness. Ten small translucent skylights in the top created a diffused natural lighting. The floor was a concrete slab covered with durable cork tiles. A network of hot water pipes beneath the floor exuded radiant heat.

The dome's one large bedroom, shaped like a half moon, had five doors. Two led to closets, two to bathrooms, and one to the kitchen. One of the bedroom's two windows was behind a closet next to the front door.

A 45-foot, semi-circular ventilation shaft in the bedroom ceiling came out underneath a bookcase cradling a loft that was Fuller's study. The loft overlooked a larger crescent-shaped room, with a 16 1/2-foot-high ceiling, that was the living room, dining room and kitchen. The dominating feature of the living room was its three sets of glass patio doors spaced 20 feet apart. Beyond the patio doors was a fenced yard with a fountain.

Shortly after moving in, Fuller described

dome life as "very secure. It's an interesting experience getting up and going out to the university in the morning from this round house. As I go from the bedroom through the kitchen and dining area, and then out through the living room and finally all the way around again out the driveway, it's like coming out of a conch shell."

The first "bug" to turn up in the dome was the one space-age material used in its construction -- a Celastic tape soaked in methyl-ethyl-ketone -- meant to seal the seams between the triangular plywood sections. Many dome dwellers say a miracle substance has yet to be developed that can take the place of shingles for keeping out water, and the Fullers added a layer of white shingles to their house a few years after moving in.

When Fuller came to SIU he said he'd be "putting down roots in southern Illinois," but it was not to be. Though in his 60s, his public persona was just entering its prime. While he was based in Carbondale, many of his writings were first published, as were a spate of books and articles about him. In 1966, Walter Cronkite visited the dome to interview Bucky for the TV series *The 21st Century*.

As Fuller's fame grew, and especially after he designed the U.S. Pavilion at Expo '67 in Montreal, he spent more time globe-trotting and only a couple of months a year in Carbondale. In 1972, he accepted a position with the University City Science Center in Philadelphia, and moved out of the dome forever.

Michael Mitchell, a 39-year-old musician and self-described "unpaid assistant to Fuller for 17 years," bought the property from the inventor in 1973 for $22,000. He lived there for awhile before moving to California and renting it to college students. A few years after the first tenants moved in, they began complaining about leaks. Instead of fixing the roof, the landlord advertised for new tenants. The old ones left, but not before alerting the city's code enforcement department, which, after an inspection, posted unfit-for-occupancy signs.

Luckily, a local Fullerphile, George Vensel, heard about the plight of the house and offered to make repairs. Vensel, who lived in a dome he built in nearby Pomona, recalled that when he inspected Bucky's dome in the fall of 1978 "it leaked like a sieve. There were buckets all over the floor to catch drips."

Vensel said the leaks came from badly-fitted skylights that had been installed over the originals when Fuller shingled the dome. The water had rotted the wood and attracted termites. So extensive was the damage that the entire south side of the shell over the living room had to be replaced. The landlord wouldn't pay for additional insulation, so to compensate, Vensel applied thick, brown, heat absorbing shingles over most of the shell, including the vented skylights.

The next tenant stayed just a few months before moving to Florida to join a religious cult. Thus it was that when I returned to Carbondale in the summer of 1979 to become a reporter at the *Southern Illinoisan* newspaper, "Buckminster Fuller's historic dome" turned up in the "For Rent" section of the classified ads. That September a co-worker and I moved in. He got the back bedroom and I took the loft.

"The loft." It sounded so urbane. What it turned out to be was cramped, stuffy and lacking in privacy. The same curved ceiling that is so cathedral-like from the living room is quite low from the loft, not unlike a regular attic. Although the curved ceiling and air shaft between the loft and downstairs bedroom had no perceptible impact on air circulation, they sure circulated sound. Not only could every toss and turn by one of us be heard by the other, but someone in the bedroom could hear the TV on the other side of the house better than someone sitting in front of it.

Many of the dome's features, including the air shaft and patio doors, were meant to utilize natural forces like sunlight and wind to control the environment. Unfortunately, they just didn't work. Even with fans it was hard to coax a breeze through the house, and unless the weather on the outside was in what the heating and cooling industry calls "the comfort zone," keeping it that way on the inside proved elusive.

Nevertheless, dome dwelling was like living inside a bubble instead of a box. One felt just the right balance of being exposed to nature and protected from it at the same time. Besides, the bragging rights alone were worth a certain amount of inconvenience.

As autumn turned to winter, however, one began to feel over exposed. In addition to being poorly insulated, the dome needed to be caulked and sealed. Gaps large enough to see through had developed between many of the plywood sections. Any hope I had that the three patio doors would contribute significant amounts of passive solar energy in winter were dashed when I discovered icicles on them -- on the inside.

The hot water pipes under the floor were meant to take advantage of another natural force -- hot air rising -- rather than ducts and blowers. I wish I could say the heating system made the house toasty, but tepid is more accurate. It was also expensive, tripling the electric bill.

Dome life became mellow again with the arrival of spring. The sounds and smells of the season flowed through the house, and the fenced backyard was perfect for sunbathing and barbecues. Spring also gave the dome a chance to showcase its great strength. On several occasions wind storms damaged trees and tore down parts of the fence. The dome stood firm, partly because of its aerodynamic shape, and partly because of its "tensegrity," a Fuller-coined term describing a dome's ability to disperse a force exerted against any part of it evenly over its entire shell.

Of all the seasons, the dome was least equipped to handle summer. Without vents in the top for hot air to escape (nor in the bathrooms, for that matter), hot weather turned the dome into a sauna. The dark asbestos shingles soaked up sun all day and radiated heat into the night.

Central air conditioning was in its infancy in 1960, but with his "natural" instincts, Fuller probably wouldn't have wanted it anyway. Sometimes I opened the patio doors and pretended subtle air currents were cooling the house. More often I covered them with sheets to keep out the sun. There was a noisy ceiling fan, but all it seemed to do was blow the hot air around.

After my co-worker moved out and my significant other moved in, we hooked up a used air conditioner in the bedroom. Feeling wimpy, we also employed an electric blanket, space heater and other "low tech" devices to assist with climate control.

The dome was never meant to be split into apartments, and living there as a couple was way more comfortable. Yet some things remained a mystery. Like that window in the closet. All it seemed good for was fading clothes and letting in bugs, dust and drizzle. Only after researching the house for this article did I learn that while Bucky designed the outside, Mrs. Fuller laid out the interior. With all his patio doors and windows, he left his more practical wife with few places to turn into closets, so she put one over a window. She also added a door from the bedroom to the guest bathroom, which was a shortcut to the front door.

Bucky's dome may have its idiosyncrasies. But give credit to the inventor for its simplicity and adaptability. Because of the geodesic dome's many unique qualities, including its strength, light weight and easy construction, some believe that when man establishes his first colony in outer space, it will be under a dome.

Ghosts of Carbondale Past

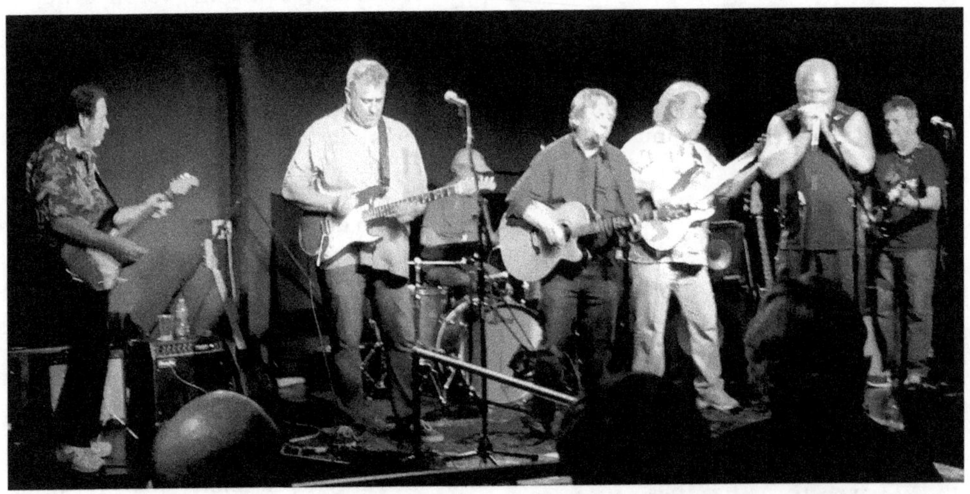

Some of Jim Bruno & Friends, from left: Terry Mueller, guitar; Mark Soljacich, guitar; Russ Ward, drums; Jim Bruno, guitar and vocals; Dean Milano, bass and vocals; Joe C Castrejon, harmonica; and Robbie Stokes, guitar.   *--Photo by H.B. Koplowitz--*

"It's great to be back in Champaign … just kidding," Jim Bruno quipped at the start of his bittersweet reunion concert Sept. 17, 2017, at the Varsity Center in Carbondale.

Billed "Jim Bruno & Friends," the line-up included surviving members of some of the hottest bands during the heyday of the Carbondale music scene in the 1960s and '70s, including Devil's Kitchen, Scuttlebucket, Pontiac Jones, and the Dixie Diesels. Bruno is a singer, songwriter and acoustic guitarist who lives in the San Francisco area. He got his start in Carbondale during the 1970s, performing with another aspiring singer and guitar player named Shawn Colvin.

Carbondale in the '60s and '70s had been a special time for a lot of baby boomers like myself -- I was born there in 1951 and graduated from Southern Illinois University in 1977. One of the best things about the '60s was its socially conscious rock music. The bands that played that music in Carbondale were a big part of what had made the town special, and the musicians performing at the concert had been a big part of those bands. Attention must be paid.

Besides, my generation has reached an age that musician Paul Simon calls "A Hazy Shade of Winter," and spending an evening basking in music and memories from the springtime of my life sounded downright cathartic. Alas, I didn't think I'd be able to attend. I'd just been to Carbondale to partake in native rituals during a total eclipse of the sun. Then Hurricane Irma struck, and I, my brother, his girlfriend, and their Yorkie, fled South Florida in my car to Atlanta. We could have continued on to St. Louis, where I could have stayed with friends and family, looked up an old girlfriend, and gone to the concert. Instead, we languished in a hotel in Atlanta for nearly a week before returning Friday. The hurricane had spared our homes.

On Saturday, perhaps suffering from car lag, I got a bad case of the coulda shoulda wouldas. I began to kick myself for not having gone to St. Louis and the concert. That regret triggered an avalanche of other regrets, which are far too numerous, banal and excruciating for me to list here. As I sunk ever deeper into my funk, I actually tried to will myself back in time and make a deal with a God I didn't believe in.

Earlier that day I'd written to my Facebook friends that I was sorry I wouldn't be at that night's concert. When I thought the show was starting, I got back on Facebook to see if anyone was posting photos or live-streaming the event. Instead, high school classmate and Carbondale guitarist Bill Carter had sent a cryptic reply to my earlier message. He said the concert wasn't until the next night.

Holy moly. If I hopped a plane, I could still make the show. I knew I'd simply made one of those "wrong day" errors that we all do sometimes. But given my agitated state of mind, it was hard for me not to read something more cosmic into the situation. Even if I hadn't willed myself back in time, or a God I didn't believe in hadn't called my bluff, I had been given one of life's most precious moments -- a second chance. A do-over. I could torture myself for another day about what might have been, or I could erase one small regret in my life.

I checked the airlines, and there was a reasonably priced morning flight that would get me to St. Louis in time for the 7:30 p.m. concert. Around 3 a.m. I texted the same "team" I had watched the eclipse with. Mark Kerwath, a high school friend and guitarist who lives on the Merrimac River, provided the transportation. Ruth Ann Levinson, the widow of Marc, another high school friend -- Ruth Ann also plays bass, sings with a group called the Free Range Chicks, and lives south of Makanda -- provided a place to stay. It was short notice, but they came through.

Mark picked me up at the airport, and around 5 p.m. we met up with Ruth Ann behind the Varsity. There, we ran into Carbondale icon and blues singer "Tawl" Paul Frederick, who was sitting on a gas meter, sipping a drink and smoking a cigarette. When someone suggested he might blow himself up, he growled that he'd done a lot riskier things and was still here. True that. The former frontman for Pontiac Jones circa 1972 still performs with Slappin Henry Blue (including townies Bill Carter, guitar; T. Thomas, bass; and Charlie Morrill, drums), which over the past quarter century had become the unofficial house band at venerable PK's on the strip. When I introduced myself to Tawl Paul, he said he'd been following my exploits on Facebook, then something about Santa Claus and sitting on his knee.

"I see you made it," Robbie Stokes, another relic of the Carbondale music scene, hollered when he rolled up in a vehicle. I think Robbie is the best guitar player in the world, but I'm biased. We both went to University High School (Pulliam Hall) in the 1960s, and I was smitten by his first band, the Viscounts, which played a combination of surf and British Invasion music. His next band was Om, and then Devil's Kitchen, with Brett Champlin, Bob Laughton and Steve Sweigart. They fused folk and psychedelic rock into a sound that took them to San Francisco in 1968, where they played in legendary venues like the Family Dog, Fillmore, and Whisky A Go Go, opening for and playing with members of the Grateful Dead and other San Fran bands. After returning to Carbondale two years later, Robbie played in a gazillion local groups including Coal Kitchen, Vision, Dr. Bombay, St. Stephen's Blues, Four on the Floor, and the Venturis. He also founded Robco Audio, which mixes sound for Hangar 9, Shryock Auditorium and many other places.

Another old school chum, Terry Mueller, let us through a back door of the Varsity to have a look around. Terry is one of the unsung heroes of the Carbondale music scene. For many years he and Bill Carter ran Golden Frets, the town's primo music store and repair shop. He's also played guitar and mandolin in a variety of bands, including the original Dixie Diesels.

The Varsity movie theater is a Carbondale relic in its own right. Built in 1940 as a thousand-seat auditorium with balcony for colored folks, it was later split into upper and lower theaters. (Late comedian and civil rights activist Dick Gregory is said to have been the first black to integrate the theater by sitting on the main floor in the 1950s.) The building also housed four storefronts and a corner grill. While installing a third screen that replaced the stores in 1981, a construction fire destroyed the main auditorium and damaged the rest of the building. Also, the building's art deco facade was replaced by an ugly stone wall. The theater closed in 2003 and was vacant until 2008, when the nonprofit Jackson County Stage Company turned it into a performing arts center. The third theater is used for plays, and the balcony theater was recently renovated and reopened for movies as well as live performances. The lobby and former grill are used for art exhibits. Some of the original features remain, including inlaid glass tiles between the balcony steps, and the striking, V-shaped marquee. The theater's board was trying to raise $3.5 million to repair the main auditorium and restore the exterior to its 1940s art deco glory.

Terry led us to the balcony theater, where Jim Bruno and Charlie Morrill were doing a sound check. Charlie is a veteran Carbondale drummer with many Carbondale bands, including the Dixie Diesels. He plays drums like a good baseball umpire -- he does his job so smoothly that you hardly notice he's there. He was using the same burgundy drum set he's had since high school, which was appropriate for the occasion.

We looked inside the ground-floor the-aters and saw the three surviving members of Scuttlebucket/Pontiac Jones: Russ Ward, drums and banjo; Dean Milano, bass and vocals; and Mike Potter, guitar, mandolin and bass. Only the late Pete Special was missing. I knew Mike, a quiet, gentle and talented musician, from childhood -- he went to Murphysboro High. I'd never met Dean and Russ, who now live and play music in the Chicago area, but in recent years we'd become Facebook friends.

In high school, Dean, Russ and Pete crossed paths playing in bands in the west suburbs of Chicago. Dean and Russ were in a high school band called Grope, while one of Special's first bands included a drummer named John Belushi. After Dean enrolled at SIU in 1972, and inspired by groups like The Band, and Crosby, Stills, Nash and Young, the three moved into a dilapidated house in Carterville, their own Big Pink, where they became Pontiac Jones. They also played bluegrass as Scuttlebucket. After southern Illinois native Terry Ogolini (tenor saxophone), and Chicago Vietnam vet Tawl Paul Frederick (charisma) joined the band, it took off. In addition to playing downtown bars and out-of-town roadhouses, they opened for Paul Butterfield and Leo Kotke at Shryock Auditorium, and for Luther Allison at Kilo's (Carrie's), a rowdy roadhouse outside Murphysboro.

The band split up in 1975, partly because the bars went disco and replaced bands with deejays and recorded music. Dean returned to the Chicago area and became a folksinger. Russ and his wife, Diane, also returned to the burbs, where they started a family. Mike helped start the country swing band Dixie Diesels with Brad Davis, a former drummer turned guitarist and singer from the country music trio Ronnie and the Bossmen. When the Diesels, including Brad Valentine, Willie Wainright, Ralph "Radar" Hurst, and Shawn Colvin, moved to Austin, Mike went along. He still lives there, where he's a musician and paints pictures of music legends.

In the early '70s, Special and Ogolini discovered "300 pounds of heavenly joy," Larry "Big Twist" Nolan, playing drums and singing in a three-piece country/R&B band at a rural honky-tonk called Lyin' Sam's; he was one of the few blacks on the roadhouse circuit in southern Illinois. After Twist died in 1990, Special told the *Chicago Reader*, "When we saw Twist we said, 'My God, that's the real thing!' ... He was everything we admired and looked up to; he had that magic."

Twist, who is believed to have been born in 1937 in Terre Haute, Indiana, had been living for many years in Murphysboro. He began sitting in on some of Pontiac Jones' gigs, and when the band broke up, Special and Ogolini started a new band with Twist, drummer Denny Best, and a group of black musicians -- including singer Martin "Big Larry" Allbritton, keyboardist Ronald West, Sr., and bass player Ron "Tango" West, Jr. -- who called themselves the Mellow Fellows. In the 1950s, the Mellow Fellows had been the house band at the New Orleans Bourbon Street Night Club, a famed bawdy house in Colp owned by Ma Hatchett and her son Junior.

Big Twist and the Mellow Fellows became Carbondale's premier band until they moved to Chicago in 1978, where they played at blues clubs, toured with The Band and released several R&B albums. After Twist died of complications from diabetes in 1990, the band continued for a few years with Big Larry out front. Then Special got to play with The Band and fronted his own band before his untimely death from a heart attack in 2014. Other Mellow Fellows, including Ogolini, formed the Chicago Rhythm and Blues Kings.

The reconstituted Pontiac Jones/Scuttlebucket were doing some last-minute rehearsing, so after a brief conversation, my team headed up to Thai Taste in the historic Brush building at Main and Illinois Avenue, where we had a tasty meal despite the fact that a car had recently crashed through the wall facing Main Street. By now you are probably wondering if I'll ever get around to reviewing the concert. But before I do, let me say that by this point in my mini odyssey, I had realized the show wasn't going to be as epic as I had built up in my mind.

First of all, it was being held in the balcony theater, which was too small for there to be a mass gathering of Carbondale blasts from the past like I had imagined. Second, there had been a similar reunion show, organized by Bruno and with many of the same musicians, plus a few more, the year before, at the Old Feed Store in Cobden, so it wasn't a singular event. (Many of the musicians also performed the day before at Blue Sky Vineyard in Makanda and Yellow Moon Cafe in Cobden.) And third, the quality and quantity of Carbondale band members from the 1970s who would not be there meant it could never be the ultimate harmonic convergence, so to speak.

The number of Carbondale musicians from that era who have passed on is enough to fill an Academy Awards Show obit reel, starting with Big Larry (1937-2017), who died just days before the concert. As mentioned, Twist (1937-1990) and Special (1952-2014), had been the soul and heart of Big Twist and the Mellow Fellows. Others no longer with us include the voice of the Dixie Diesels, Brad Davis (1952-2009); Skid City Blues Band guitarist Jack "Slo-Jack" Soljacich (1953-1999); and Coal Kitchen vocalist Carla Peyton (1947-2005), who would have added some gender as well as color diversity to the lineup.

Those still alive but not at the show included saxophonist Kevin Cox of Springfield, IL, who also performed with Coal Kitchen and just about every other Southern Illinois band since the Egyptian Combo; the aforementioned Bill Carter; T. Thomas, who had played with Katie and the Smokers; Greta Mitchell (Tristram), harmonica and keyboards for Skid City, among others (she still performs in New York City); and Billy Desmond, also of Skid City, who now fronts for Billy D and the Hoodoos out of Portland, Oregon. Also: Russell "Radar" Hearst (Dixie Diesels); Terry Ogolini (Big Twist, Pontiac Jones); Alfredo Jahn, (Vision); keyboardist and high school friend and keyboardist Gus

Pappelis (oom pah music at Das Fass); and, of course, Grammy winner Shawn Colvin.

No matter. From the moment Bruno and his band walked on stage, he set a mellow mood with his Champaign quip and laconic patter. The smaller venue had great acoustics and provided a more intimate listening experience for the audience. In addition to Bruno, who sang and played acoustic guitar, his cousin, Mark Soljacich (brother of the late "Slo-Jack" Soljacich) played electric guitar; Brian Sandstrom, who was in the Shawn Colvin Band and Skid City, played bass, and on drums, steady Charlie Morrill.

The first set showcased several songs Bruno wrote for his latest album, *Long Short Story*. With a voice that's not as hard as early Bob Dylan, nor as soft as Paul Simon, Bruno writes what I would call existential love songs. He started the set with a tune appropriate for the occasion, "We'll Always Remember Tonight," and later followed up with a song about regret, called "Don't Listen." Especially strong was a lyrical ballad called "Marie," which was enhanced by Soljacich's note-bending guitar work. Midway through the set, Bruno announced that the author of *Carbondale After Dark* was in the house, prompting a smattering of applause as I slouched down in my seat, embarrassed and pleased beyond joy.

Scuttlebucket took the stage for the second set, with Russ Ward on banjo, Dean Milano on bass, Mike Potter on acoustic guitar, Terry Mueller on mandolin, and Charlie Morrill on drums. They began with "On the Banks of the Ohio," but I got chills when they next performed "They Call the Wind Maria," with Terry's nimble mandolin playing and powerful vocals by Dean. The song comes from the Lerner and Loewe Broadway musical *Paint Your Wagon*, but of course my generation remembers The Smothers Brothers folksong version best. To honor Brad Davis of the Dixie Diesels, they covered a couple of Merle Haggard tunes, "White Line Fever" and "The Fugitive."

For their Pontiac Jones tribute, Russ moved to drums, while Mike, Terry, and Robbie Stokes played electric guitars to compensate for the absence of Special and Ogolini. To excited applause, out strode Tawl Paul, and the band launched into "St. James Infirmary Blues." Tawl Paul has a unique delivery style, which is part Cab Calloway and part Joe Cocker. Nowadays he sits for some of his performances, but this night he stood. The all-too-short set included two other Pontiac Jones standards, Howlin' Wolf's "Wang Dang Doodle," and "The Weight" by The Band. (Later, Russ reminisced that "St. James Infirmary" had been their "show stopper." "We started it slow, sort of like this impromptu version, but then kicked it up into a fast rocker. Mike, Pete Special and Terry Ogolini used to tear up the solos," he recalled.)

Bruno returned with his acoustic guitar for the third set, which was a Carbondale all-star jam that included Mueller, Soljacich, and Stokes on electric guitars, Sandstrom on bass and Morrill on drums, plus Joe "C" Castrejon on harmonica. Castrejon owns the current music store in Carbondale, Sound Core.

They limbered up with "I Ain't Got You," the much-covered 1955 R&B classic by Jimmy Reed, and then played the dance song "Hand Jive," fittingly, because that had been the last song The Band played at their reunion concert in 1983. Some of the women in the audience began to freestyle on the stoop next to the projection booth, and when the band played another feel-good song, "Hey Baby" (I want to know if you'll be my girl), a few danced to the front of the stage, to the delight of the crowd.

Next came the highlight of the evening for me. "All Along the Watchtower" was not only a Dylan song, but my favorite tune the Shawn Colvin Band played back in the day. It was the one song I had hoped to hear that night, but thought it would be too cheesy to request. When I recognized the opening chords I grabbed my iPhone, which had about 7 percent battery left, and

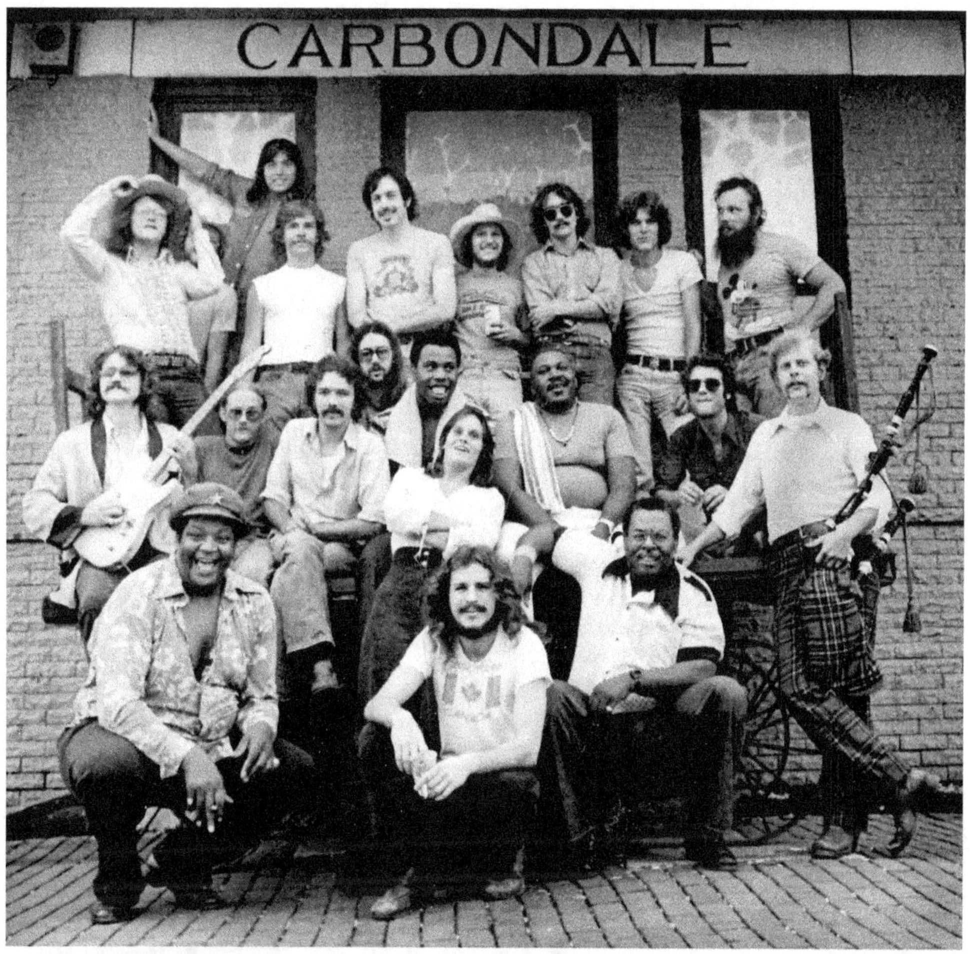

Carbondale's "honky tonk heroes" posing for the cover of *nonSequitur* magazine in the summer of 1976. 1st row: Larry "Big Twist" Nolan, Jackie "Slo-Jack" Soljacich, Ronny West, Sr. 2nd row: Robbie Stokes, Mick "Rock", Terry Ogolini, Bob Valentine, Ronald "Tango" West, Jr., Shawn Colvin, Martin "Big Larry" Allbritton, Pete Special, Scott Koerting. 3rd row: Rusty "Radar" Hurst, Kirk Opyt (obscured), Willie Wainright, Mike Potter, Randy Bradle, Denny Best, Bill Desmond, Mark Kerwath and Steve Rodely.

--Chuck Fishman--

began to shoot video. Upside down. But I got it.

It had been a Trump-free evening, thankfully. No jokes and no allusions to the president. On the other hand, the times they weren't a changin'. The country was as polarized as it was in the 1960s, split over issues such as civil rights, guns versus butter, and a president some say was a crook and a liar. Apocalyptic times. And when the band at the Varsity launched into a seven-minute rendition of the apocalyptic "Watchtower," I was transported, if not in time, then in spirit and in passion.

Jim sang the verses and Charlie and Brian kept the beat, while Terry, Mark and Robbie traded guitar licks, and Joe C riffed on his harp. The players were loose and kept improvising, extending the song beyond its expected end. Soljacich and Bruno shared a laugh, then Dean Milano appeared on stage, whispered to

Bruno, and stepped up to a mic. He raised his arms to get the guitarists to let him take a verse. They almost sputtered to a stop, but were immediately lifted as Dean growled, "All along the watchtower, princes kept the view…" Sounding more like Jimi Hendrix than Bob Dylan, he poured himself into the lyrics. And when he got to "the wind began to howl," he let loose with an Old Testament howl that brought down the house. Reinvigorated by Dean's singing, the guitarists reached another crescendo that continued until Charlie finally ended the revelry with a crash of cymbals.

By the end of the concert, the performers had given their all. But I still wanted more. Throughout the evening, I had been inquiring, "where's the party?" and nobody seemed to know. Then, I think it was Russ, said he heard where there might be a gathering, and I rolled my eyes at my own stupidity. Where else could an after party for a reunion of old Carbondale bands possibly be held except at the strip's ultimate relic, the unsinkable PK's? So my team toked up, I mean walked up, to PK's, which was nearly empty on a Sunday night. Then the various band members and entourage trickled in, and we partied like it was 1969, if you can believe that.

At one point I was sitting at the bar next to Bruno, and we got to talking about Shawn Colvin. Back in the 1970s, he'd helped Shawn get her start. He set up her first gigs, played in her bands and wrote her songs, in Carbondale and the Bay Area, before she relocated to New York and began writing her own songs. They were also a thing for a while.

Anyway, Bruno told me about the first time he met Colvin, which was around 1975, at an annual musician campout at SIU ethnomusicologist and folk museum curator Dale Whiteside's farm. "Lots of music around campfires," Jim recalled. The future Grammy winner was 19 and Bruno was 24. It got late, and cold, and he found himself stranded on the farm without a coat or a sleeping bag. Shawn and her female roommate had a cozy tent, so he went up to her and asked if he might bunk with them for the night. Bruno's eyes twinkled as he recounted Shawn's reply: "dream on."

Dream on indeed. I reckon I'll just have to live with my regrets, just as I'll never be able to recapture my youth. But for one night I could wallow in some '70s flashbacks, hear the music, share the memories, and mingle with other ghosts of Carbondale past.

Was it worth the trip? Hell yes!

1959

I Killed a Man

<u>I Killed a Man</u>

I killed a man,

    Yet I'll never be tried.

For though he's dead,

    He's still alive.

He entered my store ~~################################~~

    With his pride at his side.

One of them seven,

    One of them five.

They noticed not their poorness,

    Nor blackness of skin.

They saw not the shape,

    In which they were in.

It wasn't my toys,

    That gleamed in their eyes.

It was but their father whom they idolized.

    I looked to his clothes,

I looked to his skin.

    I called him a niger,

And ne'er come back again.

    They turned to him with hope,

With hope and dismay.

    But stoopshouldered and defeated,

He could only turn away.

    Gone was their fortress,

Their nice wonderland.

    And as they went out the door,

They didn't take his hand.

    I killed a man,

But I'll never be tried.

    For though he is dead,

He is still alive.

by Harold Koplowitz

www.ingramcontent.com/pod-product-compliance
Lightning Source LLC
Chambersburg PA
CBHW051116050726

47592CB00002B/847